Architecture and the Novel under the Italian Fascist Regime

Francesca Billiani • Laura Pennacchietti

Architecture and the Novel under the Italian Fascist Regime

palgrave
macmillan

Francesca Billiani
School of Arts, Languages and Cultures
University of Manchester
Manchester, UK

Laura Pennacchietti
School of Arts, Languages and Cultures
University of Manchester
Manchester, UK

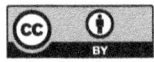

ISBN 978-3-030-19427-7   ISBN 978-3-030-19428-4   (eBook)
https://doi.org/10.1007/978-3-030-19428-4

© The Editor(s) (if applicable) and The Author(s) 2019. This book is an open access publication.

Open Access This book is licensed under the terms of the Creative Commons Attribution 4.0 International License (http://creativecommons.org/licenses/by/4.0/), which permits use, sharing, adaptation, distribution and reproduction in any medium or format, as long as you give appropriate credit to the original author(s) and the source, provide a link to the Creative Commons licence and indicate if changes were made.

The images or other third party material in this book are included in the book's Creative Commons licence, unless indicated otherwise in a credit line to the material. If material is not included in the book's Creative Commons licence and your intended use is not permitted by statutory regulation or exceeds the permitted use, you will need to obtain permission directly from the copyright holder.

The use of general descriptive names, registered names, trademarks, service marks, etc. in this publication does not imply, even in the absence of a specific statement, that such names are exempt from the relevant protective laws and regulations and therefore free for general use.

The publisher, the authors and the editors are safe to assume that the advice and information in this book are believed to be true and accurate at the date of publication. Neither the publisher nor the authors or the editors give a warranty, express or implied, with respect to the material contained herein or for any errors or omissions that may have been made. The publisher remains neutral with regard to jurisdictional claims in published maps and institutional affiliations.

Cover illustration: Joaquin Torres Garcia - Catedral Constructiva (1931). Mariano Garcia / Alamy Stock Photo; all rights reserved, used with permission.

This Palgrave Macmillan imprint is published by the registered company Springer Nature Switzerland AG.
The registered company address is: Gewerbestrasse 11, 6330 Cham, Switzerland

Grazie Alistair, grazie Georgios

Preface

The Book and Its Designs

This book forms part of a wider research project entitled, *Modernism, Modernization, and the Arts under European Dictatorships*, funded by the UK's Arts and Humanities Research Council (AHRC). Drawing on a wide-ranging set of modernist journals and artefacts—spanning public building, films, theatre plays, artworks and novels—this research project explored how the Italian Fascist regime's participation in an aesthetic movement (modernism) and in its transformation into a social phenomenon (modernization) created a distinctive system of the arts, which, in the 1930s, also had a profound influence across the whole of Europe. Specifically, this book analyses the relationship between the novel and architecture as one of the key expressions of the system of the arts under the dictatorship.

The project as a whole started from several working hypotheses which have been tested across the Fascist system of the arts and are visible in the website. As it has been established, during the Ventennio, not dissimilarly from what it did happen in other 1930s totalitarian regimes, the Italian Fascist regime created totalitarian aesthetic apparatuses together with new forms of social and cultural patronage for the control of the individual/citizen in the social sphere, seeking mass consensus and the constitution of the 'New Man' as the foundation of a modern collective social identity. In its claims, the regime adopted modernist aesthetics in a variety of forms and across various artistic fields, albeit not unproblematically and unilaterally, as the privileged paradigm for the modernization of the public sphere. In doing this, the idea of modernity encompassed progressive as well as reactionary forces.

Taken as a whole and despite their different ideological orientations, the official debate on State art as well as that on liberal arts shared a similar concern: the imperative of using the arts as a platform for fostering social modernization in the civic sphere to accommodate the new Fascist Man shaped by the regime's anthropological revolution. In the theory and in the practice of the modernist/Fascist dialectics of modernity and modernization, architecture, the novel, the visual arts, realism, the theatre, the newsreels and the futurist avant-gardes functioned for the regime and for Italian writers, artists and intellectuals, as core drivers for building a new society. In this project, we therefore argue that these debates and artistic expressions were of key importance for the existence of the regime, for they played a foundational role in shaping the aesthetics orientations of Italian culture, in creating its transnational profile, and in strengthening the power of the arts during political repression. Realism across these artistic fields in particular was the key aesthetic principle for such a construction and for creating a new national novel embedded within the international field.

To fulfil its aims, the project produced several outputs, including this book, and a website-database which collects, displays and more importantly connects information about circa 180 artefacts. The website also features five interpretative hypotheses about the role the novel, architecture, visual arts and cinema played in the construction of the arte di stato. The hypotheses function as the project's conceptual framework since they describe the main lines of enquiry developed throughout. The general and overarching hypotheses and the individual artefacts analysed in short essays are connected through a set of 12 cardinal principles, two or three associated to each hypothesis. Each artefact has been selected as representative of one of the hypotheses, and is linked to an essay in which it is analysed in light of the appropriate principle. Such principles are shaped in the total work of art, which was designed to represent modern forms of total power and technologies different from those championed by the avant-gardes. In the 1920s and 1930s, the total work of art found its implementation in: (1) the new theorization of the relationship between subjectivity and objectivity; (2) the sacralization of the new man's total politics though the arts; (3) the construction of the new man's urban reality; (4) the new man's/citizen's media manipulation; and (5) the legitimization of the artist/intellectual participation in the civic sphere.

The website also contains a database of journals, which have been used as sources for the project and the chapters of this book. The website functions as a collective book which has been written by Francesca Billiani, Silvia Colombo, Gianmarco Mancosu and Laura Pennacchietti.

This book and the website-database share a similar conceptual design, which is at the same time rhizomatic and dialectical. The book and the website-database are arranged according to a clear-cut and linear structure, which is organized around a series of conceptual kernels and principles spanning all chapters. The book then can be read as a stand-alone reflection on the intersections between architecture and the novel during the Fascist regime; but it can also be read alongside the website, which can provide further background illustrative examples of these artistic interconnections. It is a manifold and versatile book, both in its conception and in the way it can be read and understood, and it addresses multiple audiences who can navigate its various levels. Finally, readers can enter the virtual space of the book and of the website through various entry points. The online book has direct links to pages and sections of the website-database. In short, the two can exist separately or they can form part of a wider discourse on the dialectics of modernity and the role of the arts under a totalitarian regime.

Manchester, UK
Francesca Billiani
Laura Pennacchietti

Acknowledgements

This book came to life thanks to the support of the Arts and Humanities Research Council and the School of Arts, Languages and Cultures at the University of Manchester, and a special note of thanks goes to Delia Bentley for her generosity. Manchester IT research team has also contributed to the project by developing a website that can be consulted alongside the book, and a special thanks goes to Philip Bradbury and Louise Lever. We thank many people who have offered their help but in particular we mention those who have read the manuscript in parts or in its integrity: Chiara Costa, Costantino Costantini, Wissia Fiorucci, Patricia Gaborik, Martino Marazzi, Mila Milani, Jonathan Hensher, Monica Jansen, Gigliola Sulis, James Scorer, and Sara Sullam. A special thanks also to Francesco de Cristofaro and his students and colleagues at the University of Naples Federico II, to Massimiliano Tortora and the Fondazione Caetani in Rome for their interest in the project, to the Fondazione Prada and Chiara Costa for having discussed this project with us, and to Sara Sullam and Luisa Finocchi and the staff at the Laboratorio Formentini in Milan for their hospitality and fruitful discussion about the project. We are grateful to Shaun Vigil and Glenn Ramirez at Palgrave, and to the anonymous reader who has commented constructively on the project. Paola Pettenella and the archivists at the Museo d'Arte Moderna e Contemporanea di Trento e Rovereto (MART) in Rovereto have offered us more than generous support since the beginning of the research. We also thank Prof. Vittorio Anceschi and the Fondazione Mondadori, Tiziano Chiesa and Anna Lisa Cavazzuti specifically for allowing us to consult their papers and Katrin Albrecht for allowing us to use her photo of Angiolo Mazzoni's post office in Pola. We extend out thanks to Chiara Berrani, Silvia Colombo, Anna Lanfranchi and Gianmarco Mancosu, who have contributed to the creation of the website-database. Our colleagues in Italian studies and in modern languages at Manchester have been patient and have given us the time and trust we needed. And, finally, a note of unfailing gratitude to the many friends, family and colleagues who have helped in more than one way, but have nonetheless always made sure they did express their reservations.

Contents

1	National Novel and New Architecture	1
2	The Regime and the Creation of an 'Arte di Stato'	15
3	Constructing the Novel	31
4	Fascism and Architecture	61
5	*900* and *Quadrante*: Theorizing an Interdisciplinary Aesthetic Model	97
6	State Art, the Novel, and Architecture: Intersections	125
7	Novels and Buildings	149
8	Conclusion	201
	Bibliography	207
	Index	223

About the Authors

Francesca Billiani was the principal investigator of the project and Laura Pennacchietti the main research assistant. Billiani is the author of Chaps. 3, 4, and 6 and Pennacchietti of Chaps. 2, 5, and 7. The introduction and conclusion have been written by Billiani with the support and input of Pennacchietti. Both authors have read and commented on each other's chapters and on the overall structure of the book.

List of Figures

Fig. 4.1 Casa elettrica di Luigi Figini e Gino Pollini alla IV Esposizione Internazionale d'arte decorativa e industriale moderna di Monza (1929–1930). Veduta dell'esterno, 1 fotografia Mart, Archivio del '900, Fondo Luigi Figini e Gino Pollini, Fig.Pol. 3.1.1.6.1. 8 — 72

Fig 4.2 (a) La cucina della Casa elettrica di Luigi Figini e Gino Pollini alla IV Esposizione Internazionale d'arte decorativa e industriale moderna di Monza (1929–1930), 1 fotografia, ante/retro; (b) Mart, Archivio del '900, Fondo Luigi Figini e Gino Pollini, Fig.Pol.3.1.1.6.1.4 — 74

Fig. 4.3 Angiolo Mazzoni, Palazzo delle Poste di Pola (Croatia), courtesy of Katrin Albrecht — 81

Fig. 7.1 Drawing of Florence railway station, Gruppo Toscano project. *Architettura* 13, no. 4 (April), 1933: 201 — 174

Fig. 7.2 Drawing of Florence railway station, Gruppo Toscano project. *Architettura* 13, no. 4 (April), 1933: 203 — 176

Fig. 7.3 Drawing of Florence railway station (with detail), Gruppo Toscano project. *Architettura* 13, no. 4 (April), 1933: 203 — 178

Fig. 7.4 Drawing of Florence railway station (foyer), Gruppo Toscano project. *Architettura* 13, no. 4 (April), 1933: 205 — 179

Fig. 7.5 Luigi Figini e Gino Pollini, Ampliamento delle Officine Olivetti a Ivrea, fronte lungo via Jervis, 1939–1940 — 183

Fig. 7.6　Progetto per il Danteum, view towards the Colosseum, 1938, Archivio Pietro Lingeri　188
Fig. 7.7　Progetto per il Danteum, Inferno, 1938, Archivio Pietro Lingeri　189
Fig. 7.8　Progetto per il Danteum, Paradiso, 1938, Archivio Pietro Lingeri　191
Fig. 7.9　Progetto per il Danteum, Impero, 1938, Archivio Pietro Lingeri　192

1

National Novel and New Architecture

Modest methodological proposal for the cultural-historical dialectic. It is very easy to establish oppositions, according to determinate points of view, within the various 'fields' of any epoch, such that on one side lies the 'productive', 'forward-looking', 'lively', 'positive' part of the epoch, and on the other side the abortive, retrograde, and obsolescent.
—Benjamin (*Arcades*, [N1a, 3], 459)

This book traces the relationship and the intersections between the theory and practice of the novel and architecture in Italy during the Fascist regime (1922–1943), a period which saw an institutional body actively trying to shape the artistic world through a series of political choices and a system of patronage, which had distinct aesthetic reverberations.[1] Our initial hypothesis is that the aesthetic urgency of renewing the novel runs parallel to that of reconstructing a new architecture with the aim of creating an *arte di Stato*, or 'State art'. This monograph considers these issues over the entire duration of the regime, with particular focus on the first half of the 1930s, the moment in which these aesthetic projects, the structural reforms planned as well as the consensus enjoyed by the regime were at their height.

Throughout the arch of its lifespan but more so from the late 1920s to the mid-1930s, the regime presented itself as a modern, totalitarian political apparatus seeking to modernize the country's infrastructures, and the arts had to offer their contribution to these endeavours. Thus, our general argument is that an effort of construction, or reconstruction, was the main driving force behind the advocated 'revolution' of the novel form (realism) and of architecture (rationalism) called for by commentators and practitioners, both sustaining the 'anthropological revolution' brought about by Fascism, and creating spaces for the 'New Man'. As far as the arts were concerned, on the one hand, there was general consensus amongst novelists, publishers and intellectuals that the national novel needed to be rebuilt as a solid narrative form, reversing the nineteenth- and early twentieth-century trends towards Decadentism, art for art's sake, solipsism and the *prosa d'arte*, to address the demands of the growing Italian reading public. On the other, a generation of critics and relatively young architects explicitly argued that architecture had to be refounded and deployed in the service of building collective spaces for the New Fascist Man within a modernized social sphere. These aesthetic projects, then, both aimed at the cultural and social transformation of the new nation through a reconstruction and rationalization of artistic forms, and were marked by a strong belief in the moral and social role of art, which should sublimate individual experience into an anti-bourgeois collective narrative and spectacle. Both projects, catalysts as they were of the Fascist way to modernity, drew inspiration from foreign sources, and in this way, they were both instrumental in the process of the internationalization of Italian culture, while reclaiming the collective and nation-specific sense of artistic expression.

The fields of the novel and architecture became the subject of extensive discussions in public fora and in literary and cultural journals of different political orientations, as one can see throughout our analysis. These debates were at once theoretical, technical, aesthetic and political in nature, and on occasions intersected with each other to a remarkable degree. The journals hosting these arguments acted as spaces to theorize first and construct after a modern cultural infrastructure on which to base a process of modernization of the public sphere (e.g. publishing industry and State-commissioned public buildings), with the debate on the realist novel and rationalist architecture at its centre. Despite the different perspectives from which they were conducted, these debates on the novel and architecture tended to focus particularly on the need to rationalize current aesthetic practices—in terms of both formal structures, stylistic renderings and thematic repertoires—in order to respond to a widespread need to modernize the cultural and social spheres and make them more suitable to the needs expressed by the citizens (the new New Man), who had been shaped by the Fascist regime. To this end, from 1926 the regime started a campaign to support the arts both financially and politically, which is discussed in Chap. 2.[2] The regime not only produced the *libro di Stato* but also entered into profitable dialogue with the publishing industry in order to gain mutual benefit; this became even more prevalent in the 1930s.[3] Not dissimilarly, prominent cultural agents and architects wanted architecture to be elevated to the status of official State art. If this was a difficult task as far as private housing was concerned, from the early 1930s onwards, the collective dimension of the art of building was supported by the State and a specific architectural language (the *stile littorio*) was progressively developed.[4]

By returning to these topics in a concerted and consolidated fashion and not as individual projects, the main point this book seeks to make regards the importance of looking at a cultural system, in this case the system of the arts during the Italian dictatorship, as a series of intersections of cultural, political and aesthetic discourses in order to understand both how the arts could contribute to the political and cultural discourse of the regime and how a cultural system was designed and needed to work as an integrated whole rather than as self-defined fields of cultural production. Once this is established, it is crucial to determine how and why this is the case, and the degrees of such interconnectedness. To this end, we have chosen to analyse these connections in relation to the debates on State art. The creation and shaping of a Fascist *arte di Stato* became a major concern for the regime after the Matteotti affair in 1924, following the 1927 Discorso dell'Ascensione, in which Mussolini called for the *andata al popolo*, and particularly in the years of consolidation of consensus after the Patti lateranensi in 1929 and the proclamation of the Empire in 1936. In this context, debates on State art, on the form and content of the novel, and on new architecture often assumed a performative tone: in other words, they assumed a meaning not only when realized in practice but also when articulated either in writing or verbally. The system of the arts understood as such became a space where political and aesthetic aims could meet not only to produce forms of propaganda but also to create a discursive apparatus, which could embody the regime's ideology through experimental and anti-representational iconologies, designs and poetics. The arts and their intersecting theorizations did not necessarily aim at achieving a practical result, but rather at supporting the building of an aesthetic apparatus engendered by the regime with the political ambition of transforming the lives of Italian citizens; this was especially the case after 1932 and the Mostra del Decennale.[5]

Having identified similarities between the two projects under examination, it is necessary to reflect on their respective differences. The novel was never directly sponsored by the regime. Publishers (including Mondadori) did not receive systematic financial support: rather, the agreement between the parties was on a mutual understanding of each other's needs and priorities in order to avoid the publication of subversive, or even too controversial, material, as was made explicit in the case of translations. There were exceptions of course. In contrast, architects took part in public competitions and received direct financial support from the regime when engaged in the construction of public buildings: train stations, post offices, corporativist cities, the Sapienza University, public buildings for State functions and the E42 as a final attempt at building a new Rome are some of the most obvious examples. Public competitions attracted great interest and were the subjects of extensive debates. Architectural achievements were reviewed and discussed in literary journals and weekly cultural magazines alike. The novel performed its role as traditionally understood within the structures of an expanding publishing industry, while architecture gained unprecedented popularity because of its visibility and because of the public role it performed. The other difference worth mentioning here concerns the respective ways of reception and enjoyment of the two art forms. Architecture was a visible product that was immediately accessible and which everyone could see and comment upon: it was the product of the conflation of space and concept (see also Tschumi 1996, 39–44). The novel instead remained a much more difficult product to enjoy. It needed financial commitment on the part of the reader and it was often not simply a pleasant distraction, but required sustained intellectual attention. Otherwise put, if the Italian 'Fascist' novel was in many ways a failed project because it could not reach a wide enough audience and was eclipsed by translations, the regime's architecture was more successful. Following from what we have just stated, a fairly obvious statement would be to say that the book takes an interdisciplinary approach: the novel and architecture not only belong to rather distant disciplinary fields, but they also reach their audiences through different channels, languages and functions, employing disparate aesthetic practices.

Because of the differences between the two projects we have outlined above, we have decided to focus on how they were theorized in public fora, rather than on the ways in which they were sponsored by the State or enjoyed by the audiences they targeted and addressed. However, in order to paint a coherent picture, we have sampled our sources widely: we have looked at journals of diverse orientations, we have chosen a pool of famous and less well-known examples of novels and of buildings as representative cases embodying the principles we have identified, and we have consulted several archives. The book combines more obvious examples with less obvious ones, since we believe that patterns of cultural production function only when tested across a series of diverse cases spanning high and popular culture, avant-garde and mainstream artefacts. However, if we scrutinize them as interconnected efforts, if we theorize the ways in which they existed within the system of the arts, and, significantly, if we do so under the overarching rubric of State art, we can see similarities emerging across the four main principles that guide these endeavours and share in their aesthetic and political programmes. From scrutiny of the many aesthetic-political debates and theoretical statements, we have identified four cardinal principles, around which we have built our analysis of the 'atlases' of the novel and of architecture, the reading of periodical press and the dissection of the artefacts. These principles are the rationalization of aesthetics, the necessity for morality in the arts, the call for a social and collective mission for the arts, and the need for a new brand of realism. We understood the rationalization of aesthetics as a practice whereby the shaping of an artwork was based on a process of simplification of the subject matter in order to produce a unitary construction, while we interpreted the call for morality as an underlying ethical meaning of a given work of art. Principles three and four, concerning the social meaning of art, and the adoption of new forms of realism, are closely connected. Both envisage the work of art as the result of an exchange between subjectivity and objectivity, which has to take place with reference to a social context. They both call for an engagement with objectivity, which instead can give weight to a historicist approach. All principles question the idea of the autonomy of the arts traditionally conceived as detachment from the real, and propose to view autonomy and heteronomy as mutually connected.[6] The work of art is an autonomous product of the imagination, carefully constructed, which is also closely connected and heteronomous to the contexts of its production.

From a methodological perspective, a few points need to be explained by way of introduction: the definition and understanding of the arts, or the system of the arts under an anti-liberal regime; the distinction between the arts per se and the arts as a system (Cioli 2011, xi); and the overall design of the book. Firstly, we do not view an artistic field in isolation, and we are not interested in any of their individual developments during a particular historical period. We are interested in how distinctive fields interact with each other when occupying different positions within their fields of cultural production. Secondly, our field of cultural production, in this particular case, is shaped by the presence of a dictatorship, which at least from the mid-1920s engaged in the definition and construction of the concept of State art, as discussed in Chap. 2. The presence of an overarching debate on State art called for by a totalitarian State fundamentally changes the modes of production and exchange within any cultural landscape, since it acts as a governing mechanism that cannot be disregarded. By looking at these phenomena as intersecting fields within the overarching project of the State art, we can ask questions which exceed traditional disciplinary boundaries while following a clear conceptual trajectory defined by the key principles outlined above. Thus, in order to assess the relevance of the interconnections between the novel and architecture for the profile of Fascist culture and the culture produced by and within the regime, the main questions we ask are: how and why did the new novel and architecture assume such a privileged position within the Fascist system of the arts? What is the relationship between the aesthetic principles governing the theorization of the new novel and those guiding the development of architecture? How did the novel and architecture contribute to shaping the idea of Fascist modernity? To what extent were the arts instrumental to the process of social modernization initiated by the dictatorship? Finally, to what extent did the arts, specifically novel and architecture, contribute to forming the identity of the Italian way to totalitarianism?

Having said that, this book is neither about architecture nor about the novel. Its aim is rather to develop a methodological perspective which is, in turn, neither comparative nor historicist. We are not comparing two distinct phenomena in order to assess what they might have in common, nor are we looking to determine their modes or points of comparison. We are, perhaps, closer to adopting a historicist approach, both when we place the artefacts we analyse in close dialogue with the historical landscape and when we focus on their modes of representation rather than on their 'real' existence. Or else the book aims 'to tread the shadowy paths' that connect artistic and cultural practices, which were juxtaposed under a political banner (Greenblatt 2004, 12). If anything, however, by analysing two distinct cultural fields, the book proposes a way of thinking about culture as a polymorphous field of action, which can be more productively analysed by creating junctures across phenomena that occur simultaneously but belong to diverse artistic fields. This can be achieved by choosing an overarching narrative, which gives coherence to the overall argument and which, in our case, is the narrative concerning the construction of State art under the regime.[7] One can therefore read this book as a contribution to the cultural history of the Fascist period in Italy from the point of view of the debates on architecture and the novel. We are less concerned with the history of the novel or the history of architecture taken as independent experiences than we are with an interdiscursive analysis of their relations, which can tell us about the aesthetic and political system of the day. In this respect, the book is not about individuals but about projects per se, which assume a relevance if placed within a given historical, political and aesthetic context. We hope to have made a contribution to advancing further the understanding of how the arts interacted with each other under the umbrella of the *arte di Stato* and how such participation has shaped the idea of Italian totalitarianism during the age of the European totalitarian regimes along the pathways identified by academic colleagues in Italy and across the Atlantic from the early 1990s to the present day.

In our analysis, we have relied heavily on architectural historians and critics of Italy, as well as on literary critics, and historians of Fascism, as we indicate throughout. To date, both architecture and the novel in the Italian Fascist period have received significant critical attention as distinct spheres of research, but have not been extensively analysed in close dialogue; rather they have been studied as isolated endeavours, which seemed to have very little aesthetic and political overlap. In particular, there have until now been no studies that examine them over the long term. As is discussed in every chapter, the theoretical foundation of the project draws on Emilio Gentile's work on modernity and on the anthropological revolution pursued by the regime (1982, 1990, 2003). The anthropological revolution of (imperfect) totalitarianism had to shape an individual capable of being a social and collective subject; and in order to achieve such a shift in perspective, it had to redefine the very parameters of the concept of realism. This was intended to support the process of the modernization of the public sphere. Arguably, the regime wished to elaborate a system of the arts capable of formulating just such a new expression of a modern and modernized subjectivity: from literature to the visual arts, theatre, architecture and, obviously, to the most powerful weapon, cinematography, what had to be achieved was a system of interdisciplinary arts, which proved to be at the same time official State art but also Art in the Fascist era.[8] Similarly, the past 20 years have seen a reassessment of the relationship between Fascism and culture in both Italian and Anglo-American scholarship, and especially so from the 1990s onwards. Walter Adamson (1993, 2001), Mark Antliff (2002), Ruth Ben-Ghiat (2001), Emily Braun (2000), Roger Griffin (1998, 2007), Mario Isnenghi (1979), Aristotle Kallis (2014), Jeffrey Schnapp (2003, 2004, 2012), Marla Stone (1998) and Pier Giorgio Zunino (1985) have amply demonstrated the key role played by cultural apparatus in shaping the Italian way to totalitarianism and introduced a new critical vocabulary to discuss culture and fascism: cultural modernities, palingenetic rebirth, the third way, cultural representations as complementary to historical fact, Fascism as a 'discourse', the Fascist regime as the patron State, and the patterns of aesthetic pluralism. They have all contributed to furthering our understanding of the complex ideological positions occupied by intellectuals, of the importance attributed to the process of modernization of the country through forms of cultural production which were not exclusively propaganda, of the complex nature of the regime's formulation of the idea of modernity, and of the connections between cultural formations of the pre- and post-Fascist regime. Fernando Tempesti (1976), Sileno Salvagnini (1988, 2000, 2015), Laura Malvano (1988a) and Monica Cioli (2011) have analysed the steps taken by the regime in the artistic sphere and have produced detailed accounts of the various cultural fronts in this war at any given time. Salvagnini and Cioli in particular have addressed with an impressive wealth of archival material the problem of the system of the arts as a concerted whole, including the issue of state patronage, within a broader interpretative framework which was at the same time historical, cultural and sociological. If Cioli has given prominence to the Futurist participation in the design of the *arte di Stato*, Salvagnini instead has painted a detailed picture that moves from the grand designs of the exhibitions to State-run local initiatives and the role of private galleries.

Architectural historians have been no less active, and we wish to mention the seminal work by David Rifkind (2012) in the journal *Quadrante* as an example of cultural analysis of a key phenomenon of the *Ventennio*, namely rationalist architecture and its politicization. Furthermore, Aristotele Kallis has discussed the matter from the point of view of a historian of culture and thus he has emphasized the importance of the cultural fabric in the reconstruction of an historical landscape of analysis. Of profound significance to our argument too have been the histories of architecture during the regime written by such scholars as Doordan (1988), Ciucci (2002 [1989]), Etlin (1991), Nicoloso (2008), De Seta (1998) and Ghirardo (2013), because of the detailed ways in which they have reconstructed the history of architecture while focusing on its political and technical aspects, problematizing without judgment its complex relationship with the regime. Finally, the work of some art historians, art critics and curators has pioneered the understanding of the arts during the regime as a complex, intersecting system to be studied as such rather than as individual, yet very detailed, discrete occurrences (Danesi and Patetta 1988; *Anni Trenta* 1982; Pontiggia 1990; Fagone 2001; Celant

2018).⁹ These scholarly works have provided methodological examples from the visual arts, which we can apply to fields of the novel and of architecture. 2018 has been a particularly fruitful year, with two major exhibitions centring on the arts under the dictatorship. The first one was organized by the Fondazione Prada in Milan and showcased more than 600 artworks covering the visual arts, architecture, literature and cinema from 1918 to 1943. The aim of the exhibition was to show an interdisciplinary scenario, while putting the system of the arts into the context in which it had been produced. Another major exhibition on Futurist art from 1909 to 1939 'Universo futurista' was curated by Jeffrey Schnapp and Silvia Evangelista and opened at the Fondazione Cirulli on 21 April 2018. It featured over 200 artworks belonging to the Fondazione Sonia and Massimo Cirulli, and because of its chronological span it reinforced the importance of looking at Futurism not only as a pre–World War I (WWI) phenomenon, rather as a more flexible and overarching cultural, political and aesthetic project. Two further exhibitions will open shortly, one to be held contemporaneously at the Museo del Novecento in Milan and at the Mart (Museo d'Arte Contemporanea di Rovereto e Trento) in Rovereto on Margherita Sarfatti, and the other in Pordenone at the Galleria Harry Bertoia on Mario Sironi's early works. This book is the result of an ongoing dialogue, real or virtual, with all the scholars, practitioners, curators and institutions listed above and in the bibliography.

Chronologically speaking, because of the 'battle for consensus' fought by the regime, we have paid particular attention to the first half of the 1930s, when the debates around the role of the arts for the totalitarian regime as well as those around the new Italian novel and the new Italian architecture peaked in intensity and incisiveness. We have focused primarily on the journals *900*, *Quadrante, Occidente, Orpheus, Critica fascista, L'Italia letteraria* and *Il Saggiatore*, because they engaged most systematically with the debate on the novel and architecture, and that on realism and the new culture. In order to offer a comprehensive picture, however, we have when necessary made references to other journals which addressed similar issues (e.g. *Architettura* from the point of view of leading architect Marcello Piacentini and the official architecture of Italy, and *Interplanetario* and *La ruota dentata* as expressions of the avant-gardes, before these were hegemonized by the regime). We have examined archival material as well as a set of novels and buildings, which can be taken as representative of the principles shared by the twin projects of renovating architecture and reconstructing the novel, as well as a series of intersecting points in the trajectory towards a modern *arte di Stato*. After 1936, across both fields, the international isolation faced by Italy as a consequence of the Ethiopian war caused a sea change. The novel continued to be theorized in terms of 'realism', but the architectural field became progressively less experimental and more dominated by the broad umbrella known as the monumental *stile littorio*. Finally, as World War II (WWII) began to loom, these debates died down and the major manifestations of State art in the field of architecture collapsed into crude monumentalism.

Chapter Outline

The book follows two main trajectories: the debate on the novel and the debate on architecture under the overarching discourse of State art. Chapter 2 engages with the notion of *arte di Stato* as an Italian peculiarity and thus identifies the main traits and singularities of the Fascist system of the arts, as well as of the relationship between the arts and politics under Fascism, as articulated in the various cultural and political debates on the matter which took place from the mid-1920s onwards. Chapter 3 focuses on the shape of the Italian novel in the period under scrutiny and assesses the debates concerning it. In particular, it discusses the importance of the realist novel in the construction of State art while juxtaposing the Italian novel with the phenomenon of translation, which supported the publishing industry during the whole duration of the regime. The chapter looks not only at well-known novels but also at others that have been progressively forgotten. Chapter 4 discusses the architectural debates across the two decades in order to extract the main discursive lines which defined them. From the analysis of these architectural debates, we can see how important architecture was for the shaping of the novel form. It emerges that there were many similarities with debates surrounding the novel and all focused on the morality of art, the need for construction and the social imperative, which the arts needed to acknowledge as part of their identity under the regime. Chapter 5 examines debates and discourses on the journals *900* and *Quadrante*, and we argue that they were two of the main platforms for the construction of the novel and architecture as two interlocking projects working towards the construction of a modern and interdisciplinary Fascist culture, based on the shared principles of the rationalization of style, the morality of art and the engagement with the real. Chapter 6 turns to the analysis of three journals published in Rome and Milan—*Occidente*, *Il Saggiatore* and *Orpheus*— which engaged in the debate on realism as well as on the importance of morality and social engagement in the arts. These journals associated themselves with the cultural fringes of the youth culture produced by the regime and sought to offer a pragmatic solution to the debate on the new culture initiated by *Critica fascista* and Giuseppe Bottai and indirectly to the shape of the novel in realist terms. Chapter 7 applies the principles identified in the previous chapters to the analysis of a set of novels and buildings. These artefacts have been chosen because they epitomize the structural and conceptual intersections between architecture and the novel in more or less well-known novels and buildings. In this chapter we demonstrate how the convergence between the two artistic fields worked in practice and contributed to shaping the aesthetic, social and political meaning of the artworks in question.

Notes

1. We have not taken into consideration the last two years of the regime's history, since the political configuration of the Republic of Salò and of occupied Italy were different and the cultural debates were silenced by WWII.
2. Some key works in this field we are indebted to are: Isnenghi (1979) and Mangoni (1974, 1999) on the profile of Italian intellectuals, Turi (1995) on Giovanni Gentile, and on Stone (1998), while for the history of the institutions which promoted the arts, see Carli and Pontiggia (2006), De Sabbata (2007, 2012), Sagramora (2008), Salaris (2004), Salvagnini (2000) and Toffanello (2017).

3. For a historical assessment of the relationship between the regime and the publishing industry, see Turi (1980), and on the Einaudi publishing house, Turi (1990), as well as other landmark publications, such as Finocchi and Gigli-Marchetti (1997), Tranfaglia and Vittoria (2000), and Cadioli and Vigini (2004).
4. We will return to this topic in Chap. 4, but we would like to mention some important contributions which highlighted how the regime orchestrated the staging of a particular architectural language for the display of the symbolic order it had created. See, for example, Nicoloso (2008, 2012) and, as far as rural architecture was concerned, Sabatino (2010).
5. 1932 is a turning point in the history of the regime, and the fusion of Futurist aesthetic patterns with rationalist ones on the façade of the Mostra is quite indicative of the ways in which cultural matters would be dealt in the decade to follow. On the exhibition, see Ciucci (1982), Schnapp (2003, 2004) and Ghirardo (1992).
6. We understand autonomy as an aesthetic practice which takes the subjective experience both as its main expressive form and as its point of refraction. On the contrary, we intend a heteronomous aesthetic practice as one that conceives of the aesthetic experience in relation to an external objective reference point.
7. We are not aware of any other publication which proposes an extended analysis of these two phenomena as intersecting ones from the point of view of two artistic practices. Often, interdisciplinary analysis is collected in edited volumes or as journal articles. Finally, we are not using the categories of modernity and Modernism as overarching ones.
8. We can certainly list Albertina Vittoria's (1983) work on Fascist periodicals as a frontrunner of this trend because of how she intersected historical and cultural discourses. Similarly, Luisa Mangoni's (1974) work on Italian intellectuals at the thresholds between the nineteenth and twentieth centuries is giving significant prominence to cultural matters vis-à-vis historical ones.
9. These works grouped together the work of architectural critics, visual art scholars, art and literary historians, historians, intellectual and cultural historians in order to offer the reader a very detailed, yet angular, view of the arts under the regime. They all acted scientifically from an interdisciplinary perspective and without privileging one perspective over the other, thereby showing the complexities, while making rather bold claims about their significance as a concerted whole. Such an approach avoided the pitfalls of a potentially reductionist ideological assessment of the arts under the dictatorship.

Open Access This chapter is licensed under the terms of the Creative Commons Attribution 4.0 International License (http://creativecommons.org/licenses/by/4.0/), which permits use, sharing, adaptation, distribution and reproduction in any medium or format, as long as you give appropriate credit to the original author(s) and the source, provide a link to the Creative Commons licence and indicate if changes were made.

The images or other third party material in this chapter are included in the chapter's Creative Commons licence, unless indicated otherwise in a credit line to the material. If material is not included in the chapter's Creative Commons licence and your intended use is not permitted by statutory regulation or exceeds the permitted use, you will need to obtain permission directly from the copyright holder.

2

The Regime and the Creation of an 'Arte di Stato'

The expression 'arte di stato' (literally 'State art'), which is crucial to understanding Fascism and its aesthetic politics, refers to the Italian context in which it arose and was almost exclusively used.[1] There is no exact equivalent for the expression in English, and the art officially supported by totalitarian regimes is referred to mainly as 'official art', or more specifically 'totalitarian art', the title of the best-known and most influential book on the subject, written by art historian Igor Golomstock. In *Totalitarian Art*, Golomstock claims that 'in a totalitarian system art performs the function of transforming the raw material of dry ideology into the fuel of images and myths intended for general consumption' (1990, xii), a statement which holds for all the twentieth-century totalitarian regimes that he examines (Germany, Italy, Russia and China). However, significant differences existed between these regimes' approaches to national art, and Italian Fascism certainly stood somewhat apart in this landscape, as Golomstock acknowledges, for, while he takes 'total realism' as the sole truly defining art form sponsored by totalitarian regimes, he recognizes that in Italy 'the process of its formation stretched out over two decades and was never fully completed; it was not until 1938 that Fascist culture ever came close to total realism' (1990, xiv).

In point of fact, Fascism's attitude towards the arts was never one of repression, imposition or the election of one single 'official' style, but rather one of inclusion, diversity and even the encouragement of antagonistic aesthetic styles, as several scholars have argued (e.g. Malvano 1988a; Fagone 1982, 44; Schnapp 1993; Stone 1998; Adamson 2001; Cioli 2011). In general, the regime took pride in supporting 'good' art, with the aim of educating the masses and helping forge them into a new civilization, and also of promoting the achievements of Italy's 'national genius' (Bottai 1992, 76; Bottai 1943, 16, 85). Critics have used various terms to describe this distinctive approach to cultural politics, from Marla Stone's 'hegemonic pluralism' (1997, 207), to Roger Griffin's 'totalitarian pluralism' (1998, 20), and Affron and Antliff's simple statement that it was 'heterogeneous in nature' (1997, 17). This chapter will explore the notion of *arte di stato*/State art, the type of relationship established under the regime between the arts and politics, and the system of the arts that was put in place by it, in order to demonstrate the relevance of State art to the existence and legitimation of the dictatorship. The Fascist 'system' of the arts is to be conceived as a network of interconnected parts and positions, not existing independently, but rather in constant interdependence both between each other and with the regime. These positions were determined by a social functionality attributed to the arts, linked to a moral obligation to 'build' a Fascist culture (see Billiani 2018, 382).

Fascist art, or art supported and advocated by the regime, occupied an intermediate position between autonomy and heteronomy. While not totally independent of the regime, the autonomy of artistic creation would be at least partly preserved during the dictatorship, in accordance with the dominant Crocean tradition, which prioritized artistic autonomy (Ben-Ghiat 2001, 23–24), and also with Italy's unique artistic tradition, which was exceptionally rich, prestigious and deep-rooted. In the view of the most prominent Fascist intellectuals and officials in the field of culture, such as Bottai,[2] and indeed Mussolini himself, if art were to be made subordinate to politics, on a German or Soviet model, it would become mere propaganda. This would not only deprive art of its very nature (see Malvano 1988b, 56–57), but also render it ineffective for the purposes of the regime, because in order to be 'effective', convincing, and

2 The Regime and the Creation of an 'Arte di Stato' 17

therefore instructive, art had first to be of high quality and aesthetic value (see Bottai 1992, 146; Ben-Ghiat 2001, 23). While the complete autonomy of art and artists was out of the question, included as they were in a totalitarian project in which everything was subordinated to the superior interests of the State, belief was nevertheless widespread that the need for the arts to maintain a certain degree of autonomy coincided with the interests of the State. At the end of a topical survey on Fascist art carried out in the journal *Critica fascista* between 1926 and 1927 (discussed below), Bottai inveighed against mediocre and grotesque propaganda artworks filling 'the headquarters of *fasci*, trade unions, and many town halls', 'bringing great disgrace to our artistic civilization' (Bottai 1927, reprinted in Bottai 1992, 74).[3] The attacks by less progressive and more extremist members of the Fascist party, like Roberto Farinacci and Telesio Interlandi, against modern art and against such a 'permissive' artistic policy were for the most part rejected, or not taken seriously. Their attempts at introducing conservative aesthetic models and repressive measures, following the German example, were generally considered unsophisticated and inappropriate by authorities in the field, and were never very successful (Fagone 1982, 50–51; Stone 1998, 179–90).

The regime's intervention in the field of culture was more directed towards the control and management of the networks and institutions that enabled artists to perform their activity than the indication of a specific style or aesthetics to follow—a major undertaking that art historian Sileno Salvagnini has defined as 'the colossal Fascist project of integrating Italian art into the apparatus of the state' (Salvagnini 1988, 7; see also Masi 1992, 22; Cioli 2011, 209–13; Salvagnini 2000). The regime sought to exercise control over the means, contexts and 'occasions' involved in the production and enjoyment of art, first and foremost through a coordinated system of exhibitions, ranging from the 'mostre sindacali', on a local level, to major events like the Biennials, Triennials and Quadrennials (Maraini 1934, reprinted in Cazzato 2001, 43–46; Salvagnini 2000, 13–45; Cioli 2011, 209–311; Fagone 1982, 47–49). This attempt at management and control also included various forms of direct financial support for artists (besides that provided through exhibitions), such as grants and prizes, like those awarded by the Accademia d'Italia (Ben-Ghiat 2001, 24; Masi 1992; on prizes, see Salvagnini 2000, 87–126).

This system of material aid also sought to win the support of intellectuals and artists and lead them to engage with the regime, in an effort to build a solid consensus among the intellectual classes, seen as instrumental to the legitimation of Fascism and to the consolidation of its power. As late as 1939, well into the more authoritarian (or totalitarian) phase of the regime, Bottai—the main driving force behind Fascist cultural policy— reiterated an idea which he had consistently put forward since the 1926–1927 debate on *Critica fascista*:

> The State neither formulates aesthetics nor accepts any given aesthetics. The State simply acts so that artistic work is serious, concrete, and productive; and wants artists' conditions to be such as to grant them the necessary ease of work. (Bottai 1939, quoted in Bottai 1992, 37)[4]

Art critic and historian Vittorio Fagone, one of the curators of the 1982 exhibition *Annitrenta, arte e cultura in Italia*[5]—which first challenged the widespread post-Fascist consensus that the Fascist regime had produced no culture worthy of the name—has defined the culture of Fascism as a 'pragmatic culture', reprising an expression used by Karl Mannheim (Fagone 1982, 44). This more practical and less normative approach undoubtedly enabled Fascism to carve out a much more extensive and rooted presence for itself in a country with a prominent artistic tradition like Italy, than would have probably been the case had it adopted a normative and repressive approach. Whether or not the Fascists succeeded in reforming the artistic system in Italy and gaining control of Italian artistic culture,[6] they certainly managed to enrol many artists and intellectuals in the cultural 'mission' of the dictatorship (Stone 1998, 65; Cioli 2011, 209–13; Salvagnini 2000, 330–54; see also Isnenghi 1979), thanks largely to this 'tolerant' approach to the arts, which allowed the regime to include and absorb within itself very different artistic forms and movements (Fagone 2001, 11–12). Indeed, a key objective of these movements would increasingly be to prove that they, and not others, were the main representatives and interpreters of the values of the Fascist revolution and of Fascist modernity.

Defining Fascist Art

In 1926, Mussolini made two key speeches on the question of art and its relationship with Fascism: on 15 February, at the opening of the first exhibition of the Novecento group, in Milan; and on 5 October, at Perugia's Accademia di belle arti (Mussolini 1934, 279–82, and 427). In the former, Mussolini stated that Fascist art would not need to figuratively depict Fascist 'subjects' or scenes, but rather embody Fascist values, a theme revisited frequently in later debates, as will be shown in this book. He argued that the 'marks' of recent events, like the war and especially the advent of Fascism, were not immediately visible in the vast majority of the works, insofar as these were not direct representations of historical-political events (and were therefore not works of explicit propaganda); but the 'mark' was nevertheless present in the values and moral qualities embodied in the artworks' aesthetic characteristics. Specifically, the new art showcased at the exhibition distinguished itself from that of the previous period, and was therefore innovative; it was the result of strict inner discipline and deep, even painful, effort, rather than easy craftsmanship; it was 'strong', like Italy after two wars. Mussolini identified certain common aesthetic features: sharp, clear lines; rich, vivid colours; and the 'solid sculptural quality of things and figures', which all point to an effort towards construction and rationalization that would be the hallmark of processes of artistic modernization in the Fascist period, in particular, as our analysis here will show, those relating to architecture and the novel. Yet, while these features unquestionably defined the Novecento style, they were also intentionally left rather loose and generic. More than anything else, they seem to point to the anti-impressionistic and anti-subjective turn that would, in broad terms, characterize Italian interwar art. The qualities of an artwork belonging to the Fascist era were thus to be found more in its 'morality' and the values it embodied, than in its subject matter or in any clearly defined aesthetic style. These artworks 'did not celebrate the regime *tout court*, but the very essence of the regime: Italy's genius, tradition, and modernity' (Cioli 2011, 48). The importance of the notion of 'morality' to the development of Fascism and its value system would be unequivocally stated by Mussolini in his first cogent attempt at defining an ideological framework for Fascism, *The Doctrine of Fascism*, published in the *Enciclopedia Italiana* of 1932. There, he claimed that 'whilst the fascist state did not have its own theology, it did have its own morality' (Gentile 1990, 229). Accordingly, the moral aspect of art was a key question around which the debate on Fascist art revolved, as we will be arguing in this book.

At Perugia's Accademia delle belle arti, Mussolini unequivocally affirmed the crucial role and importance that Fascism ascribed to the arts, although in his usual rhetorical and formulaic terms. He claimed that 'art marks the dawn of any civilization' and stated the need to create 'the new art of our times, Fascist art'. He defined this simply as 'great art, which can be traditionalist and modern at the same time', giving a foretaste of the ambiguity and 'inclusiveness' that would mark Fascist artistic policy over the course of the regime. This speech gave rise to an open debate published in the pages of the journal *Critica fascista* that can be taken as a pivotal moment in the definition and development of Fascist cultural policies, and in the strengthening of the relationship of interdependence between the regime and intellectuals, which Fascism had sought to achieve since its inception (Schnapp and Spackman 1990, 236). *Critica fascista* was a periodical founded by Giuseppe Bottai in 1923 as a forum for intellectual and artistic discussion.[7] According to historian Albertina Vittoria, Bottai and his collaborators were those most aware among Fascist officials of the need for a 'nexus between culture and cultural policy', and *Critica fascista* incorporated the question of culture into the broader project of construction of the State and the formation of the ruling class (Vittoria 1980, 327–28). In October 1926, Bottai launched a survey on Fascist art, asking artists and intellectuals to express their opinions on what Fascist art should be. The debate drew wide participation from artists and intellectuals, including Ardengo Soffici, Mino Maccari, Gino Severini, Massimo Bontempelli, Cipriano Efisio Oppo, Curzio Malaparte, Filippo Tommaso Marinetti, Anton Giulio Bragaglia, Umberto Fracchia and Emilio Cecchi. Their contributions were published in the journal between 1926 and 1927.[8]

Echoing Mussolini's speeches, most contributors seemed to agree that Fascist art had to be engaged and socially meaningful, but without being propagandistic or explicitly political; it had to be unmistakably Italian

2 The Regime and the Creation of an 'Arte di Stato' 21

and connected to the prestigious Italian tradition, yet modern, and not a mere imitation of the past; and it had to be 'national', 'of the people', placing the artist in a new relationship with the collectivity. Alessandro Pavolini, who had been a Fascist activist since the very beginning, and was at that time collaborating with several Fascist journals, called for a *rapprochement* between artists and the people (Pavolini 1926). Maccari, artist and director of *Il Selvaggio*, and writer-journalist Malaparte rejected the idea of Fascist art as an aesthetic school or tendency, declaring that it should instead be the interpreter of a specifically Italian modernity (Maccari 1926; Malaparte 1926). Writer and intellectual Bontempelli reprised the principles of his Novecento movement (see Chap. 5), and stated the need for an anti-subjective art concerned with 'building things' ('costruire cose'), telling stories and creating new myths and tales (Bontempelli 1926a). Bragaglia, the director of the Roman Teatro Sperimentale degli Indipendenti, maintained that the profile and reputation of a dictatorship are built through the arts, more than through an 'exemplary administration' ('una amministrazione esemplare') (Bragaglia 1926, 417). For him—and his particular focus was on theatre and cinema—Fascist art should be, first and foremost, modern, innovative and revolutionary. The architect Alberto Jacopini, focusing on architecture, described Fascist art as being marked by 'frankness, clarity, simplicity, order, and truth' ('schiettezza, chiarezza, semplicità, ordine, verità') (Jacopini 1926, 455); in short, by morality and rationalized aesthetic means. It is worth pointing out that nobody tried to define Fascist art in terms of style and subject, nor provide 'aesthetic guidelines' (apart, perhaps, from Marinetti, who of course advocated Futurist art, but without really discussing aesthetics). Fascist art could only be defined negatively, by what it should not be: not Romantic (Pavolini); not academic, and against any style taking inspiration from past traditions, like neoclassicism (Bragaglia); not decadent (Fracchia); not cosmopolitan and not 'French' (Malaparte).

Bottai continued to pursue this line in his final article 'Resultanze dell'inchiesta sull'arte fascista', in which he attempted to draw some conclusions (Bottai 1927, reprinted in 1992, 71–79). Significantly, the first section was entitled 'How Fascist art must not be' ('Come non deve essere l'arte fascista'): summing up the majority view, Bottai concluded that it should not be 'fragmentary, syncopated, psychoanalytical, intimist, or crepuscular' ('frammentaria, sincopata, psicoanalitica, intimista, crepuscolare') (Bottai 1992, 72). He drew a parallel with architecture to describe the only real tendency he could see in Fascist art thus far, alluding to the notion of art as reconstruction—a notion which forms the basis of our argument in this book—visible in the tendency towards 'more solid, more full, more powerful constructions', generated in turn by the same tendency at work in the political field, and in line with the native Italian tradition (ibid.). He thus established a direct connection between aesthetics and politics, both of which were driven by an urge for reconstruction. As Roger Griffin has demonstrated in his study on 'generic Fascism', palingenetic myths were foundational to Fascist ideology: 'fascists believe the destruction unleashed by their movement to be the essential precondition to reconstruction' (Griffin 1993, 47).

Bottai did, however, express disappointment that most contributions had not gone beyond vague and generic discussions, and had not considered whether manifestations of Fascist art already existed, and what the regime could do to encourage them; in other words, the practical aspects of establishing an artistic system under Fascism, which he deemed crucial. He stated the need for artists to be integrated into society, unlike in the liberal state. Artists 'need[ed] the State', firstly in terms of economic support, which according to Bottai, they would receive through the system of trade unions,[9] and secondly, and most importantly, in terms of 'artistic, moral, and spiritual assistance' (Bottai 1992, 75). He alluded to a process of evaluation and selection of artists and artworks, which would take into account their value as artists and intellectuals of Fascism, based not only on aesthetic but also on ethical criteria. This task would be entrusted to the Accademia d'Italia—founded in January of that year, but only inaugurated in November 1929—which despite its name would be an anti-academic institution, dynamic and creative. Its duty would be that of

> encouraging any form of intellectual and artistic expression and manifestation, which [...] reflects the historical and immutable nature of the Italian genius, and is able to recreate this genius into a style that is its own, and is unmistakable from that of any other people. (Ibid., 76)[10]

Who would be the judges in this *Accademia*—a task that, even in the view of its promoter Bottai, would be 'extremely hard'? (ibid., 75). Again, Bottai's indications were quite indeterminate: 'The academics will be chosen among the lively, distinguished Italian Fascist personalities of the Nation' (Ibid., 78).[11]

This crucial debate in *Critica fascista* can be taken as emblematic of the ambivalence and contradictions that the regime fuelled and never resolved in its cultural politics, as highlighted by Schnapp and Spackman (1990, 237). The debate, and the contributions of artists and intellectuals, revolved around certain key words and themes like 'Italianness', 'national', 'revolutionary', 'classical', 'tradition', and 'modernity'. Not only were some of these words antithetical, but they were also versatile terms, which could be interpreted in different ways. Their vagueness was exploited to maintain a certain level of ambiguity while formulating the pompous and highly rhetorical statements typical of Fascism, as some of the excerpts previously quoted demonstrate. The idea of 'Italianness', for instance, was a highly rhetorical concept, and one that each artist or movement could claim for themselves, bending it towards modernity or tradition, according to their aesthetic beliefs. This ambiguity was not exclusive to Fascist discourse on the arts and culture. Fascism's versatile cultural politics were rooted in the regime's ambivalent attitude towards the key notions of tradition and modernity, which generated a simultaneously anti-modern and modernizing rhetoric. Fascist ideology consisted of a powerful, but sometimes contradictory, combination of revolutionary and reactionary values. An emphasis on the idea of revolution and the palingenetic myth of the construction of a new world and a new civilization coexisted with the idea of a 'return to order', a cult of Romanness, and various anti-modern myths, found for instance in the regime's ruralist, anti-urban propaganda, and its conservative views of family, gender relations, morals and social life in general (Griffin 1993, 47; Gentile 2003, 59–62).

In the artistic field, where Fascist myths were supposed to be produced, this self-contradictory ideology generated the 'pluralist' aesthetic approach referred to above. More specifically, it translated into the regime's endorsement of diverse, and even antithetical, artistic movements, which fought for hegemony, that is to say, for the right to be proclaimed the regime's official 'State art' (Cioli 2011, 160). The most famous of these 'battles' opposed the dominant aesthetic movements Futurism and Novecento.[12] The connection between Fascism and Futurism was foundational, owing to the Futurists' role in the creation of the *Fasci di combattimento* (Gentile 1982, 152–158; 1988; 1996 [1975], 167–87; Cioli 2011, 21–24). For this reason and for the many ideological elements they shared with Fascism[13]—at least its early, revolutionary version, the so-called *fascismo diciannovista*—the Futurists expected to be automatically elected as the exclusive artists of the 'revolution'.[14] For them, 'it was not Futurism which should be labelled Fascist, but the exact opposite, because it was Fascism that had originated from Futurism' (Cioli 2011, 171). However, the regime never elected one movement, or style, as official Fascist art, and intermittently supported both Novecento and Futurism.[15] Futurism embodied the revolutionary side of Fascism, its leaning towards modernity, while Novecento—whose 'creator', Margherita Sarfatti, defined *Novecentisti* as 'the revolutionaries of the modern restoration' ('i rivoluzionari della moderna restaurazione') (Sarfatti 1925, 127)—represented its conservative and populist side, expressed in the return to order and to the Italian tradition, and in a legible figurative language. A similar battle for hegemony happened in the field of architecture, chiefly between the proponents of rationalism and monumentalism (see Chap. 4). Fascism's ambition, expressed in its eclectic cultural politics, was to absorb these conflicts within itself, without seeking a resolution, in an attempt to reach 'concord',[16] a national style which would encompass these different factions, so that all good Italian art would be Fascist art.

The Role of Artists and the Arts in the Public Sphere

The debate in *Critica fascista* highlighted the belief of many artists and intellectuals that art was the most important, effective and noble instrument for the education of the masses, for bringing about spiritual renewal and a change in mentality. We find this idea expressed very clearly, for instance, in Maccari's article:

2 The Regime and the Creation of an 'Arte di Stato'

It cannot be denied that art is the most delicate and formidable political instrument for the development of a people. It is certainly the purest spring from which the sentiments of national pride, of sacrifice for the motherland, of love for the traditions of race, boldness, and civic consciousness flow down to the nation. [...] Any excellence in any field of intellectual activity is art. (Maccari 1926, 397)[17]

This was very much the role that Fascists ascribed to, and expected from, intellectuals and artists. At the same time, 'excellence in any field of intellectual activity' would bring prestige to the regime, and be the 'final nail in the coffin' of the democratic era ('l'ultimo colpo d'ascia da vibrare all'età democratica') (Aniante 1927). These, then, were the principles that inspired the regime's extremely keen interest in the arts and guided the steps of the Fascist 'azione per l'arte'.[18] The ultimate goal of the regime was the modernization of the Italian nation, not only in political and social terms, but also morally and culturally. Mussolini envisaged a process of national regeneration in which political revolution and social modernization were to be accompanied by a 'revolution of the mind', which would, in Emilio Gentile's words, 'form the sensibility, the character, the consciousness of a new Italian, who would comprehend and confront the challenges of modern life' (Gentile 2003, 46). This cultural and moral revolution would be brought about through the creation of myths for the new modern civilization, a 'palingenetic mythology' of Fascism that would undermine 'the modernity of enlightenment reason' as another undesirable element of bourgeois society, favouring a different model of modernity grounded in 'activism, instinct and irrationalism' (Braun 2000, 6).

Artists and intellectuals were enrolled in this mission and given the critical role of 'demiurges' and educators for the regime. They were entrusted with the central palingenetic process of the creation of myths for the new Fascist era and the constitution of the regime's symbolic space. The case of Mario Sironi and his aesthetic-visual mythology grounded in the themes of the nation, work and the family, and stylistically, from the 1930s onwards, in mural painting, provides the archetypal example, extensively examined by Emily Braun in her seminal work (Braun 2000; see also Griffin and Feldman 2004, 129–30). Therefore, as

Gentile aptly pointed out, Fascism cannot only be understood in terms of the 'aestheticization of politics', as famously theorized by Walter Benjamin (1939, reprinted in 2003, 251–83), but also in terms of the specular process of the 'politicization of aesthetics' (Gentile 2003, 43), and of culture. The regime, with the expectations it placed on producers of art and culture, changed both their role and their relationship not only with power, but also with society. Artists and intellectuals renounced the complete autonomy and separation from society and power that had been their goal since the Romantic age, and became absorbed in the totalitarian mission of the regime, playing an active and central role in it (Iannaccone 1999, 37–38; see also Isnenghi 1979).

Art was no longer valued as the privileged means of expression of the artist's subjectivity, instead becoming the highest embodiment of the thrust and the spirit of the collectivity. Artists and intellectuals were thus expected to leave their ivory towers and engage with the people, the masses, whom they were supposed to guide and educate. In so doing, they would become instruments for the mass legitimation of the regime, but in return, they would receive the material and symbolic rewards (financial support and enhanced social status), which they craved. The following, for instance, is an excerpt from an article written in 1932 by eminent artist Carlo Carrà, praising the regime's actions in support of artists:

> To artistic problems, Fascism gave more than mere platonic support. It gave hundreds and hundreds of thousands of Lire; it reorganized the International Art Exhibitions in Venice; it ensured the Milan Triennials of Decorative and Industrial Arts could continue; it established the Rome Quadrennials. It placed representatives from the ranks of artists, architects, painters, musicians, and writers in the Chamber of Deputies and the National Council of Corporations. In short, it gave Italian artists something that no liberal democratic government had ever given them: that positive recognition and moral vigour that are the foundational elements of dignity and human decorum. (Carrà 1932, cited in Cioli 2011, 209)[19]

The debate in *Critica fascista*, as well as the other sources and debates analysed in this book, including this quote by Carrà, prove that most artists and intellectuals were willing and happy to take on this social, even 'messianic' role. This epochal shift in the role of artists and intellectuals did not end with Fascism, but on the contrary continued to shape postwar Italian culture, despite the social and political change brought about by the Second World War (Iannaccone 1999, 11–30). Our particular focus in this book, however, will be to show how architecture and the novel, in their synergy and intersections both with each other and with the political sphere, are the artistic forms which best exemplify this collectivist, constructive and rationalizing aesthetic effort.

Notes

1. The expression '*art d'Etat*' exists in French (see, for instance, the recent exhibition at the *archives nationales*: 'Un art d'Etat?' http://www.archives-nationales.culture.gouv.fr/un-art-d-etat).
2. Giuseppe Bottai held several important positions within the regime, and was one of the key figures engaged in the conception and construction of Fascist art and culture. The most important posts he held were Minister of corporations, governor of Rome and of Addis Ababa, and Minister of national education (for further detail, see Mangoni 1974 and De Grand 1978).
3. 'Decorazioni pittoriche incredibili sulle mura, busti orribili di gesso colorato ad ogni cantone, emblemi e stendardi a colori pugno negli occhi per arazzi, fasci littori di stucco dorato che sembrano fastelli di legna da ardere, cromolitografie del Duce in atteggiamenti impossibili […] ecco le sedi dei Fasci, dei sindacati e di molti comuni. […] con gravissimo disdoro della nostra civiltà artistica'.
4. 'Lo Stato non fa dell'estetica e non accetta alcuna estetica determinata. Lo Stato si preoccupa, soltanto, di far sì che l'operare artistico sia serio, concreto, produttivo; e vuole che le condizioni di vita degli artisti siano tali da consentire loro l'indispensabile serenità di lavoro […]'.
5. See the voluminous catalogue of the same title. The exhibition received praise for commencing a re-evaluation of artistic production during the Fascist regime, free from the ideological bias that had previously prevented an objective assessment (see e.g. Lucie-Smith 1985). However, it was also criticized for providing a limited and misleading representation of the 1930s in Italy that excluded political, social and economic problems, while claiming to give a comprehensive account (Rochat 1982).

6. On the failure of the system of artistic trade unions, see, for instance, Cioli (2011, 224–27).
7. On the journal *Critica fascista*, see Vittoria (1980, 327–34), Malgeri (1980), and Sechi (1980).
8. Several scholars have discussed this crucial episode in the history of Fascism and the arts. See, e.g. Schnapp and Spackman (1990), Salvagnini (2000, 346–48), Cioli (2011, 54–56), and Ben-Ghiat (2001, 25–26). Some of the most relevant contributions have been reprinted and translated into English in Schnapp (2000, 207–41).
9. On artists' trade unions, see Salvagnini (2000, 13–25) and Cioli (2011, 213–27).
10. '[…] Incoraggiare ogni forma di espressione e di manifestazione intellettuale ed. artistica, giudicate dall'Accademia perfettamente rispondenti al carattere storico ed. immutabile della genialità italiana, capaci di riportare e di confermare questa genialità nello stile che le è proprio ed. è inconfondibile con quello di ogni altro popolo'.
11. '[…] gli accademici saranno scelti fra le personalità artistiche vive, egregie, italiane, fasciste della Nazione'.
12. This 'battle' was thoroughly reconstructed and analysed by Monica Cioli (2011).
13. According to historian Emilio Gentile, the cultural and ideological basis that Fascism and Futurism shared is located in 'modernist nationalism', a cultural orientation centred on the myth of the nation and an optimistic attitude towards modernity, which in social and political terms meant 'a crisis of traditional aristocracies, an epoch of new masses and the rise of new elites, the predominance of collectivities over individuals, renovation of the State, and political and economic expansion' (Gentile 2003, 46). See also Cioli (2011, in particular 117–54).
14. See in particular the article 'Futurismo e fascismo' by the Futurist artist Fillìa, who argued that 'only Futurists, a group of artists who were precursors and collaborators of the Fascist Revolution, have the right to speak of State Art' ('Soltanto I futuristi, come raggruppamento di uomini artisti preparatori e collaboratori della rivoluzione fascista, hanno diritto di parlare sull'Arte di Stato' (Fillìa 1929, reprinted in Patetta 1972, 258).
15. The relationship of Futurism with Fascism, and the question of whether Fascism supported or marginalized Futurism, has generated a heated debate among art historians and historians of Fascism. We subscribe to the balanced view of Cioli (2011, 169–75) and Salaris (1985, 190–91),

according to whom the Futurists were strong and loyal supporters of Fascism, at least of what they perceived as its dynamic and revolutionary part (Ibid., 172), and in turn, Fascism supported Futurism and considered it among the most important artistic movements of Fascist Italy. Equally, we endorse the claim that Novecento, despite being a dominant artistic movement of the period (especially in the 1920s and early 1930s), cannot be considered the official Fascist *arte di stato* (Fagone 2001, 17–18).

16. The 'courage of concord' was a famous expression used by Bottai, which gave the title to an important article on *Primato* (Bottai 1940a, reprinted in Bottai 1992, 229–31).

17. 'Né si può negare che l'arte sia forse sia forse il più delicato e poderoso strumento politico dell'espansione d'un popolo: è certo la fonte più pura, dalla quale scendono alla nazione i sentimenti dell'orgoglio nazionale, del sacrificio, per la patria, dell'amore verso le tradizioni della razza, della fierezza e della coscienza civiche. [...] Tutto quello che eccelle in ogni campo dell'attività intellettuale, è arte'.

18. This famous expression of Giuseppe Bottai can be found, most significantly, in an interview published on *Corriere della sera* on 24 January 1940 (Bottai 1940b, reprinted in 1992, 222–28), and as the title of a work written in 1940 by Marino Lazzari, the General Director of Antiquity and Fine Arts, and prefaced by Bottai himself (Lazzari 1940). See also Salvagnini (2015, 175) and Cioli (2011, 211).

19. 'Ai problemi artistici, il Fascismo ha dato qualcosa di più di un semplice appoggio platonico. Ha dato centinaia e centinaia di migliaia di lire; ha regolato le Esposizioni Internazionali d'arte di Venezia; ha dato modo di continuare le Triennali dell'arte decorativa e industriale di Milano; ha istituito le Quadriennali di Roma. Alla Camera dei Deputati e al Consiglio Nazionale delle Corporazioni ha messo i rappresentanti degli artisti, architetti, pittori, musicisti e letterati. In una parola, ha dato agli artisti italiani, quello che nessun governo demoliberale aveva mai dato: quel riconoscimento postivo e quel vigore morale che sono gli elementi base della dignità e del decoro umano'.

Open Access This chapter is licensed under the terms of the Creative Commons Attribution 4.0 International License (http://creativecommons.org/licenses/by/4.0/), which permits use, sharing, adaptation, distribution and reproduction in any medium or format, as long as you give appropriate credit to the original author(s) and the source, provide a link to the Creative Commons licence and indicate if changes were made.

The images or other third party material in this chapter are included in the chapter's Creative Commons licence, unless indicated otherwise in a credit line to the material. If material is not included in the chapter's Creative Commons licence and your intended use is not permitted by statutory regulation or exceeds the permitted use, you will need to obtain permission directly from the copyright holder.

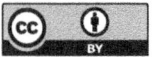

3

Constructing the Novel

> *Delvau believes he can recognize the social strata of Parisian society in flânerie as easily as a geologist recognizes geological strata.*
> —Benjamin (*Arcades*, [M9a, 1], 434)

As we have seen in Chap. 2, within the discourse on and debate over State art, two main lines of enquiry have emerged: the first concerned the protracted aesthetically oriented discussions surrounding the need for a rationalization of forms, often through the use of straight lines, simplified decorative patterns, and an adherence to the real; the second voiced the demands for a political reconfiguration of the role played by the arts within the social sphere, to be achieved by placing increased emphasis on the moral message they are expected to articulate when brought into a wider public discourse involving writers, publishers and intellectuals more generally. From different perspectives, we have so far discussed how, since the mid-1920s, the core problem—namely of creating a modern social, cultural and aesthetic system of the arts resting upon new totalitarian State apparatus and of rejecting the individualism upheld by the liberal State—became a prominent bone of contention throughout the entire system set up by the Fascist regime in Italy. However, such a broad issue needs to be broken down into several smaller questions addressing, respectively: the aesthetic process of the rationalization of narrative and architectural forms, the syntactical renewal of artistic expression, the emphasis on morality in the arts, and the use of the arts in the process of social modernization that the regime, as a self-professed ethical and omnipotent State, sought to engineer. These conceptual landmarks guided the debate on State art: in what follows, we will analyse them vis-à-vis the discursive patterns articulated in the novel.

Towards a Fascist Modernity

From 1926 onwards, prolonged discussions about a possible definition of Fascist modernity—or more precisely about what it meant to be 'modern' according to the doctrine and stance of the Fascist regime[1]—punctuated many debates in literary, cultural and political journals of various orientations, ranging from politically conservative journals to official Fascist organs, from those at the fringes of the political arena to seemingly neutral publications.[2] In sum, even though no conclusive definition was arrived at, it was recognized that to achieve this result, the arts would have to function as an integrated system, through what, in the twilight of the regime, Minister Giuseppe Bottai described in his preface to General Director for Antiquities and Fine Arts Marino Lazzari's book of the same name, as *L'azione per l'arte* ('action for art'), a concerted practical effort to save the national artistic system (Lazzari 1940, X–IX).[3]

It would be beyond the scope of this monograph to enter into a full-scale theoretical discussion about Fascist modernity, since this issue has been dissected by historians as well as by cultural historians.[4] The need to be modern, or more precisely to be perceived as not lagging behind compared to the great achievements of the other European nations, had dominated the Italian imagination for some time, and had increased in the 19th and 20th centuries as outlined by Emilio Gentile in his 1997 monograph, *La grande Italia*. Both Emilio Gentile and Jeffrey Herf, discussing the specificities of the Italian and German case respectively, have highlighted the heterogeneity of the phenomenology of the concept of modernity under totalitarian rule, where the notion became at once imbued with a desire for renovation—be it in aesthetic, cultural, political or social terms—but also with a deeply reactionary, irrationalist character in similarly aesthetic, social, cultural and political terms (Gentile 2003; Herf 1986).[5] In a similar vein, Roger Griffin in particular has put forward the idea of 'palingenetic' rebirth as foundational to the understanding of Fascist modernity, whereby he dissects the role played by mythologies and by the imaginary in its construction (2007, 73–74, 187). As an abstract concept, therefore, the 1930s' version of modernity, and of totalitarian modernity, encompassed a wide-ranging set of propositions, which included a drive towards experimentalism, often through technological progress and theoretical debate, and through a simplistic and grandiose—yet utopic—view of the future, which had to be in line not only with the regime's doctrine of the rejuvenation of the Italian nation, but also with Italy's illustrious past, as well as with the country's own reactionary and technocratic views.[6]

This conceptual, clashing plurality can also be very clearly seen in action throughout the debates and polemics centring on the configuration of State art and on the supremacy of one movement over all the others in the ensuing struggle for hegemony, as, for example, in the wars for intellectual hegemony between the Novecento and Futurist movements, both active across literature, architecture and the visual arts and both politically in close dialogue with Mussolini himself. Devoting specific attention to cultural movements, Mark Antliff has conducted a sustained analysis of modernity, modernism and modernization in relation to the arts and architecture. In his analysis, Fascism and modernism are not to be treated as separate categories but rather as propositions in constant dialogical flow, which can neither exist independently nor in opposition to each other (2002, 165). According to Walter Adamson (1993), in fact, the artistic origins of Fascist modernity are to be traced back to the pre-WWI Florentine avant-garde, since they articulate the very same contradictions and oppositions, which would define the cultural politics of the dictatorship over the whole arc of its existence. In a more recent article, Adamson returns to the cultural dynamics of the dictatorship in order to assess which of the movements and their actors (again: Margherita Sarfatti and Novecento[7]; Filippo Tommaso Marinetti and Futurism[8]; Mino Maccari and Strapaese) finally won in the competition for artistic hegemony. Adamson concludes that none of them did, all failing in different ways and to varying degrees (2001, 244–45). Jeffrey Schnapp has talked about 'eclecticism of spirit' as far as the regime's take on cultural production is concerned (see also Malvano 1988a). By formulating this definition, Schnapp highlights Mussolini's encouragement of the proliferation of expressions of cultural modernity to be used by the regime as it saw fit: every expression of modernity was legitimate if it was used appropriately and if it performed a useful function (1993, 91). We accept the critical assessment that plurality was a key feature of Fascist modernity, and our contention is that no artistic movement either succeeded or failed in gaining hegemony in the race to embody modernity, since they all need to be understood as a concerted system where every part functioned in relation to the others (Cioli 2011, 5–27, 45–56; see Chap. 2 on pluralism and on the definition of the system of the arts).

In addition to recognizing this artistic plurality, we must also briefly discuss a possible definition of modernity, a term which is central to explaining the intellectual context of the ideas under discussion. As far as the regime and its artistic theorization were concerned, modernity was a mixture of innovation and passéism: of new political statements and reactionary and dogmatic thinking paired with the ambition of modernizing the country socially and culturally.[9] Crucially, however, modernity was seen as a new social, cultural and political configuration, which would not only create an anti-bourgeois, anti-individualist Fascist Man,[10] but also produce a vision of a future controlled by anti-liberal politics. Emilio Gentile has often stressed the ways in which the anthropological revolution of Fascism has shaped and substantiated the New Man, a psychic and social subject at the same time (2009). The New Man was so in many respects: in terms of a renewed energy, vigour and pragmatism, for instance, but also with regard to the relationship between subjectivity and objectivity which such an individual had to embody, as an aesthetic political statement and as the expression of aesthetic policies (2009, 103). In short, with regard to the arts, modernity was a process driven by progressive statements coupled with experimental aesthetics and media technology, increasingly oriented towards the needs of a 'mass' society within the functioning mechanisms of a repressive political apparatus. In relation to the novel and architecture, however, modernization involved the structural transformation of the public spheres driven by social projects centring on a set of aesthetic principles associated with the very idea of modernity and championed by State patronage and the publishing industry.[11]

Modernity as theory and modernization as practice were synergic responses to a set of technological innovations geared to transforming the perception of the individual (publishing, cinema and radio being the most obvious examples), which the regime could use as a means of propaganda as well as a means of turning citizens into a collective being, directed by a super-State.[12] The relationship between those two fields—modernity and modernization—and likewise between the novel and architecture, is often based on 'heteronomous as well as autonomous' principles and statements, which allowed for pluralism[13] within practices, often going beyond the boundaries both of State art and art for art's sake.[14] Such aesthetic projects, catalysts as they were for the regime's aspirations towards modernity and social modernization, not only exerted strong pressure in the direction of the internationalization of Italian culture but also strengthened the national tradition both at elite and at popular levels by reinforcing politically the collective sense of individual experience, the anonymity of artists and their creations, and the need for a wholesale renewal of the Italian tradition (see Chap. 5).

The heterogeneous configuration of Italian politics regarding the arts under the regime has led scholars to speak of aesthetic 'pluralism', hoping through such a definition to account for (and vindicate) the relative tolerance of the regime towards aesthetic as well as aesthetic/political expressions which, though seemingly heterodox when compared to the official party line, were nevertheless accorded political credibility.[15] In this regard, the two great debates on State art examined in Chap. 2—the discussion of Fascist art which appeared between 1926 and 1927 in the pages of *Critica fascista*, and a similar survey published in *Primato* in 1940 before the 2% bill—show how modernity was, throughout this period, simultaneously a political and an artistic question. They highlighted right from the beginning the regime's awareness of the importance held by intellectual labour, youth culture, popular culture and the education of the masses for its very survival.[16] Intellectuals from across the political spectrum took part in these (Anton Giulio Bragaglia, Massimo

Bontempelli, Giuseppe Bottai, Mino Maccari, Curzio Malaparte, Umberto Fracchia, Alessandro Pavolini, Mario Puccini), a heterogeneous convergence which exemplifies the eclecticism typical of this decade and of the avant-gardes in the 1910s, prior to the imposition of stricter organizational control through State-sponsored exhibitions and acquisitions, public works and investment in urban regeneration which would define the second half of the 1930s (see Chap. 4 for more details, and Chap. 6 on youth culture). Although no definition of State art could be found, there was agreement on some crucial concepts: Fascist art had to be modern and totalizing, but also ethical/moral, so as to be an expression of the New Fascist Man. Art had to be State art because the State was an ethical and corporative[17] entity, and hence also a moral and a civil entity which created coercive spaces for the individual. This coercion had to contribute to the completion of the Fascist revolution, which was an 'intellectual and social' revolt.[18] The arts were crucial in defining the modes of existence of the totalitarian apparatus, especially when functioning as an orchestrated machine[19] and not simply as a propaganda tool.

The question of this ethical front recurs in the question of modernity, too: art has to speak for a new morality as its first duty, but it also needs to be 'technical' since 'its principal purpose would be this unity of the arts referred to time and again, which the bourgeois revolutions had shattered and which, the argument went, only architecture would be able to restore'.[20] Above all, however, this discussion of modernity coincided with an invitation to Italian artists to start a process of rationalization of current aesthetic practices, both in terms of formal structures and of thematic concerns, and to consider the moral aspect of artistic creations as foundational to their execution, while at the same time acknowledging the irrational side of creativity (see Chap. 6 for these debates and Chap. 7 for narrative examples).[21] Novelists in particular were expected to contribute to the creation of a Fascist model of modernity, by producing works championing the values of Fascism or a new morality and by constructing a narrative space which could accommodate 'reality' and a sense of collectivity in place of solipsism and self-referentiality, and which could adopt a prose style that embraced stylistic essentiality and a geometrical organization of plot structures.[22] This had to be sought in order for the novel to speak to wider, growing and assorted reading publics as required by a more modern publishing industry. Likewise, modern architecture had to share with the novel a similar technical desire for rationalized and functional forms, morality and commitment to social integration and a collective ethos, and so contribute theoretically and practically to the modernization of the public sphere.

From Fragmentation to Construction

The turn of the century saw the rise of the avant-gardes across Europe, with Italy at the vanguard of the Futurist movement in dismantling structures and grammar and fragmenting the novel.[23] Meanwhile, the book market was expanding in ever more varied directions, encouraging both popular culture and new writing, through the support of publishers such as the Edizioni della Voce, Carabba, Treves, and Sonzogno and the newly founded Mondadori (Tranfaglia and Vittoria 2000, 156–73). Overall, subjectivity was replacing straightforward nineteenth-century objectivity (e.g. realism), whether in heroic and sensationalist or more intimist, memorialistic and solipsistic works. Having said this, while this attitude was evident in popular fiction, Pericles Lewis has convincingly argued that the modernist novels of Conrad, D'Annunzio, Proust and Joyce materialized their consciousness of the crisis of political, ideological and economic systems, such as liberalism and nationalism, by giving space to a wider, factual, if not explicitly historical, dimension, which ultimately provided an external means of decoding internal logics (2000, 4, 11).

The end of WWI halted experimentation of the avant-gardes and closed down what had been hailed as a new literary beginning by the likes of the Florentine avant-gardes of *La Voce* and *Lacerba*, by Renato Serra's quasi-economic analysis of the book market in *Le lettere* (1913), and by the omnipresent, chameleon-like Futurists. Furthermore, with the Milanese publishers Treves and Sonzogno leading the way, the Italian publishing industry was essentially still in its infancy and there was no consolidated structure at a national level which could help rebuild the novel itself and allow it to reach a wider audience (Tranfaglia and Vittoria 2000, 191–224, see also Borgese 1923, 86–89).[24] If the 1920s saw the ferment of the Weimar republic in Germany and the rise of New

Objectivity, in Italy the situation was rather different, dominated as it was by various manifestations of the 'return to order', such as De Chirico's metaphysical painting, the Novecento movement in architecture and the visual arts, and *prosa d'arte* and *elzevirismo* in literary writing hailed from the pages of the Florentine literary reviews, *La Ronda* (1919–1923), and later *Solaria* (1926–1936) and *Letteratura* (1937–1947) (Billiani 2013, 849–54). This pervasive and interdisciplinary 'return to order', then, was a return to classically composed forms which did not necessarily map directly onto the novel—if the latter is understood as a form of storytelling or a form that constructs a plot and a story for the reader.

A notable exception to this trend was Giuseppe Antonio Borgese's novel *Rubè*,[25] insofar as it problematized the relationship between subjectivity and politics, between freedom and ideological choice during the tumultuous years of the *biennio rosso* (red biennium) of 1918–1920. The novel was first published in 1921 by Treves and then reissued by Mondadori in 1928, the year before the publication of Moravia's *Gli indifferenti*[26] by Alpes in Rome (see Chap. 7). During the 1920s, the status of Italian literature had become particularly problematic owing to the sharp separation between a popular literature (supposedly educational, but more often simply propagandistic) and a literature for the elites.[27] In 1930, Luigi de Crecchio Parladore makes this point explicitly in *Il Saggiatore*: Julien and Filippo are both marginal characters because they fail to engage with reality constructively. Sorel is a man of action, while Filippo Rubè cannot act and produce social transformation (1930, 'Giuliano Sorel e Filippo Rubè' *Gli Esclusi*, 1 (1–2): 32–41). *Rubè* sits on the threshold between the old liberal regime and the new Fascist order. It is a novel about a man, Filippo Rubè, split between two worlds and between action and passivity. It is a realist novel with a strong historical drive, which spans WWI and the Red Biennium. At the beginning of his life, just like in Gadda's *Il castello di Udine*,[28] Filippo Rubè is an enthusiastic supporter/advocate of WWI: he sees it as a way of changing the status quo for the better. But he very quickly becomes disillusioned, and after the end of the war, like many men across the country, he struggles to find a place in the new social fabric of the country. His relationship with the socialist movement is equally accidental and lacks any real engagement and commitment. The novel draws a clear connection between economic precarity and social frustration, presenting these conditions as a prelude to the dictatorship. In this respect, *Rubè* is a social novel centred around a very particular individual, an indecisive character who fluctuates between existential ineptitude and social opportunism. Told in four parts and twenty-four chapters, *Rubè* represented the need for a new Italian novel with a 'constructive' dimension, which rejected the 'frammentismo' of artistic prose. Moreover, it called for a reassessment of the failure of a generation and the need for social and, crucially, political change. It should be also read in relation to the collection of short essays entitled *Tempo di edificare* published by Borgese two years later, in 1923. *Rubè* is therefore another novel which marks the need for modernity and modernization, understood as a transformation of the social sphere. Such a shift is necessary to accommodate the needs and aspirations of Filippo, the average man (l'uomo medio) who has intellectual aspirations, but lacks a clear ideological drive. This is a social and political situation which in 1921 was yet to be clearly defined but which will come to an end by the mid-1920s with the regime's consolidation into power after the murder of socialist politician Giacomo Matteotti on 10 June 1924.[29]

In 1923, Lorenzo Viani published *Gli ubriachi*, a novel about the living conditions of the lower classes, while Federigo Tozzi published *Con gli occhi chiusi* (1919), *Tre croci* (1920) and *Il podere* (1921), a trilogy of modernist texts set in the Tuscan countryside. In 1923, Umberto Fracchia, editor of the leading *La fiera letteraria*, released *Angela*, another example of realist narration with a strong, subjective focal point embodied in the viewpoint of the main character (a young woman who has to become a prostitute to protect the son she had with an older and powerful man) from which to dig down into the unforgiving existence lived by the other characters (Zìmolo, Pietro and Emilio), who have no choice but to face a cruel destiny. Fracchia's novel is an interesting example of early 1920s' realism, because it combines a psychological exploration of the humble lives of the individual characters with choral, interweaving narratives that in style are between nineteenth-century feuilleton, late Decadentism and an early return to realism. Every character, from the old Zìmolo to the young Angela or Emilio, follows a typical trajectory of coming of age and at some point acts as an independent self. However, because of their strong links to their historical moment and social milieu, they can only be understood in their complexity if we take the whole story as a closely knit system. Fracchia adopts a lucid prose, which is very precise and devoid of excess, to picture both the characters' interiority and the ways in which reality acts upon them. There is no redemption or happy ending for anyone and the lyricism and naiveté of the beginning become bitter disillusionment. *Angela* is, however, an important example of the coexistence of intimism and realism against the backdrop of a carefully constructed and chronologically consistent plot.

In the same year though, Italo Svevo completed his modernist, experimental masterpiece, *La coscienza di Zeno*, and Bruno Cicognani finished his bestselling naturalist novel *La Velia*, thereby showing the variety of narrative performances and styles of the 1920s which were yet to be formalized under the rubric of either the 'Italian, national novel' or the 'return to realism of the 1930s'.[30]

The year 1929 saw the *cause célèbre*[31] of *Gli indifferenti* and the beginning of a distinctively anti-bourgeois movement in literature, while the *rondista* Vincenzo Cardarelli won the Premio Bagutta with his far more conventional *Il sole a picco* (see Chap. 7). In Moravia's scandalous novel,[32] the Ardengo family embodied a social problem, a microcosm of collective middle-class indifference, while Leo Merumeci represented a loutish yet successful Fascism. Above all, however, we have a solid diegesis—the Aristotelian unity of time, place and action—as well as a linguistic precision, almost surgical in its eschewal of manneristic psychologism. The failure of Carla and Michele can be seen as a result of their inability to escape from themselves and assume full responsibility in their enlarged social sphere (see Chap. 7 for a detailed analysis).

As this selection of significant, yet diverse, examples suggests, just as was the case in the publishing industry, which lacked a centre and a clear direction, the literary field in the first half of the 1920s was equally divided up between the few remaining *elziviristi*, for example, Emilio Cecchi (*Pesci rossi*, 1920), *La Ronda*, the modernist, europeanist, francophile intimism[33] of *Solaria*, the developing naturalist tradition of sensationalist novels and the ever-ebullient pseudo-Futurist underground milieu of the Rome-based avant-gardes of Anton Giulio Bragaglia et al. (Mondello 1990, 67–88).

3 Constructing the Novel   41

The 1930s were the decade of the industrial development of the publishing industry, led by Mondadori, and supported by a regime which needed a 'realist' novel to represent the Italian-Fascist tradition nationally and internationally (Tranfaglia and Vittoria 2000, 249–57). More generally, however, as observed by Paolo Buchignani, the attempt to rebuild the novel is evident not only in the celebrated *Gli indifferenti*, but also in Corrado Alvaro's *Gente in Aspromonte*[34] (1931) and in his dystopian novel *L'uomo è forte* (1938) (1987, 727).[35] The book was published in 1931 by the Florentine publisher Le Monnier. Set in the author's native Calabria, the narratives delve into the difficult realities of post-unification rural Southern Italian life. The collection's powerful exploration of the poverty, exploitation and injustice endemic to the Italian South renders it one of the finest examples of the return to realism of the 1930s. The eponymous opening story (and the longest, at just a little short of half the length of the whole book) sets the scene and tone of the whole collection. It recounts the desperate plight of the peasant Argirò and his family, left 'by history and reality' to a destiny of poverty and marginalization. Published just two years after Moravia's *Gli indifferenti*, Alvaro's novel also focused on the everyday reality of its protagonists, but in the radically different setting of one of the most deprived areas of the country. *Gente in Aspromonte* addressed another crucial issue for the regime: the question of regionalism, which split the art world into two camps (Sabatino 2010, 129–64). On the one hand, there was the ultra-nationalist Strapaese movement led by Mino Maccari, and on the other, the cosmopolitan Stracittà, pioneered by Massimo Bontempelli. From the early 1930s onwards, regionalism was also a bone of contention in architecture, with different schools of thought similarly divided into advocates of the national/regional tradition and those looking at the European scene (see Chap. 4).

As Sabatino observed, Giuseppe Pagano was one of the most ardent admirers of rural architecture (*architettura rurale*[36]). Pagano's understanding of *architettura rurale* 'as an antidote to classicizing monumentality was not encumbered by the appeal of *rusticity*, but instead fuelled his interest in the rational process underlining affordable housing[37] and the role that industrialization could play' (130). Just like *architettura rurale*, *Gente in Aspromonte* responded to the call for a novel which was in touch with reality, but also wanted to simplify the narrative structure and language of prose writing in line with Bontempelli's magical realism and that of *900* Alvaro was a regular contributor to. It was also characterized by a firm moral imperative, seeking to bear witness to the harshness of peasant life and to promote social change. The collection deals with the themes of emigration, illness, marginalization, sexuality, social ambition, resentment, resignation and social injustice. Alvaro observed the lives of peasants in the region of the Aspromonte in the documentary style typical of the 1930s, refusing any ornament in a text punctuated by essential dialogical exchanges (again, like Moravia). There is no oneiric evocation of the past in Alvaro's writing. Rather, the hope for a change is a *trait d'union* across the thirteen short stories. Contrary to previous *letteratura meriodionalistica*, Alvaro's text had an almost militant ambition coupled with an interest in the mythological dimension that the act of telling can impose on reality: by turning objects and people into universal symbols, his writing was an effort to record and raise awareness of the social condition of those obscured, not seen by history.

Such an ideological aspiration was in line with the idea of modernity as progress, able to change the social sphere, and therefore as part of a wider process of modernization and with the desire of preserving the specificity of the Italian tradition: this theoretical (if not always applied) position was not radically different from Pagano's *architettura rurale* or the aspiration of the Novecento rationalist moments in architecture.[38] The characters, from the Argirò family to the prostitute, the priest, the immigrant, la Signora Flavia, Teresina, are all individuals but, at the same time, are part of a collective history. The link between writing, social context and pedagogical/ethical mission was also a prominent theme in the youth culture related to the regime, especially in journals, such as *Il Saggiatore, Orpheus, L'Universale* and *Occidente* to which Alvaro contributed as discussed in Chap. 6. Finally, it is important to note that Alvaro's brand of realism was distinct from the experimentalism of the avant-gardes; to him the idea of writing as a social construct with a clear moral message was more relevant than any form of writing understood as an experiment in representation.

Having said this, we could argue that this return to the real is pervasive and equally evident in some post-avant-garde fringes, such as the Roman *immaginismo* of 'Bolsheviks' writer Umberto Barbaro[39] in *Luce fredda* (1931), or in Dino Terra's realist novels *Ioni* (1929) and *Metamorfosi* (1931), or even in Marcello Gallian's anarcho-fascist novel *Pugilatore di paese* published by Carabba with its impoverished setting and atmosphere, but which nonetheless won the 1932 Premio Mediterraneo and the collection of short stories *Comando di tappa* (Premio Viareggio, 1934).[40] A new brand of realism was also theorized by the architect, theatre choreographer and theorist of the *Manifesto dell'Immaginismo*[41] Vinicio Paladini, or in the works of painter Ivo Pannaggi and in the debates of the intellectual groups revolving around journals such as *Interplanetario*, *I lupi* or the overtly Fascist *Impero*, all championing their anti-bourgeois spirit and willingness to get closer to reality through experimental aesthetic practices.[42]

The year 1933 saw the first three instalments of *Garofano rosso*,[43] Elio Vittorini's censored *Bildungsroman*, published in *Solaria* (only appearing as a single volume in 1948), while *Tre operai* by Carlo Brenari, a full-scale call for realist narration, was published in 1934. Between 1933 and 1934, Carlo Emilio Gadda wrote *Il castello di Udine*,[44] again published by Solaria edizioni in 1934, which won the Premio Bagutta (1935), while Dino Buzzati completed *the Bàrnabo delle montagne*[45] for Treves. The *Castello* collects prose writings of various inspiration, but which are always experimental and expressionistic in nature. The book is dedicated to the former *rondista*[46] Riccardo Bacchelli. From this first publication, Gadda's propensity towards linguistic experimentation, which translates into a grotesque and sarcastic transformation of reality, is already clear. The work's language is such an experiment in distortion that the collection of stories opens with a glossary to help readers navigate the linguistic complexity displayed by the *Ingegnere*. It is entitled 'Sinossi delle abbreviazioni usate annotando' and it is signed by a certain Doctor Feo Averrois, who introduces himself as the translator of the whole work, thereby adding a meta-literary layer to expand the reach of Gadda's experimental writing. It is, therefore, a highly stratified book, which nonetheless rejects the idea of construction to propose a fragmentation of reality through an expressionistic use of languages, as well as also through a sarcastic view of the everyday reality and aspirations of the bourgeoisie (Barberi-Squarotti 1982, 4934; Guglielmi 1963). And, in this respect, it sits squarely within the expressionistic wave in the development of the twentieth-century Italian novel.

In 1934, the former Futurist Aldo Palazzeschi published *Le sorelle Materassi*,[47] an eloquent but crude exploration of the lives of three sisters and their emotional exploitation, thereby renouncing his previous surrealist, humorous writings. After his Futurist phase, Palazzeschi wrote a book that is again a satire but which is also a dissection of the precarious and miserable lives of those living in provincial Santa Maria a Coverciano near Florence. Three hard-working sisters, who have devoted all their lives to working as embroiderers, eventually find some joy in the arrival of a nephew, who, however, is only interested in exploiting them. Palazzeschi's realism could be placed between that of Verga in the nineteenth century and the intimism of early twentieth-century literature. Within 1930s realism, *Le sorelle Materassi* pointed towards the domesticity of the provinces not as a locus amoenus but rather as a suffocating space which prevents growth and personal development: Remo, the nephew, is narcissistically preoccupied with his physical health and beauty, which he uses to take advantage of everyone around him. Compared to the values of Strapaese upheld by Mino Maccari, the Tuscan provinces are a place of suffering—without redemption—and are therefore removed from the regime's ideals of ruralism and purity. Palazzeschi paints a realistic portrait of the individual subjectivities of the protagonists, which is transfigured comically to tone down the looming tragedy but, more importantly, to alleviate the feeling of a collectivity in crisis. Palazzeschi's characters are caricatures as we see in the three ladies and their attachment first to their work and then to their young and lively nephew. The nephew represents disempowered subjectivity, unproductive and unethical. In contrast to a nineteenth-century tragedy, the story does not end and remains suspended in a sort of modern 'waiting in vain' for Remo who will never materialize other than in his photograph (see Bo [1958] 1982, 5256–257). *Le sorelle Materassi* shapes collective identities that can relate neither to each other nor to the external reality in a meaningful way, while also describing the limitations of modernization as well as of ruralism. Palazzeschi's iconoclastic vein turns a seemingly realist novel into a moment of reflection on modernity and modernization and on their inevitable crisis.

Until the mid-1930s, narrative realism, like architecture, could construct and constitute itself within a new artistic morality as well as through a new compositional syntax, allowing degrees of variation in experimentalism, detail and topicality, while still focusing on the social aspect of writing. It is worth remembering that from 1929 to 1933, the literary field was split into two camps because of the famous battle between *calligrafisti* and *contenutisti*. The former group represented the establishment who wanted to preserve the idea of writing as an act driven by a stylistic mission, while the latter was calling for a prose in tune with the shapes of reality. Gramsci summarizes it very clearly when he dismisses Croce and the *calligrafisti* idea of the autonomy of the arts by stating that the aesthetic and literary question is a problem of 'the historicity and perpetuity' of the arts ('storicità e perpetuità) to ascertain whether the 'bare fact' ('fatto bruto') has been transformed and has evolved into a work of art. Gramsci is, of course, concerned with the 'purity and autonomy of aesthetic practices', but they can only be comprehended if understood as a result of an ongoing historical development (Gramsci 2014 [1933], Notebook 15 (II): p. 1777). As Massimo Bontempelli too stressed, realism could no longer be understood as a mimetic process, since it had to go hand in hand with the process of myth construction, of the deformation of reality, which was also, coincidentally, one of the requirements of the dictatorship as a religion geared towards the construction of a New Man and citizen and a new society ('Spazio e tempo.' January 1928, *L'avventura novecentista*, 27, see also Chap. 5).[48]

As Bontempelli, a member of the Italian Academy and co-editor with Pier Maria Bardi of the journal *Quadrante*, also suggested in a letter to Minister Giuseppe Bottai, the Italian novel needed to be rebuilt on three crucial premises:

Dear Bottai,
I am not quite sure whether you are aware or not that your conclusions about the so-called 'fascist art' are terribly twentieth-century, in the worst sense of this word.
I am keen to point out to you that my two prefaces and the theoretical excerpts in the 'caravana immobile' in the two issues, rather than being, as it is being reported to you by Malevilparts, the soft Soffici and the many Longanesi, have already outlined a series of ideas that are very detailed: they might be debated, of course, if there is anybody around, who might

be educated enough as well as in good faith; but they are rather fecund anyway, and as Italian as can be. Let me point them out:

1. My position again aestheticism (decadence of the classical spirit)
2. My position against psychologism (analysm, intimism, Freudianism and so on, decadence of the Romantic Spirit)
3. The Art of Writing when considered in the manner of architecture, and therefore as a modification of the inhabitable world. Hence with the aim of inventing myths and fables for our new times.

   Corollary:—antilyricism, antimetrics, antistyle
   More:—the condition of cinema in this regard has been assessed

4. The difference between imagination as we see it, and the old "fairy-tale", has been cleared
5. The "avant-garde" mode, which has been judged neurotic and soaked in 'literature' has been overcome. Setting in motion an art for the audience.
6. A clear primacy of Italy in the new civilization: a new Mediterranean revival.
7. Specific consequences (condition of the theatre: orientation of music, and so on...

[...]
Faithfully
Yours
Bontempelli[49]

This is a *sui generis* manifesto of an epoch, but Bontempelli also intended it to be a theoretical and conceptual blueprint going beyond the boundaries of the novel. In order to complete the programme of Fascist art and of Fascist State art,[50] some things needed to be discarded, such as aestheticism, characterized in terms of the static accumulation of objects, introspection—now seen as psychic stasis—and the rejection of bodily movement as action (and implicitly also that of Bottai's idea of culture as action). What needed to be supported instead was the image of artistic creation and of aesthetic experience as constructive phenomena. Although Bontempelli's letter to Bottai is not dated, we can compare it with writings of a similar nature published in *Avventura novecentista* around 1933–1934, during his collaboration with *Quadrante*. According to Bontempelli, the regime's aesthetic project entailed the construction of myths and fables. Therefore, Fascist art had to avoid any form of nineteenth-century psychologism or the cerebral, abstract avant-gardism of the early twentieth century, as both were incapable of engaging with the everyday contemporary reality of people's lives. Fascist art should not be individualist but rather directed towards the collectivity, in order to produce a full representation of Mediterranean civilization. Yet, what exactly was it that led Bontempelli to write to Bottai on themes connected with art and the novel and architecture, under the aegis of constructivism (a type of soviet constructivism *à la* Vinicio Palladini or a type of Immaginism *à la* Dino Terra, editor of *La ruota dentata*)?[51] How could such art be realized? It came about through a series of crucial stages, which involved writers, intellectuals, publishers and politicians.

In October 1932, in the first issue of the Rome-based journal *Occidente*, founded by Armando Ghelardini but affiliated to the Immaginists and the Casa Bragaglia in Rome, a short note appeared in the regular column on the publishing industry, 'Idee uomini opere attraverso la stampa internazionale':

> Book publishing has seen a very noticeable increase in output. The statistical data that I have to hand, taken from the *Bollettino delle Pubblicazioni Italiane* show that the classes of novels, music and the social sciences alone count for an increase of around a thousand units compared to previous years. The growth in the number of novels is significant. From 1920 to the present, the number of monthly publications has gone from 511 to over 1,500. [...] The total number of book titles printed in Italy has reached 11,949. The number of translations has risen to 1,135. The *Libro di Stato* experiment, which had made life very hard for publishers, can now be considered complete. (121)[52]

In this short piece, in a rather marginal journal, some key issues emerge regarding the profile of the novel and its relationship with regime's consensus-building programme. According to the anonymous reviewer, the novel is growing both in quantitative and in qualitative terms, together with music and social sciences publications.[53] From 1922 to

1943, the number of novels published annually ranged from 6336 in 1922 to 8162 in 1943. These figures excluded the *libri scolastici* (school textbooks), which ranged from 554 in 1922 to 381 in 1943. In 1932, we see book production peaking at 12,304 titles, a figure which remains stable until 1941, with 10,762 books published, only to decrease again during the war period. The same can be said for the *libri scolastici*, with an average of 1300 titles per year throughout the 1930s (Santoro 2008, 392–33). Novels maintained a steady share of around 20% of the book market from 1922 to 1933 (Santoro 2008, 395). In terms of its market share, then, the novel was not a significant phenomenon in itself.[54] It assumed a more stable position within the literary field if paired with the social sciences and with the two major singularities of the decade: translations and the *libro di Stato* (unique textbook for all Italian schools). The Italian novel has a value if compared with other types of books, such as the social sciences, which have an average of 35% of the book market. Or if we read these figures in more abstract terms, the novel has a 'symbolic' value if placed within the boundaries of the Fascist project of building a State art which comprised also other arts and types of books. Crucially, this project had to involve writers and publishers simultaneously.

In 1932, the now Rome-based *L'Italia letteraria* (formerly *La fiera letteraria* led by Umberto Fracchia) published an 'Inchiesta sul romanzo'. Directed from 1929 onwards by writers Giovanni Battista Angioletti and Curzio Malaparte, *L'Italia letteraria* was, de facto, the official regime-sanctioned national newspaper for the arts. Bruno Cicognani, author of the bestseller *La Velia*, contributed to this debate, reiterating how important it was to build a novel around a solid architecture, while lamenting the fact that many Italian men of letters were excessively individualistic (1932, 4, no. 4 (24 January): 1). The Imaginist Umberto Barbaro,[55] meanwhile, in his article on Dostoyevsky, stated that the loss of an ethical stance and increasing 'fragmentism' were traits shared by both a certain type of Italian literary production of the time and by Croce's idealism, while he called for a change of direction which could embrace a more constructive narrative mission (1932, 'Nuovi occhi per Dostoievschi.' *Il Saggiatore* 3, no. 3 (May): 98). In the same vein, the editor-in-chief Angioletti praised the inaugural award of the 1932 Bagutta Prize to Giovanni Titta Rosa for his *Il varco nel muro* because of his vivid portrayal of 'ordinary people' and of their real lives (1932, 'Il premio Bagutta a G. Titta Rosa.' 4, no. 5 (January): 1).[56]

The notion of the arts as a collective social enterprise was similarly and officially endorsed by Minister Bottai in his opening speech given at The Third Arts Exhibition of the Syndicate of Lombardy.[57] Just as the visual arts had benefitted from the widespread system of exhibitions and art galleries so, albeit in a much lower key, 1927 had seen the first book fair (festa del libro) held in Rome under the auspices of the Ministry of Education. The same period also witnessed a proliferation of literary prizes to support the fortunes and misfortunes of the novel. The Mussolini Prize (Academy of Italy, 1931), the Viareggio Prize (1930) and the Bagutta Prize (commissioned by Fracchia, the former editor of *La fiera letteraria*, in 1927) were all attempts to fill a gap in the market and to promote well-written, realist and carefully constructed Italian prose, which had the main function of addressing 'modern' and new groups of readers.[58]

From various perspectives (writers, critics, party officials, publishers), it seems evident that the novel was increasingly closely associated with an interdisciplinary outlook, and not merely in avant-gardist or experimental terms, but also in connection with the social sciences, the sciences of a modern society. More explicitly, the novel was becoming associated with State art, in an attempt to create a reading public which would support the regime in its totalitarian objectives.[59] As in every nation-formation process, or in this case the Fascist revolution, which was first officially celebrated in 1932 with the Mostra della Rivoluzione[60] held at the Palazzo delle Esposizioni, the novel had to occupy in theory, if not in practice, a higher position compared to other artistic genres because it would be instrumental in defining the New Fascist Man, a pivotal element of the Fascist anthropological revolution and, in order to do so, it would have to change its status and profile: it needed to be turned towards the social and become closely connected with the contemporary process of technological transformation.[61] What, then, was this new regime of the novel?

In his contribution to young and up-and-coming publisher Valentino Bompiani's well-known call for the collective novel along the lines of John Dos Passos's trilogy *The 42nd Parallel* (1930), *1919* (1932) and later

The Big Money (1936), Bontempelli dismissed the apocalyptic, self-destructive novel, fraught with anguish and subjectivism, in the following terms:

> And we all remember *Berlin Alexanderplatz* (by Döblin, who is a cut above the others) which, two years ago swept across Germany and then overflowed as it were onto the whole of Europe. The new German novelists are replacing the old myth of the pedantic German by the myth of the anguished German. (Even France, a few months ago, hailed Céline's *Voyage au bout de la nuit*). We are thus besieged by a type of literature which proclaims itself as the mirror of the epoch, and which can be summed up by that tetra chord pronounced by one of *Fabiano*'s characters: crime, poverty, lust, fraud. But without any of the forces of redemption, whether individual or social, which lighten the darkness of Dostoyevsky and even that of Zola. ('Romanzo apocalittico.' March 1933, *L'avventura novecentista*, 169)[62]

Bompiani established his publishing house in 1929. He followed in Mondadori's footsteps but was more innovative in outlook, trying to combine in his catalogue popular literature with more experimental products, and of course with translations of foreign novels from Europe, the US and the Far East. From an ambitious publisher's perspective, and one with distinct echoes of the architectural debate, Bompiani singled out the problematic hiatus between national and international literary production and implicitly called for a collaborative, European effort. He also insightfully stressed the importance of the real in the construction of all literary production which, in order to be useful (i.e. sell), cannot be solipsistically conceived and must instead retain close contact with the materiality of the everyday. He hence aligned the novel with the broader discourse on the arts as a whole and on architecture as a privileged form able to reach the new mass public and build a nation (Ben-Ghiat 2001, 113).

In 1934, Bompiani started a campaign for the collective novel, again inspired by John Dos Passos' trilogy. According to Bompiani, the collective novel had to assume its place as the new Italian novel, and embrace a new brand of *verismo* aiming at building a new collective consciousness ('Invito editoriale al romanzo.' 14 March 1934, *Gazzetta del popolo*: 3).⁶³ The ensuing debate is interesting in many respects: Bontempelli was sceptical regarding the initiative because he saw it as excessively documentary, while other voices expressed doubts about the ability of Italian writers to produce a national novel. Bompiani's vision of, and call for a collective⁶⁴ novel is also important in relation to the wider picture because of his openness towards Europe. He placed Italian literature's existence in relation to other cultural landscapes on a competitive basis, as was also the case for the architectural project and for Bontempelli and *900*, since, as a professional, he was rightly aware of the growing success of translations, which overshadowed a still weak national novel (Billiani 2007, 139–40).

Translating the National Novel

Seen purely as a marketable product, the Italian novel was, arguably, never a major concern for the regime, or at least not in terms of censorial control or mass distribution. Such a situation lasted until 1938, when the racial laws were introduced, and deteriorated during WWII. Hostility towards translations was rather a matter of debate, which opposed foreign texts in favour of authentic Italian novels (Billiani 2007, 141–43). Censorship was exercised with care, preferably before publication and in agreement with the publishers themselves, and it started to be systematized only in 1934 and later in 1937 with the establishment of the Ministry for Popular Culture (Ministero della Culture Popolare) (Fabre 1998, 18–39). The reason for such a delay in taking official action against foreign influence was that the Italian novel as such never managed to reach a wide enough audience to become a visible problem, and was never in a sufficiently culturally hegemonic position to be able to disseminate values that contradicted those promulgated by the regime; translations, however, were in such a position. Yet, if the regime treated translations, like the novel, with 'tolerant indifference', at least until 1938, and the racial laws, in public it sought to appear distinctively less laissez-faire in this respect. Gramsci's analysis of the literary market provides one possible explanation for this attitude. Wondering why readers preferred foreign texts, Gramsci argued that Italian literature was incapable of creating a communication channel between the leading and the subaltern classes. This type of communication was, much in evidence in foreign works, and this also accounted for their economic success (*I quaderni del carcere*, Notebook 21 vol. 3, (XVII, 1934–35), 2108 and ibid., vol. 3, Notebook 19, (X), 2116–120). Gramsci also suggested that Americanism fostered a new model of realism able, through the use of a shared language, to transform a literary country into a literary nation. The national novel, incapable of speaking to the middle classes, who craved realistic well-written adventures, could now help out an industry which complained of being in a continuous state of crisis—even if the *libro di Stato* had kept Mondadori afloat. The publishing industry was increasingly becoming an important ally for the regime as it was able to provide the link with the masses that it increasingly needed, especially as the 1930s went on, and it sought to construct a panopticon-like controlling State apparatus.

The novel needed to sell, and the 'scandal' novels of Guido Da Verona and Pitigrilli were the Italian bestsellers of the early twentieth century, yet the success of foreign novels would continue uninterrupted until the end of the regime because these books filled a gap in national production insofar as they told realistic stories with captivating, modern plots, and also put forward an ethical message, however dubious this might be, which could bring readers together (Tranfaglia and Vittoria 2000, 314–16). The Italian bestsellers were often sensationalist, page-turning stories or biographies: *Mammiferi di lusso* (1920) by Pitigrilli, *Il giornalino di Gian Burrasca* (1920) by Vamba, *Storia di Cristo* by Papini (1921), *Le scarpe al sole* by Paolo Monelli (1921), *La Velia* by Bruno Cicognani (1921), *Il mestiere di marito* by Lucio D'Ambra, *Mussolini* by Giorgio Pini (1926), the bestselling *Dux* by Margherita Sarfatti (1926), *Piccolo alpino* by Salvator Gotta (1926), *Ma che cosa è questo amore* by Achille Campanile (1927). A print run of 20,000 was enough to make a novel a bestseller. As for translations, the bestsellers of the 1930s were the novels published in Mondadori's 'Medusa' series, with a bestselling print run, followed by the 'Romanzi della Palma' (1932–1943) with their exotic locations, risqué illustrations and seemingly neutral stories set amongst social and cultural contexts that were profoundly different from Fascist Italy, and their low price.[65] The 'Medusa' (1931–1977) and 'Biblioteca

3 Constructing the Novel 53

Romantica' (1931–1942) collections embodied exactly what Gramsci had described: high-quality literature with well-assembled plots and clarity of style (see Billiani 2007, 118 for figures regarding translations and individual series). Margaret Mitchell's *Gone with the Wind*, published by Mondadori in 1937, sold 100,000 copies and former rondista Riccardo Bacchelli's *Il mulino del Po*, published by Garzanti, achieved similar sales in 1943. Across the whole publishing field, foreign literature was able to provide quality and also popular appeal, and thus reach the elites, common readers, and, also occasionally, the middle classes.[66] In terms of sales and sustained success, detective stories, *i libri gialli*, were unrivalled, selling a cumulative total of 10,000,000 copies by 1943.

It would therefore be rather safe to assume that the novel, as indicated in cosmopolitan *Occidente*, occupied a relatively marginal position within the Italian literary system of the 1920s and 1930s, which was numerically dominated by translations of elite and popular foreign fiction. The Italian novel, in line with tradition, was nonetheless the privileged means of representing a nation (as had been the case since unification), and therefore could not simply be treated or addressed as a minor phenomenon; on the contrary, it had to be firmly included in the State's propaganda machine as a vessel of true *italianità*, and this promotion would be carried out through press campaigns, however ineffective these proved in practice. The novel functioned and assumed relevance and meaning when placed within the cogs of the project of constructing a State art, while it exercised a relatively weak influence if taken as a stand-alone venture.

To conclude, as a working definition for our analysis to follow, from the early 1920s until the end of the 1930s, and in the powerful wake of *Gli indifferenti*, realism was to be understood as a recalibration of the relationship between subjectivity and objectivity as interconnected moments, and as a move towards a rationalization of prose writing as either expressionist linguistic experimentation à la Gadda or as a reduction to 'naturalezza' as suggested by Bontempelli. It was of course no longer possible to take a nineteenth-century view of realism whereby the real was placed solidly in front of the subject—Verga's famous 'clod of earth'—for the real had now entered the realm of the subject, moulding him or her along with itself, in a constructivist process of mutual reshaping. The subject could not stand as a self-sufficient item, whether heroic or intimist, for it had become necessary for it to be reconstructed in relation to an objectivity which had, like in a post-expressionist painting, the power almost to penetrate and disfigure the subject. Yet, while subjectivity as a filter of reality was certainly possible in the 1920s with some notable exceptions, as the regime expanded its State patronage of the arts through firmer control mechanisms and press campaigns, the theorization of aesthetic rationalization as a path towards modernity and social modernization changed the balance of the equation. This paradigm shift is visible in many artistic fields from the second wave of Futurism to mural paintings in the early 1930s. Thus—and just like other forms of artistic, visual and literary expression—the novel privileged a literary mode that embraced varying degrees of realism (including magical realism and spiritual realism) and which was oriented towards social matters. Finally, in doing so, it directly mirrored the contemporaneous Fascist architectural project, which sought to rebuild and reconfigure the foundations of the discipline in order to accommodate a social space for the New Collective Man.

Notes

1. Only formalised in 1932 with the publication of the *Doctrine of Fascism* and the *Italian Encyclopaedia*.
2. The debate on Fascism and modernity has been discussed in detail elsewhere, but for a persuasive analysis of its cultural specificities concerning literature, the visual arts, cinema and the role of literary journals, see Adamson (1993), Ben-Ghiat (2001), Cioli (2011), Tarquini (2011).
3. For more details on this specific debate, see Chap. 2. The idea of art as action was also a constant preoccupation for the Futurists since their early days; see, for example, the manifesto 'Ricostruzione futurista dell'universo', signed by Giacomo Balla and Fortunato Depero and published in Milan on 15 March 1915.
4. We refer back to the critical discussion about critical contributions to the definition of 'Fascist culture' or culture under a dictatorship in the introductory chapter.
5. In this regard, David Roberts has explained that the modernist dimension of art should not be intended simply as an attempt to tame the

irrational and romantic tendencies of society through processes of technic and productive rationalization (2011).
6. Key to our argument is the notion of 'multiple modernities' as multiple cultural programmes contributing towards the same result: e.g. modernity in this particular instance (Eisenstadt 2002).
7. http://dialecticsofmodernity.manchester.ac.uk/artefact/117; http://dialecticsofmodernity.manchester.ac.uk/essay/486; http://dialecticsofmodernity.manchester.ac.uk/essay/505
8. http://dialecticsofmodernity.manchester.ac.uk/essay/450
9. Futurism, Novecento, Strapaese, Stracittà, Corporativism, New Urbanism, for example, all these movements belong to this rather vague category in some aspects of their thinking. See Sechi (1984, 34–44) and Parlato (2000, 18) for details. See also Chap. 2.
10. http://dialecticsofmodernity.manchester.ac.uk/artefact/143; http://dialecticsofmodernity.manchester.ac.uk/essay/419; http://dialecticsofmodernity.manchester.ac.uk/artefact/106; http://dialecticsofmodernity.manchester.ac.uk/essay/500
11. This discussion is particularly explicit in the case of architecture, with the *case popolari* (public housing), *colonie estive* (summer camps) and railway stations. See Chap. 5 on *Quadrante* for further examples of such interventions.
12. An interesting discussion regarding this specific point can be found in Cioli (2011, 80–116).
13. http://dialecticsofmodernity.manchester.ac.uk/artefact/111; http://dialecticsofmodernity.manchester.ac.uk/artefact/114; http://dialecticsofmodernity.manchester.ac.uk/essay/376
14. For a discussion of the notions of autonomous and heteronomous practices as far as the avant-gardes and modernism are concerned, see Murphy (1999, 23–33). See also Chap. 2 on this point.
15. For a sustained analysis of arts policies and the structures of the apparatus for State patronage devised by the regime, see Braun (2000) on Mario Sironi; Salvagnini (2000) on the system of the arts; Stone (1998) on national and international exhibitions, and Malvano (1988a) on policies regarding the visual arts.
16. The Decree of February 9, 1942 (D.M. 9. 2.42) rationed the use of paper and forbade any new publications as well as the resumption of those which had been suspended or suppressed.
17. http://dialecticsofmodernity.manchester.ac.uk/artefact/120

18. See Giovanni Fiorioli della Lena, 1932, 'Individualismo e collettivismo.' *Critica fascista* 10, no. 6 (1 August): 314–15; Ugo D'Andrea, 1933, 'Politica e arte nella rivoluzione.' *Critica fascista* 10, no. 5 (1 March): 83–84; Vitaliano Brancati, 1933, 'La prosa nell'Italia moderna.' *Critica fascista* 11, no. 7 (1 April): 132–33; Gherardo Casini, 1933, 'Elementi politici di una letteratura.' *Critica fascista* 11, no. 9 (1 May): 161–62.
19. http://dialecticsofmodernity.manchester.ac.uk/artefact/220
20. Salvagnini (2000, 350), discussing the article by Mario Tinti, 1928, 'Arte e sindacalismo.' *Critica fascista* 6, no. 17 (1 September): 328–30. See also by Mario Tinti, 1927, 'Arte di popolo e non arte di Stato.' *La fiera letteraria* 3, no. 13 (27 March): 1.
21. See further interventions G. B. A, 1932, 'Fascismo e letteratura.' *L'Italia letteraria* 4, no. 11 (13 March): 1–2; Mario Attilio Levi, 1933, 'Dottrina del fascismo.' *L'Italia letteraria* 9, no. 8 (19 February): 1.
22. For an extended discussion on these points, especially in relation to Fascism, realism and youth culture, see Chap. 6.
23. See Salaris (1985: 30–35), for a discussion of the nuances of Marinetti's take on prose writing in the early days of the movement.
24. The total number of books published in 1926 was 6300 units, compared to 10,000 in 1940. The maximum was reached in 1932–1933 with a total of about 12,000 books, with the percentage of novels ranging from 7% to 12%. In absolute terms, the publication of novels went from 617 in 1926 to around 1000 in 1939, peaking in 1933–1935 with almost 1500 titles per year.
25. http://dialecticsofmodernity.manchester.ac.uk/essay/440
26. http://dialecticsofmodernity.manchester.ac.uk/essay/456
27. With Slavia, Frassinelli and Ribet in Turin for high culture, Sonzogno in Milan for popular literature, along with the declining Treves, increasingly replaced by the more modern Mondadori, for middle-brow literature.
28. http://dialecticsofmodernity.manchester.ac.uk/essay/488
29. For a reading of the novel which explores the political and existential themes and divides, see Biasin (1979).
30. It is worth remembering that Joyce published *Ulysses* in 1922, Mann *The Magic Mountain* in 1924, Woolf *Mrs Dalloway* in 1925 and *To The Lighthouse* in 1927, Döblin *Berlin Alexanderplatz* in 1929 and Faulkner *The Sound and the Fury* in the same year.
31. http://dialecticsofmodernity.manchester.ac.uk/essay/456

32. http://dialecticsofmodernity.manchester.ac.uk/tag/modern-realism
33. http://dialecticsofmodernity.manchester.ac.uk/tag/elite-culture
34. http://dialecticsofmodernity.manchester.ac.uk/essay/437
35. On Alvaro's ability to shape everyday characters which are quite unlike Michele in *Gli indifferenti*, and thus create a 'national novel' with 'Italian content', see Giorgio Granata, 1932, 'Significato di Alvaro.' *Il Saggiatore* 3, no. 2 (April): 78–84.
36. http://dialecticsofmodernity.manchester.ac.uk/essay/494
37. http://dialecticsofmodernity.manchester.ac.uk/essay/418
38. http://dialecticsofmodernity.manchester.ac.uk/artefact/18; http://dialecticsofmodernity.manchester.ac.uk/artefact/27; http://dialecticsofmodernity.manchester.ac.uk/essay/514; http://dialecticsofmodernity.manchester.ac.uk/essay/404; http://dialecticsofmodernity.manchester.ac.uk/essay/417
39. http://dialecticsofmodernity.manchester.ac.uk/essay/454
40. For an account of the selection process and Bontempelli's role, see Enrico Emanuelli, 1932, 'Il Premio Mediterraneo è stato vinto da Marcello Gallian.' *L'Italia letteraria* 4, no. 19 (8 May): 3.
41. http://dialecticsofmodernity.manchester.ac.uk/essay/495
42. For more details on *La ruota dentata*, see Carpi (1981, 111–38), while on Gallian, see Bignamini (2012, 133–52, in Cremate 2012) and Bouchard (2009, 39–52, in Marcheschi 2009). The novel *Ioni* was published just a few weeks before *Gli indifferenti* by Alpes, and it was influenced by Bontempelli's poetics (Marcheschi 2014, XXV).
43. http://dialecticsofmodernity.manchester.ac.uk/essay/464
44. http://dialecticsofmodernity.manchester.ac.uk/essay/488
45. http://dialecticsofmodernity.manchester.ac.uk/essay/443
46. http://dialecticsofmodernity.manchester.ac.uk/essay/472
47. http://dialecticsofmodernity.manchester.ac.uk/essay/464
48. Dino Buzzati, for example, published two important works which mixed realism and early existentialism in 1935, *Il segreto del bosco vecchio*, Treves, and in 1940, *Il deserto dei Tartari*, Rizzoli.
49. Caro Bottai, Non so se tu ti sia reso conto quanto le tue conclusioni circa la cosiddetta 'arte fascista' siano terribilmente 'novecentesche', proprio nell'aborrito senso della parola. Ci tengo anche a farti osservare che le mie due prefazioni, e i brani teorici nella 'caravana immobile' dei due numeri, lungi dall'essere delle 'boutades' come ti van dicendo i Maleparti e i Soffici e altri Longanesi grossi e piccini, hanno già delineato una serie di idee assai precise: discutibilissime sì, se c'è qualcuno abbastanza

preparato e in buona fede, ma fecondissime in ogni modo, e italiane quanto si può essere. Lascia che te le additi:

1. Posizione contro l'estetismo (decadenza dello spirito classico).
2. Posizione contro lo psicologismo (analismo, intimismo, freudismo, ecc. decadenza dello spirito romantico).
3. L'arte dello scrivere considerata come l'architettura, cioè modificazione del mondo abitabile. Cioè con lo scopo di inventare miti e favole per i tempi nuovi.

   Corollario:—antilirsmo, antimetrica, antistile.
   Altro:—valutata la situazione del cinema a questo riguardo.
4. Chiarita la differenza tra immaginazione nel nostro senso, e il vecchio 'fiabesco' (antiorientalismo).
5. Oltrepassato l'atteggiamento 'avanguardista', considerato come nevrotico, e imbevuto di 'letteratura'. Avviamento ad un'arte di pubblico.
6. Situazione nettamente preminente dell'Italia nella nuova civiltà: nuova ripresa mediterranea.
7. Conseguenze particolari (situazione del teatro: orientamento della musica, ecc.) [...]

   Affettuosamente
   Tuo, Bontempelli. (Archivio Mondadori, folder 'Amici e Prs', f. 29, undated typescript.)
50. http://dialecticsofmodernity.manchester.ac.uk/tag/statalization; http://dialecticsofmodernity.manchester.ac.uk/tag/totalitarian-art; http://dialecticsofmodernity.manchester.ac.uk/hypothesis/1
51. For a fuller discussion on the influence Bottai exercised on *Quadrante*, see Rifkind (2012, 79–80).
52. 'La produzione libraria è in sensibilissimo aumento. Dai dati statistici che abbiamo sotto mano, forniti dal *Bollettino delle Pubblicazioni Italiane*, le classi del romanzo, della musica e delle scienze sociali rappresentano da sole un guadagno di un migliaio di unità sugli anni precedenti. L'aumento del numero dei romanzi è significativo. Dal 1920 ad oggi, le pubblicazioni mensili da 511 ammontano ad oltre 1.500. [...] I libri stampati in Italia hanno toccato il totale di 11.949 volumi. Il numero delle traduzioni è salito a 1.135. L'esperimento del Libro di Stato, che aveva messo a dura prova la vita delle aziende editoriali, si può considerare compiuto.'

53. According to Rundle's calculations, from 1930 to 1935, the number of translations as a percentage of all published titles increased from 19.19% to 47.53%. This percentage remained constant until 1941, to decline in 1942 (27.52%), because of the imposition of a quota (2001: 159).
54. See also, Nicola Perrotti, 1930, 'Perché la letteratura italiana non è popolare in Europa.' *Il Saggiatore* 1, no. 9 (November): 285–87. Perrotti argued that Italian literature had to become 'modern' and reflect a collective unconscious.
55. http://dialecticsofmodernity.manchester.ac.uk/essay/454
56. *Il Saggiatore* is also positive about the novel because it reads well 1931, '*Il varco nel muro* di G. Titta Rosa.' 2, no. 9 (November): 345–46.
57. Giuseppe Bottai, 1932, 'Arte nel nostro tempo.' *Italia letteraria* 4, no. 9 (28 February): 1; see also the editorial by G.B.A, 'Fascismo e letteratura.' *L'Italia letteraria*, cit.: 1.
58. The reading public was slowly growing since the literacy in the country was also on the rise (see Palazzolo 1993: 287–317).
59. *Critica fascista* published several interventions on the debate on the novel, such as Editorial, 1932, 'Esortazione al realismo.' 10, no. 4 (15 February): 61–62; Domenico Carella, 1932, 'Coscienza collettiva e coscienza individuale'; Valentino Piccoli, 'Babbitt o l'uomo standard.' 10, no. 23 (1 December): 448–49 and 456–57; and Domenico Carella, 1933, 'Nostro realismo.' 11, no. 7 (1 April): 133–34.
60. http://dialecticsofmodernity.manchester.ac.uk/essay/466; http://dialecticsofmodernity.manchester.ac.uk/artefact/23; http://dialecticsofmodernity.manchester.ac.uk/essay/492
61. A similar trajectory would be followed by the 1930s incarnation of Futurism in terms of the attention it dedicated to the everyday, such as in advertisements, e.g. in Fortunato Depero's 1932 Campari campaign, and in the *aerofuturismo* and *aeropittura* before and during WWII used as a means of propaganda.
62. 'E tutti ricordiamo *Berlin Alexanderplatz* (di Doeblin, parecchi gradi più su) che due anni sono ha inondato la Germania ed. è poi traboccato un po' per tutta Europa. Al vecchio mito del tedesco pedante, i nuovi romanzieri germanici stanno sostituendo il mito del tedesco angosciato. (Anche la Francia ha esaltato, sono pochi mesi, il *Voyage au bout de la nuit* di Céline). Così siamo assediati da una letteratura che si proclama specchio dell'epoca, e può riassumersi in quella quadriade dichiarata da un personaggio di Fabiano: delitto, miseria, lussuria, frode. Ma senza gli impeti di redenzione, o individuale o sociale, che accendono il nero di

Dostoevski e perfino in Zola.' *Fabian* is the eponymous title of Erich Kästner's 1931 semi-autobiographical novel.

63. See 'Medusa', *Corriere Adriatico*, 7 April 1934, 'Passaggi a livello. Ancora del romanzo collettivo.' *Tribuna*, 19 April 1934.
64. http://dialecticsofmodernity.manchester.ac.uk/essay/448
65. These novels sold up to 20,000 copies, see also Billiani (2007, 125–26) for the negotiations with the regime about this risqué series.
66. For further details on the small-scale publishing industry, especially in relation to translations and the book market, see Tranfaglia and Vittoria (2000, 364–79) and Billiani (2007, 137–49).

Open Access This chapter is licensed under the terms of the Creative Commons Attribution 4.0 International License (http://creativecommons.org/licenses/by/4.0/), which permits use, sharing, adaptation, distribution and reproduction in any medium or format, as long as you give appropriate credit to the original author(s) and the source, provide a link to the Creative Commons licence and indicate if changes were made.

The images or other third party material in this chapter are included in the chapter's Creative Commons licence, unless indicated otherwise in a credit line to the material. If material is not included in the chapter's Creative Commons licence and your intended use is not permitted by statutory regulation or exceeds the permitted use, you will need to obtain permission directly from the copyright holder.

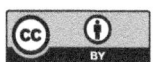

4

Fascism and Architecture

There has never been an epoch that did not feel itself to be 'modern' in the sense of eccentric, and did not believe itself to be standing directly before the abyss.
—Benjamin (*Arcades*, [S1a, 4], 545)

This chapter traces the battles for national hegemony fought between key architectural movements and styles, which most notably pitted the supporters of Novecento and Gruppo 7 against their opponents, and the supporters of rationalism[1] against those of monumentalism. These struggles shaped the development of Fascist and Italian architecture over two decades, peaking during the first half of the 1930s, and they displayed clear similarities with the debates on the novel.

Following the trajectory delineated so far, our initial hypothesis is as follows: the novel—understood by writers, publishers and intellectuals as a discursive practice connected to various degrees of realism as well as to forms of aesthetic rationalization and narrative construction—and theorizations about rationalist architecture—the project forming the basis for the design of the new collective space for the individual—possess several points of convergence both at a theoretical-aesthetic and at a structural level which revolve around a set of principles. Both endeavours reinforced the collective ethos of individual experience by claiming a strong moral imperative as foundational to any artistic expression; they both also promoted a desire for construction, to be realized through a process of rationalization of aesthetic forms, advocating, respectively, the need for a simplified narrative and architectural structures anchored to their 'contextual' realities (Etlin 1991, 255). As catalysts for the regime's cultural modernity and the creation of a State art, these projects not only exerted a strong internationalizing influence on national culture, but they also strengthened the national tradition at both elite and popular levels.

As with the novel, the debate on architecture played out mostly in journals of diverse orientations, and through public interventions by architects, politicians, intellectuals and even by Mussolini himself, and had as its primary aim the theorization and construction of a modern cultural and artistic infrastructure through which to initiate a process of modernization of the public sphere. The aesthetic urgency of reconstructing the novel intersected with the equally pressing need for rationalist architecture to theorize the discipline. Unlike the Italian novel, which did not reach a large audience and often remained a matter of abstract discussion, the architectural undertaking had a distinctly practical side, was visible in various forms across the whole country, was often state-sponsored and followed a trajectory which clearly mirrored the rise and fall of the regime itself and of its consensus.[2] Finally, architecture is not only a matter of space and design, but its language has a visual component, which the novel, traditionally, lacks.

The Total Work of Art

The total work of art can be broadly defined as a synthetic work, which aspires to integrate all its parts into a coherent whole, and dates back to the nineteenth century, with the Wagnerian *Gesamtkunstwerk*, which implied the reunification of all arts.[3] In many ways the Fascist system of the arts was constructed along similar lines, privileging interdisciplinary intersections between different artistic and aesthetic fields.[4]

4 Fascism and Architecture   63

The total work of art was another notion, which had been at the centre of avant-garde artistic debate since the beginning of the twentieth century. It was vocally revived as an aesthetic and political concept by Filippo Tommaso Marinetti himself in his strenuous attempts to make Futurism the official State art, chiefly through the 1930s Manifestos of Futurist Architecture, which included Enrico[5] Prampolini's idea of totalizing architecture, and through Angiolo Mazzoni's[6] work as an employee of the regime in the Ministero delle Comunicazioni (Ministry of Communication), where he designed and signed off on projects for train stations and post offices from Agrigento to Bolzano.[7] In a political regime with totalitarian aspirations and an aesthetic regime seeking to rationalize structures in order to adhere to the real, Marinetti's desire for a total art along neo-Wagnerian lines was realized through a combination of old and new, erudite[8] and popular,[9] through a rhetoric and a type of composition which avoided the ornamental in order to distil the essence of a new society with a distinctive political ambition.[10] A total and totalizing[11] art would allow the coexistence of many artistic and political drives: the Futurism of the 1930s, with all its State commissions and its participation in Biennales,[12] Triennales, Quadriennales; the multifaceted intermedial strength of Fortunato Depero[13] and Bruno Munari[14]; the attempt at the twentieth-century modernization of Milan by Giovanni Muzio; the architectural renewal through the social experiments of the Gruppo 7 and later the architects Banfi, Belgioioso, Peressutti and Rogers (BBPR); the rationalization of matter and line in the sculpture of Thayaht,[15] RAM[16] and Arturo Martini[17]; the bourgeois realism of Alberto Moravia[18]; the anti-bourgeois realism of Vittorini[19]; the return to rural realism with Corrado Alvaro,[20] all side by side with the mixing of the arts practised by the Bolshevik Immaginists[21] and the Bragaglia brothers, together with the cosmic experimentations of Fillìa and Prampolini.[22]

The new Fascist order required a new aesthetic order of discourse, which could express the collective subject and the consistency of the real and which would be driven by an ethical imperative; this is what underlines the architectural projects by State official and architect Angiolo Mazzoni. Through its many manifestations and embodiments spanning the visual arts, advertising, cinema and theatre—and in our case, literature and architecture—the total work of art also found fertile ground in the social and aesthetic discourse upheld by the dictatorship since, as Roberts puts it: 'These projects expressed a common will to recover the lost public function of art, a will that pointed beyond the aesthetic revolutions of the avant-gardes to political revolutions as the promise of a complete reunion of art and life' (2011, 2).[23] In other words, creating a total work of art was the aim of every dictatorship, for it brought together all arts, all corners of the social sphere(s) in a concerted attempt to become modern[24] and, in so doing, functionally integral to their very same existence (Roberts 2011, 5). The arts seem to move along an arc, which Elena Pontiggia has described as a 'persistent will to construct […] a proactive and affirmative energy' to modernize (1990, 7). The new Fascist order required a new aesthetic order of discourse, which could express the collective subject and the consistency of the real, and would be driven by an ethical imperative. Out of this cultural renewal will emerge forms equal to the task of creating beauty in the musical, plastic, theatrical and literary arts.

State Art: The Struggle for Supremacy

In his *De re aedificatoria* (1443–1445), Leon Battista Alberti stated that architecture was one of the greatest of the arts because it had two souls: a practical one and a theoretical one (Prologue, 3). This alternation between the practical and theoretical sides of architecture to a large extent determined its role and position within the cultural and political Italian landscape of the inter-war period. It is precisely this Janus-like face of architecture that has shaped its history and, in the context of our study, its impact on the debates on State art, both from a political and from an aesthetic perspective. Simply put, architecture was able to contribute to the theoretical debate on the arts and power, while also showcasing its practical results and thus becoming visible to the public eye. In his *Dialoghi* with Emil Ludwig, held daily from the end of March to the beginning of April 1932, Mussolini himself notoriously declared that '[i]n my judgement, the greatest of all the arts […] is architecture, because it encompasses everything', covering the public sphere as much as it does the personal sphere of the individual (Ludwig, *Colloqui con Mussolini*, 201 cited in Nicoloso 2008, 81).[25] Up until the mid-1930s, architecture embodied the Fascist revolution because it not only created a collective space for the individual, but also theorized the way in which such space had to be occupied. This is shown, for example, most forcefully by the Casa del fascio[26] by Giuseppe Terragni (1904–1943) built in Como in 1936, Florence train station[27] (1936) by the Gruppo Toscano led by Giovanni Michelucci, the Città Universitaria La Sapienza[28] in Rome (1935), which brought together the most distinguished architects of the time (Giò Ponti, Terragni, Piacentini, Pagano to name a few), as well as numerous stadia (the Foro Italico[29] by Enrico Del Debbio or the Stadio Giovanni Berta[30] by Pier Luigi Nervi) and post offices, a residential complex designed by Mazzoni as a seaside holiday camp for the children of industrial workers[31] (Colonia Rosa Maltoni Mussolini), new corporativist cities (Littoria-Latina, 1932, Sabaudia, 1934, Tresigallo, 1934), and new working class neighbourhoods[32] (Rebbio, Como, 1938) constructed throughout the 1930s (see Chap. 7).[33] The year of the opening of the Casa del fascio in Como, with its Bauhaus-like translucent and transparent volumes and geometrical intersections, only marked the climax of a long-term struggle to determine which artistic movement would become the official arte di Stato and fly the banners of morality and construction.[34] By 1936, the history of experimental/rationalist architecture was nonetheless practically over. Conversely, the patron of Novecento, Margherita Sarfatti, vanished from the art scene with her last appearance on the occasion of the proclamation of the Italian Empire on 6 May 1936. 1936 also meant the end of the battles for hegemony amongst architects, with Rome-based architect Marcello Piacentini now leading the way towards[35] monumentalism, and the rationalist movement marginalized after leaving its signature on the history of Italian architecture.[36]

Towards an Architectural Project

From Giovanni Muzio's[37] architectural experiments in Milan resulting in the controversially modern house, the Ca' Brutta[38] and the works of the Novecento architects in the early 1920s, through to the late 1920s with the theses of Gruppo 7 on architecture, and into the early 1930s with Marinetti's polemical outbursts, one can see a concerted effort at reconfiguring aesthetics, politics and society as a total work of art in a rather obvious fashion as far as architecture was concerned. As architectural scholar Dennis Doordan has observed: 'the development of modern architecture in Italy should be viewed as the result of the interaction of three architectural movements: Futurism, Novecentism, and Rationalism' (1988, 4). Despite the ongoing battles between the other two movements, Muzio and the Novecentisti remained a constant presence during the *Ventennio*, with notable buildings which changed the urban and cultural profile of Milan (see, for instance, Maulsby 2014, 133–60, on the planning of the Palazzo del *Popolo d'Italia*, 1938–1942).[39] In this respect, these architectural expressions of the early 1920s are in line with Sarfatti's Novecento programme outlined on 11 January 1920 in *Contro tutti i ritorni in pittura*[40]: *Manifesto futurista*, signed by Leonardo Dudreville, Achille Funi, Luigi Russolo and Mario Sironi,[41] and published in Milan (for the role of Sarfatti in the debates on the *arte di Stato*, see Chap. 2 and Fagone 1982, 45).[42] Like Muzio, these artists grouped around Margherita Sarfatti rejected the return to classicism championed by the Valori plastici movement, and they too stood at a crossroads between tradition and modernity without ever conclusively choosing one over the other but aspiring to find a new aesthetic paradigm which could guarantee a hegemonic position within the construction of State art.[43] Contrary to Sarfatti however, who was ideologically close to Mussolini's political programme, in Muzio's works the principal drive is explicitly stylistic, and not political: namely, the will to express the syntactical renewal of architectural language by drawing together traditional geometrical patterns in contrasting, alternating fashions (Kirk 2005, 69–70; Etlin 1991, 174–76). For both of them, one of the key aesthetic principles guiding their artistic practices was the idea of synthesis as construction and not as 'simultaneity of forces' as for the Futurists (Pontiggia 2003, 14–19; Fossati 1972, 27–33).

At the end of WWI, young Giovanni Muzio returned from the front line in Veneto to his native Milan, after having spent time in France, England and Germany in order to acquire some experience with foreign architectural traditions. His architectural mission was always that of bringing together different traditions under the overarching Italian one (this was also the reason for his prolonged success as one of Italy's leading architects). Muzio established his own studio in Milan, with other designers and architects who gained significant prominence in the Italian cultural sphere during the *Ventennio*: Giò Ponti, Emilio Lancia and Giuseppe de Finetti together with Mino Fiocchi, Gigiotti Zanini, Alpago Novello, Paolo Mezzanotte and Vittorio Pizzigoni, all members of the Gruppo Novecento, which, as an architectural movement, was also involved in debates about the urban development of the city (Maulsby 2014, 140–46). Muzio and these others aspired to reposition Italian architecture as a national project at the forefront of the European tradition, thereby signalling one of the most distinctive traits of relationship between aesthetic and political tensions during the 20 years to follow.

Muzio's breakthrough was the thousand-unit development at the corner of the Via della Moscova, a modern apartment block intended for the Milanese bourgeoisie.[44] The Ca' Brutta consisted of seven floors divided into three horizontal zones, and it was the first house in the city to include an underground car park and a central heating system. In order to break the monotony of his Novecento design and the squareness of his planimetry, Muzio varied the patterns of the windows so that everyone could easily recognize his or her own flat. The Ca' Brutta's façade (made of seventeen individual façades) is severe but has no hierarchical organization, and there are only subtle variations in the repetition of similar patterns: the space has clearly been transformed from the house of the individual to the house(s) of the collective, and such a shift occurred thanks to a new aesthetic organization (Isastia and Pierini 2017, 478). It was an ideal example of modernity and tradition: where modernity was embodied in the linear, geometrical construction of the building and of its series of windows, and tradition was guaranteed by the attachment to both the Italian and the classical tradition. For example, the house is divided into two blocks which are joined together by an archway where a 'severe Palladian motif of an arcuated center bay framing the view of the narrow street and flanked by smaller trabeated bays recalls Vasari's use of a similar device for the Uffizi in Florence' (Doordan 1988, 32). Muzio's use of a reinforced concrete frame, of pillars, of cantilevered bays, and of an alternation of squares and archwindows gives the building an imposing aura over Via Moscova. The Ca' Brutta received at best a lukewarm reception, but its clear and linear geometry became a symbol of an era to come.

Symbolically therefore, its monumental shape stands at the crossroads of the Novecento movement and of what would become rationalism in architecture and Futurism in art as far as the interplay between lines, geometry and volumes, as well as the need to modernize the public space of the individual, were concerned.[45]

What is particularly important to our argument is that the landmark Ca' Brutta and Muzio's use of neoclassical, neo-Palladian motifs, along with his reclaiming of the straight line in a metaphysical and vertical perspective, were the first moves in a process of aesthetic rationalization, which was meant to mark a clear break with the eclecticism of the Umbertine style, with the goal of changing the very essence of urban living. Muzio wanted to create a modern palazzo which could retain the classically composed elegance of traditional architecture in a way not too dissimilar from the *prosa d'arte* (see Chap. 3, pp. 37–40). In this respect, Etlin has described the Ca' Brutta as an 'encyclopaedic' building with a 'fragmentary composition', a composition which achieves unity through a fragmentary compositional pattern but which remains subjective in its compositional order (1991, 184). The Ca' Brutta is indeed fragmentary, in the same way that the *prosa d'arte* was: both lacked that unity which could have ensured a more neutral presence within the urban fabric, but both aspired to a return to order based on classically composed formulations. Together with Muzio, Giuseppe De Finetti's Milanese Casa della Meridiana (Sundial House, 1924–1925) is another example of 'variation' within traditional forms (Isastia and Pierini 2017, 478). De Finetti had studied with Adolf Loos in Vienna and in 1934 published his translation of 'Ornament is crime' in *Casabella*.[46] The Casa della Meridiana recalled Loos' 1912 Scheu House in Vienna and, just like the Ca' Brutta with its garages, experimented with modernity by replacing the traditional staircase with an elevator. Even more, the geometry of the façades and the simple lines of the windows were ideal precursors to Gruppo 7's claim to functionality. De Finetti opted for mural architecture, or for continuity between the friezes and the patterns which run across the facade of the house. The only criminal concession could be found in the pillars on the first floor balcony.

As Doordan argues: 'the Novecento movement rejected the idea that architecture should be the result of either the personal whim of the designer or the product of narrowly defined technological considerations'; as Borgese hoped regarding the novel, the 'tempo di edificare' (time to build) had arrived (1988, 30), since 'Muzio's appreciation of the Italian tradition in building [...] included a tectonic appreciation of Italian architecture as a type of mural architecture' (1988, 33). The Novecento movement in architecture, as in the other arts, was strongly connected to the national tradition and the Novecento architects understood and interpreted muralism as a return to order in so far as it was a return to tradition as a repertoire of composed forms which could call for a straightforward interpretation of the 'real'. The *Novecentisti* did not seek to reinvent tradition, but rather to reshape it in view of a widespread theoretical drive towards rationalization, which translated in social terms into an equally powerful drive towards the modernization of the social sphere through functional living and building. In essence, the Vasari-like courtyard, the Palladian arch, the golden decorative patterns on the doorbells, and the overall 'Renaissance tradition of linear surface patterning' of the Ca' Brutta are homages to the national architectural tradition, which nevertheless needed to be standardized to become modern and thus be able to transform the urban space (Etlin 1991, 185). We could conclude that the Ca' Brutta is fragmentary in conception, but aspires to be an example of a new way for the individual to inhabit collectively the public space. In this respect, it sits squarely between tradition and modernity, in a way that resembles the trajectory of the novel in the 1920s.

The dialectical clashes between modernity, modernization, national tradition and internationalization in architecture could not be fully comprehended without making a reference to Futurism. By 1914, Futurism started venturing into architecture with the *Manifesto dell'architettura futurista* signed by Antonio Sant'Elia and written with Marinetti's input. Only a few new architectural elements were introduced: the oblique line, the importance of new materials to be used such as concrete, iron and glass to create a new synthesis between form, function and space. The oblique-errant line had to be developed in opposition to the straight and vertical line. The former was exemplified by the work of Piero Portaluppi in his contribution to a new visionary aesthetic in the Planetario Hoepli,[47] which looked at the relationship between the urban space and individuality.

More importantly, Futurist architecture is emblematic of a trajectory followed by many other contemporaneous artistic movements: shifting from the utopianism of the 1910s to the utilitarian and pragmatic view of the 1930s which, not unlike the unbalanced relationship between the national novel and translations we have already discussed, needed to account for the demands of a much wider public, since their audiences were no longer simply the affluent middle classes but the new urban populations flooding into old and new Italian cities from rural areas.[48] Unlike Futurism, which hardly realized its ideas about architecture in practice, the Novecento movement never published manifestos but concerned itself with the act of building: the Novecentisti constructed extensively and continuously. Moreover, if Muzio was the leading exponent of the movement, it was, like the Gruppo 7, or later the BBPR, very much considered a collective enterprise based on a set of buildings and not on theoretical statements. The *Novecentisti* conceptualized the architectural work as a collective effort, turning it into a profession, and wholeheartedly rejecting the Futurist idea of the lone creative genius: they saw their practice as performing the social function of providing habitable public and private spaces (Etlin 1991, 329–67). Taken together, however, the Novecento movement and Futurism are characteristic of inter-war modernity: their awareness of their own theoretical practices and cultural traditions would be deployed to reshape the Italian/Mediterranean public sphere through structures able to assist the process of modernization. These concerns went hand in hand with the process of modernization which, for the novel, was closely connected with the publishing industry and the construction of a reading public, whereas for architecture it depended on State-commissioned works and support from the industrial sector, as was often discussed in *Quadrante* (Castronovo 1988, 12–16).

From 1931 through to 1935, the rationalist movement as a whole would create some of the most interesting architecture of the *Ventennio*, putting the main principles and spirit of this architectural renewal into practice. Because of their public role and contribution to the artistic and architectural debates, architects[49] Giuseppe Terragni (1904–1943) and Giuseppe Pagano (1896–1945) and art critic Edoardo Persico (1900–1936) were to become the three most prominent figures of the period. That said, the rationalist movement did not begin as such, but it could be said to have

4 Fascism and Architecture 71

started with the manifesto of the Gruppo 7. The first group of articles published in the little-known *Rassegna italiana* directed by Tommaso Sillani, from December 1926 to March 1927, proclaiming the new movement were signed by the Gruppo 7—Ubaldo Castagnoli (replaced by Adalberto Libera[50] in 1927), Luigi Figini, Guido Frette, Sebastiano Larco, Gino Pollini, Carlo Enrico Rava and Giuseppe Terragni—all in their mid-twenties and students at the Milan Politecnico. As Droodan remarks, in the *Rassegna* articles the 'Gruppo 7 correctly identified most of the major issues which dominated the discussion of architecture in Italy for the next fifteen years: functionalism, rationalized typologies, contemporary aesthetics, respect for tradition, and the role of the individual architect' (1988, 52). Significantly, this 'new spirit' was fuelled by the likes of Cocteau, Picasso, Strawinsky and Le Corbusier, and it was the result of a new understanding of the idea of composition which had to be based on 'an harmonious resonance of simplicity and concision, which has to be clear and have a brisk rhythm' ('una risonanza armonica di semplicità, concisione, chiara e serrata'; Gruppo 7, 'Gli stranieri', op. cit. in Cennamo (1973: 52)).

Le Corbusier's *Vers une architecture* (1923) and Walter Gropius' *Internationale Architektur* (1925), together with the Peter Behrens, Heinrich Kosina, Erich Mendelshon, Arthur Korn, Hans and Wassili Luckhardt, Alexander and Leonid Vesnin or the Engelbert Mann popular houses in Vienna, were studied as seminal texts by the rationalists more generally since they provided the 'fundamental shapes' ('forme fondamentali') and the 'alphabet' ('alfabeto') for a new aesthetics (e.g. P. M. Bardi, BBPR, Gruppo 7, Pagano, Terragni).[51] These architects presented themselves as the expression of a new spirit in architecture, which favoured Corbusian simplicity of forms, if not purism, which they termed 'the rhythm of construction' and a Gropiusesque return to a new objectivity.[52] Above all, the Gruppo 7 and the rationalists believed in rationality as function, or in the perfect correspondence between the structure of the building and the purpose that it will serve.

Better housing and improved working environments for all social classes was the mission of social architecture, and especially so for Gruppo 7, but to achieve their aims they needed to develop a new architectural language.[53] Gruppo 7's central call for a united effort involving aesthetic

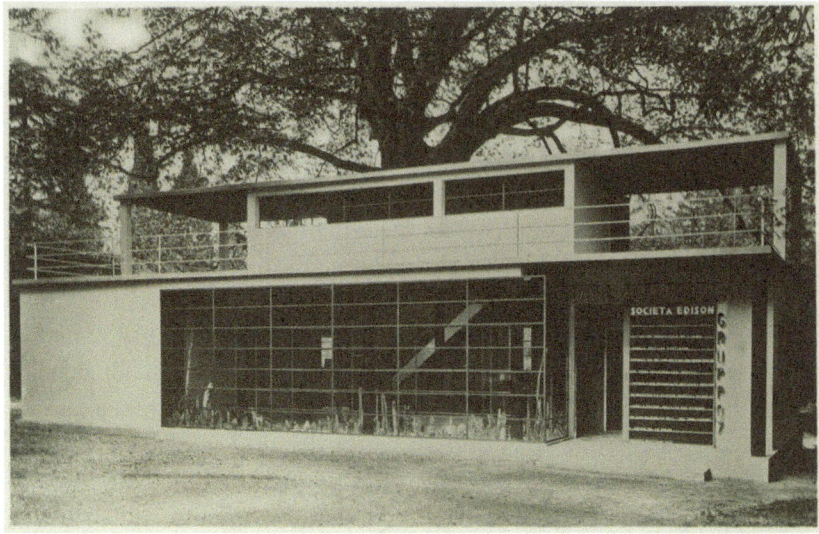

Fig. 4.1 Casa elettrica di Luigi Figini e Gino Pollini alla IV Esposizione Internazionale d'arte decorativa e industriale moderna di Monza (1929–1930). Veduta dell'esterno, 1 fotografia Mart, Archivio del '900, Fondo Luigi Figini e Gino Pollini, Fig.Pol. 3.1.1.6.1. 8

innovation and social modernization through the use of new materials and technology was realised in the Casa elettrica[54] (a 16 × 8 metre rectangular structure with a large living area). While the plans were signed by the whole group, in reality it was the brainchild of the Rovereto-born Luigi Figini and Gino Pollini, and exhibited as the part of the IV Triennale, Monza, in 1930 (Nicoloso 2008, 19) (Fig. 4.1).

The Edison electric company sponsored the project, which showcased alternative materials and paid special attention to the infrastructure surrounding the new type of house. Of particular note is the 'cucina elettrica', the electric kitchen. It featured fourteen new types of appliances and numerous new-fangled pieces of equipment, all completely unknown to Italians, which were envisaged as a means of improving daily living conditions (albeit in a house for the middle classes) by rationalizing effort and the distribution of space. Milanese architect and planner Piero Bottoni designed the kitchen and drew inspiration from the works exhibited at the 1927 Deutscher Werkbund (Erna Mayer and J. J. Oud demonstration kitchen) and from

4 Fascism and Architecture 73

Margarete Schütte-Lihotzky's Frankfurt Kitchen. As foreseen by Gropius and by Ludwig Mies van der Rohe's new architecture in Weimar as well as by Le Corbusier's machine for living, the Casa elettrica was an early example of the social transformation through technology that the regime itself was seeking in order to become a modern, modernizing nation-State (see Rifkind 2012, 91, for details of international influences and reception). Moreover, it was an example of the functional use of spaces and design in a united architectural project, featuring standardized designs (Figs. 4.2a and 4.2b).

In this respect, the description of Austrian-born architect Heinrich Kosina's plans for a power station in Berlin (1925) is a fitting example:

> Linked to the turbine shed, a bare, elemental space, devoid of shadow, is the switch house, its floor covered with a radial pattern of contrasting strips which create rhythmic horizontal rays alternating between light and dark. (*Rassegna italiana*, February 1927, in Cennamo 1973, 45)[55]

Like la Casa elettrica, with its use of glass walls, geometric lighting and *plan libre*, an industrial building had to create harmony and functional integration between external and internal spaces. Linear, open-plan design and new technology had to facilitate the exchange with nature— just as the novel had to simplify syntax to create a closer understanding of reality and gain a 'naturalezza' without ornamentation (see Chap. 7). All this had to be realized by bringing together an attention to the formal properties of materials and the building's specific context with the absolute, rationalist and self-standing forms encapsulated in the new architectural design (Etlin 1991, 227–28 on the notion of the minimum house On the use of colour in the house, see Gregotti and Marzari 1997, 255–56). In all, by the end of the 1920s, Muzio, Figini and Pollini in their conception of the house achieved something similar to what had been theorized for the novel because of their constructive ethos and their attempt at negotiating the boundaries between modernity and tradition, through a process of geometrical rationalization and stylistic essentiality. This notion of narrative rationalization combined the principles of architectural theory, which regarded construction as the rationalization of forms engineered to fulfil a specific function, upheld, for example, in Giuseppe Terragni's Casa del fascio, or glass house (1936), with those

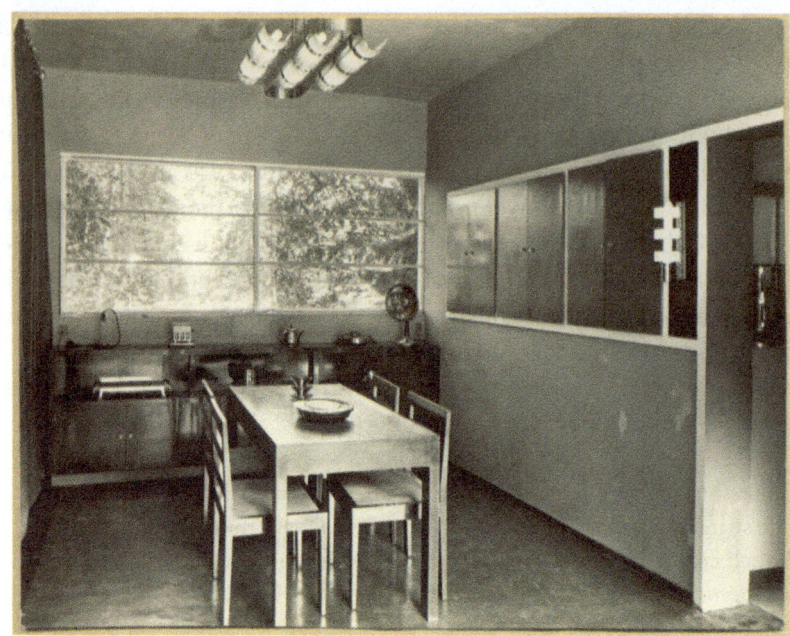

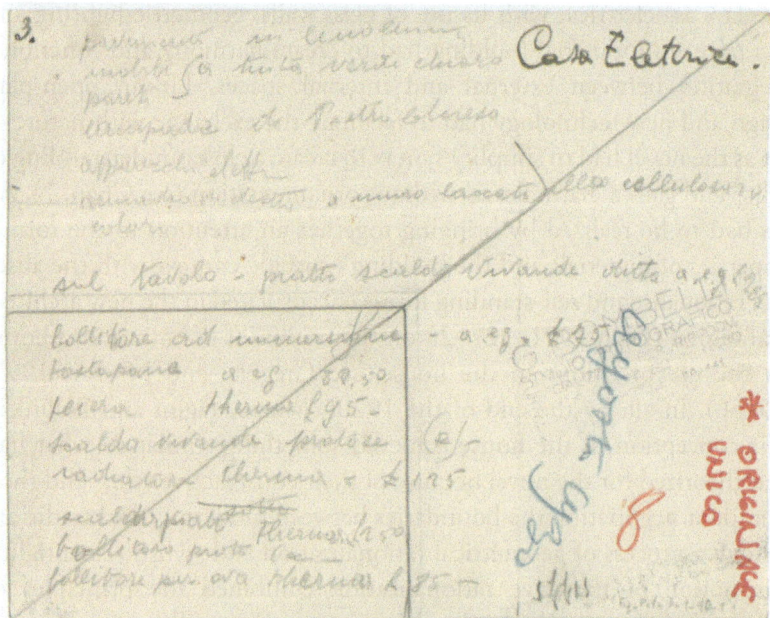

Fig 4.2 (a) La cucina della Casa elettrica di Luigi Figini e Gino Pollini alla IV Esposizione Internazionale d'arte decorativa e industriale moderna di Monza (1929–1930), 1 fotografia, ante/retro; (b) Mart, Archivio del '900, Fondo Luigi Figini e Gino Pollini, Fig.Pol.3.1.1.6.1.4

governing the novel as a national project. Both concepts fused morality and a social mission with a new understanding of the relationship between the subjectivity of the character and the materiality of external reality, no longer understood as mutually excluding entities but as mutually functional to their interconnected existences (Irace 1982, 219–20). In narrative terms, if the *prosa d'arte* was the reflection of reality within the consciousness of the character, in realist writing, external reality was part of the shaping of subjective reality and vice versa. By way of conclusion on the rationalist house and its relationship with architecture, we can mention Gadda's critique of rationalist architecture. In his collection of *novelle, I viaggi del Gulliver, cioè del Gaddus*, we find a short piece entitled 'La casa'. The story's protagonist, the architect Basletta, is a rationalist and the main target of Gadda's critique of modern architecture. Rationalist architecture for the house is self-referential and forgets the needs of those who live in these newly built dwellings in order to pursue an aesthetic and economic mission. Gadda is in favour of old-fashioned houses with thick walls and richly furnished interiors, which just like his own expressionistic use of language do reflect the unresolvable struggles of humans en large (De Seta 1982, 214–15; see Schnapp 2012, 61–62, on the affinities between Portaluppi and his cousin Gadda).

Following the exhibition of rationalist architecture held in Rome in 1928 (March–April) at the Palazzo delle Esposizioni and staged amongst others by architects Adalberto Libera and Giovanni Minnucci, July 1930 witnessed the official birth of the Movimento Italiano per l'Architettura Razionale (MIAR), founded by Libera who served as its first secretary. Presenting the first exhibition, Libera and Minnucci stressed the importance of the relationship between modern architecture and the Italian— and in particular the Roman—tradition, because they both shared a 'constructive power' and because of the parts of a building depend on the unity of its compositional patterns ('Presentazione dell'esposizione', in Patetta 1972, 155).[56] By shifting the focus onto Rome's contribution to modern architecture through its classical tradition, the two architects tried to move the scene from Milan to Rome, and thus involve Piacentini. This extension of their geographical reach would bring the MIAR wider national appeal (Nicoloso 2008, 60). Hence, in 1931, at the second MIAR exhibition—larger, more confrontational and more controversial than the first—held at the Galleria di Roma, owner and curator Pietro Maria Bardi interceded in favour of rationalist architecture and pleaded directly to Mussolini to intervene in support of it. In his 'Rapporto sull'architettura (per Mussolini)', he stated succinctly but unequivocally that architecture had to be orchestrated by the regime and the arts too had to become a sphere under regime control. With his 'Rapporto', Bardi played on various fronts: against the Italian tradition of figurative architecture, against the Futurists and their attempt to hegemonize Italian vanguard design with Prampolini, Fillìa and Depero, and with the goal of placing rationalist architecture firmly at the centre of State art as a true representation of contemporary reality. On the same occasion, Terragni expressed a view on modern architecture and State art, which was slightly different to Bardi's, as Ciucci notes: 'It is the collision between practical existence and the poetry of the architect: [...] it is necessary to ask the State to promote the conditions which will teach the public how to understand what the new architecture means' (2002 [1989], 117).[57] The movement, which sought to bring together architects from all over the country as a united national front, would be dissolved shortly after, on September 5,1931, when Gaetano Minnucci lost his university job at the Sapienza in Rome because of the strong reaction of the National Syndicate of Architects against Bardi's *Tavola degli orrori* ('Table of Horrors'). This tabletop collage mocked Piacentini's Torre Ina in Brescia and Italian traditionalist architecture more generally, especially the Italian pavilion for the Paris exposition of 1925 by Armando Brasini, whose work had been recommended to Mussolini by Margherita Sarfatti. As a consequence of Piacentini's second more violent response to the *Tavola degli orrori*, Minucci and Pollini decided to resign as secretaries of the Rome and Milan sections respectively, and no new leadership could be found ('Difesa dell'architettura italiana', *Giornale d'Italia*, 2 May 1931, XI: 3, in Pisani 1996, 168–73). Terragni had also declared that architecture needed to be promoted by the State in order to become the language used to visualize the myths created by the Fascist regime and embody them in concrete architectural terms—taking a position not dissimilar to that developed by Bontempelli in his theory of the novel and by Bardi himself (see Chap. 5). According to Nicoloso too, the problem faced by the new architecture was one of representation. In Pagano's idea of rationalist architecture, the lack of a figurative dimension prevented it from becoming State art, which primarily needed to be able to create the mythological repertoire of the revolution (Nicoloso 2008, 63).

Yet, while short-lived and soon under attack, the MIAR still represented the first attempt at creating a national organization of rationalist architects, with branches across the country (Turin, Rome and Milan) and various subsections, and also the first concerted attempt at promoting an aesthetic paradigm fusing realism (paying attention to context and tradition), morality and construction. As translations did for the novel, architecture too helped Italian culture to remain on the European map. For the most significant architectural manifestos of the twentieth century hailed, respectively, from Berlin, with a unity of technique which does not necessarily mean renouncing individuality while still remaining rigorous (Bauhaus, 1919); from Moscow, with the rejection of decorative elements (Naum Gabo and Antoine Pevsner, Constructivism, 1920); from France, with the ordering of forms and contours (Le Corbusier, 1923); and collectivist architecture in the De Stijl Manifesto V: − □ + = R4 (Paris, 1922), and finally to the rejection of all aesthetic speculation, of all doctrines, and of formalism (Ludwig Mies van der Roher, 1923). By the end of the 1920s, theoretical declarations on architecture became more frequent, from Bernhard Hoetger, who defined it as the most popular artistic form (World 1928), to the emphasis placed on its public dimension by the CIAM (Congrès internationaux d'architecture moderne) at the Chateau de la Sarraz, Switzerland, in 1928, to the declaration of the absolute authority of objectivity by El Lissitzky upon his return to Moscow from Paris in 1929. In 1932, the American architect R. Buckminster Fuller consecrated architecture as the universal art, founded upon the harmonious equilibrium between space and time. The thread running through these European experiments had been the strongly felt need to reconceptualize the relationship between aesthetics and technique in order to create new spaces and forms, which were no longer meant for the individual but rather for the individual as part of a collective project, and which could thus assume universal value.

As with the novel, the crux of the matter was to find a suitable position between foreign influences and the Italian tradition, between captivating plots and morality. This is where the Italian architectural field could meet with the international scene, as Piacentini himself admitted in 'Nostro Programma' (January 1931) published in the first issue of *Architettura*, the official journal of the national Syndicate of Architects. As we have seen in the case of translations versus the national novel, Italian architects, Piacentini wrote, must enter into dialogue with the international avant-gardes to strengthen the national tradition and eventually triumph over the other artistic movements, notably Sarafatti's Novecento (1–2). In order to preserve his influence, however, Piacentini was prepared to split the field somewhat: modern, cosmopolitan architecture was the architecture of the everyday, while monumental,[58] classical architecture was the style for public art, open spaces and State-funded projects. In January 1931, before the *Tavola degli orrori*, Piacentini had already taken an adversarial position against modern architecture spurred by *Dedalo*, a conservative journal directed by leading art critic Ugo Ojetti, who never approved of rationalist architecture ('Dove è irragionevole l'architettura razionale.' no. 3: 527–40, in Pisani 1996: 161–67). Piacentini's violent reaction in the press—with the labelling of rationalists as Bolsheviks and the demolition of the international scene (Gropius, Le Corbusier, Oud)— caused significant damage to the movement, then still in its infancy. Crucially, he denied the connection between modern architecture and national architecture, thereby dismantling the rationalists' ambition to gain a hegemonic position within the field of State art.

Despite Piacentini's attacks, from 1932 onwards, on Adalberto Libera and Mario de Renzi's rationalist-modernist façade[59] for the Mostra del Decennale, modern architecture, albeit not rationalist architecture per se, became more directly associated with State art, a State that in a benjaminesque-gropiusesque fashion sought to use technology, in particular media technology, to reproduce itself, its history, and to parade its efforts in public.[60] At the Mostra della Rivoluzione, neither classicism nor traditionalism was on display, while Terragni in the Sala O,[61] at the prestigious Sala del 1922, turned his gaze back to the pioneering work of Sant'Elia and the Constructivist movement, both understood as revolutionary directions to follow in the design of public spaces (revolution itself being the process whereby the boundaries between the public and the personal have been eroded).[62] On 4 August 1932, praising Mussolini's collective revolution, Bardi wrote how this modern political system had changed the lives of Italian citizens down to their daily habits and spaces of activity: hence, architecture had to be about clear compositional language and the sharing of collective spaces.[63] As was the case for the novel, commented the avant-gardist and true 'Bolshevik', Immaginist and architect[64] Vinicio Paladini, rationalist architecture ran the risk of becoming bourgeois if it were to follow in Piacentini's footsteps and welcome traditional monumentalism, thereby rejecting innovation.[65] Journalist, writer and *squadrista* Alessandro Pavolini instead declared in the *Bargello*, a bastion of Fascist ideas which he had founded in Florence, that the rationalist movement could help Italy to regain moral and 'aesthetic' ascendancy over other nations (1932, 'Risposta a Ojetti sull'architettura.' 4, no. 18 (1 May): 3). Simultaneously, Piacentini, again in *Architettura*, sought to annihilate rationalist architecture by describing it as a formal problem totally detached from social and moral questions, and from the reality of citizens' lives. In sum, 1932 saw the first centrifugal tendencies within the architectural movement with the return on the scene of Marinetti and Futurist architecture, but also the beginning of the realization of some of the main State-commissioned projects, which would define the *Ventennio* in architectural terms.

The Languages of Architecture

Architecture was public art *par excellence*, an art which inhabited public spaces and tried to function as a space where citizens could be more or less forcefully integrated into the State (Nicoloso 2008, 55).[66] From 1927 to 1932, the regime was moving forward with its campaign for the 'andata al popolo' and it needed visible evidence of its efforts: architecture can serve this purpose and it is one of the intriguing features of the modern movement in Italy that 'it minimized "functionalist" and "machine-age" polemics, playing up instead an abstract aestheticism' (Curtis 1982, 218).

From 16 February 1932 to 31 October 1935, another united front was formed in both aesthetic and political terms: the Città Universitaria[67] in Rome's, La Sapienza university, was the result of a compromise between rationalists and Piacentini, 'a first step towards a more organic and incisive presence for architecture within the totalitarian State'

(Nicoloso 2008, 81).[68] Crucially, Piacentini was now involved in three important projects: the Piazza della Vittoria in Brescia, the new university complex at La Sapienza, and from 1933 onwards, the first competition for Florence's train station.[69] In terms of the new architectural language, the Città Universitaria, encapsulates the unity that Bardi and Bontempelli were calling for in *Quadrante*, by tracing 'a symmetrical plan, which makes use of the classical "model" of the basilica' (Nicoloso 2008, 194). Stylistic unity was achieved through the rationalization of forms according to a shared paradigm, in this case the use of standardized window and frame designs, and the use of similar materials such as travertine marble, glazed brick and yellow and red plaster; but the function of these designs was public and collective and not individual yet socially functional as in the Ca' Brutta, or in the Casa elettrica. If stylistic unity meant a willingness to renounce individuality and to act in a socially responsible way, it needed to be deployed carefully in order to favour collectivity.

At the dissolution of the MIAR, Marinetti had leapt at this opportunity to claim that Futurist architecture was not only the one true State art, but the only real national art.[70] Particularly from the Fascist Revolution exhibition onwards, Futurism came to the fore with C. A. Poggi's *Manifesto dell'architettura* in 1933, followed in 1934 by the *Manifesto futurista dell'architettura aerea* by Angiolo Mazzoni, Filippo T. Marinetti, Mino Somezi, and publications such as *La nuova architettura* in 1931, and *La Città futurista* (1929) and *La Città nuova* (1932–1934) by Fillìa in Turin.[71] Futurist publications such as *Futurismo* (1932–1933) directed by Mino Somezi, *Nuovo futurismo* by Antonio Marasco (1934) and *Stile futurista* (1934–1935) by Fillìa and Prampolini devoted substantial attention to architecture in the context of State art and to the synergies between artistic expressions, namely aero painting and aero sculpture. Of particular interests to the Futurists is how architecture could be functional to the development of the urban fabric, if supported by the State through public competitions (Gino Levi-Montalcini, 1932, 'Architettura Arte di Stato' 1, '*Futurismo*' (11 December): 6). Meanwhile, under the banner of Futurist architecture, Angiolo Mazzoni engaged in the construction of some 20 public buildings, from Sicily to Trentino-Alto Adige, including train stations and post offices, while the rationalist movement reached the zenith of its exposure. All these experiments shared the same aesthetic premise: the recalibration of the relationship between the subjective and the objective and the rationalization of lines to construct a public space for the masses based on principles drawn from international architecture and the classical tradition. However, the Futurists insisted on the importance of the lyrical element in the act of building embodied in mural mosaics such as those in the post offices of La Spezia[72] by Fillìa and Prampolini (1935) and in Palermo a sequence of five mural frescos by Benedetta Cappa and two large paintings by Tato (1934) (Ratti 2003, 292; Lima 2003, 251–54).[73]

In the early 1930s, following in the footsteps of Sant'Elia, Futurism returned to the architectural scene with a more pragmatic and constructivist ambition (the high-rise Torre Littoria in Turin) and Mazzoni was the person to bring all these projects to fruition. The Palazzo delle poste[74] in Pula (1930–1935) coalesced rationalism, the '*edificio-tipo*' and Futurist architecture together with its cylindrical vestibule and circular staircase. The cylinder-like volume at the entrance and the ribbon windows were particularly significant elements of Futurist public art insofar as they fused experimentation with volumes, transparency and openness of public space with solidly assembled supporting structures (Fig. 4.3).

In 1933, for the first time, the V Triennale in the new Palazzo dell' Arte[75] in Milan was dedicated to architecture and not to the decorative

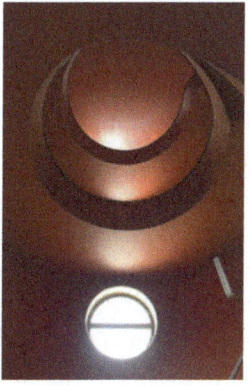

Fig. 4.3 Angiolo Mazzoni, Palazzo delle Poste di Pola (Croatia), courtesy of Katrin Albrecht

arts as had previously been the case and its name changed from Esposizione internazionale delle arti decorative to the Esposizione internazionale d'arte decorative e industriali moderna. The Casa del sabato per gli sposi by the BBPR group and Piero Portaluppi, Umberto Sabbioni and Luigi Santarella, and the Villa-studio per un artista' by Figini and Pollini with Guido Frette were examples of this call for an architecture for the everyday which was functional, and thus modern, and tailored to the needs of new social actors and sectors, as Sironi, in charge of the overall design of the Triennale, had declared in his call for collective art in the *Manifesto della pittura murale*, and now presented in terms of the necessity for collaboration across artistic fields (Sironi, 'Architettura ed arte.' 8 January 1933, *Popolo d'Italia*, in *Scritti*, 138).[76] In an anonymous article in *Casabella*, we read that the Casa per gli sposi is an example of totality in modern architecture; Marinetti (eager to promote Futurist architecture) praised it as modern, and Renato Camus in *Edilizia moderna* called it an elegant example of 'construction'.[77] The Villa studio also attracted significant attention, helped by works by visual artists: Lucio Fontana's polychrome statue of a bather reclining on the edge of the swimming pool, Angelo Del Bon's chiaroscuro fresco and Fausto Melotti's equestrian figure decorated the internal rooms, defining focal points and creating volumetric symmetries. The Villa studio showcased the intersections between the arts advocated both by *Quadrante* and the regime. Abstract artist, author of the influential *KN* (1935), Carlo Belli could not but review it positively in the second issue of *Quadrante* (Rifkind 2012, 70–71). Despite its highly abstract functionalist design, the Villa is an expression of Figini and Pollini's desire to combine classicism—in its pure abstract form as praised by Belli—with an increased focus on *mediterraneità* and the spirituality of the environment, a forerunner of the perfect consonance with the local landscape achieved by Libera with the Villa Malaparte in Capri (1937). Reality, then, had once again to be filtered through rationalized forms and in this way made 'functional' for everyday life according to the '*spirito latino*' and create a sense of metaphysical elation that was not too far removed from theorizations of the novel in this period (Trivellin 1996, 104–16, and Sironi, 'Architettura ed arte.' cit., in *Scritti*, 137 on forms of artistic cross-fertilization).[78] The courtyards (*cortile a impluvio* and *cortile del pruno*) combined *romanità pompeiana* with Le Corbusier's purist house design, especially in the floor layout, which mixed open gardens and closed internal spaces in a rationalized labyrinthine whole (Rifkind 2012, 94). The development of the design of the villa is indicative of a broader trajectory: moving from the fragmented, encyclopaedic design of Muzio's Ca' Brutta to a more cogent and coherent attempt at shaping a functional, stylistically minimal environment for the specific tasks and moments of individual life. The rationalist villa is not a collective building but a space built according to a rationalized geometry and stylized idea of modern living, a practical and conceptual turn which runs parallel to what we have seen in the theory and practice of the novel in the previous chapter.

Within the rationalist group, from 1932 to 1934, the debates took two main paths. On the one hand, there was Pagano's idea of architecture as an assembly of pure forms, embodying high morals but lacking any representational aspirations, which could mould the style and image of a modern State and a mass dictatorship; and on the other, there was Terragni's vision of architecture as principally a social construct, which could help the individual to flourish within the formal structures of the State. Terragni was not concerned with architecture as morality but rather as a social experiment, and with the 'everyday which becomes a small piece in the construction of this "new solid world" of which Bontempelli spoke' (Ciucci 2002 [1989], 148). According to Pagano, architecture was a matter of linearity, of rationalization of forms, expressed in a lucid and morally rigorous language (Ciucci 2002 [1989], 146).[79] He contested Terragni and *Quadrante*'s claim that architects can guide and control reality through their rational architectural projects. According to Pagano, modern architecture needed to distinguish itself from the past by imposing an anti-rhetorical statement about aesthetics. Modernity is anonymity; it is the voice of the new crowds, meeting in public spaces which carry the myth-making power of the regime. And this was the new language which architecture needed to develop, just as the novel, and especially Bompiani's collective novel, required an anti-rhetorical form of prose writing in order to voice collectivity over individuality (Ciucci 2002 [1989], 144–145, see Chap. 7).

Other milestones in these architectural wars were the 1933–1934 competitions for Florence's train station,[80] Santa Maria Novella, won by the Gruppo Toscano led by Michelucci (1932–1936) and for the Palazzo del Littorio (today known as the Farnesina, the Ministry of Foreign Affairs). We will discuss the project for the Florence train station in greater detail in Chap. 7. As far as the 1934 competition for the Palazzo del Littorio in Rome was concerned, 'it formed [...] the crucial point upon which to exert the leverage necessary to bolster the idea that "modern" architecture was the only possible kind of architecture for the "modern" Fascist State' (Ciucci 2002 [1989], 141; Nicoloso 2008, 63).[81] In 1934, Piacentini was amongst the judges and Pagano did not submit a project; he was himself indirectly acting an external assessor from *Casabella*.[82] In the Renaissance tradition, the Palazzo, the headquarters of the Fascist Party, needed to impose itself on the landscape of the capital city, and project authority through a monumentalism achieved by compositional unity. It is interesting to note that two projects, submitted by the Montuori-Piccinato group and the Banfi group respectively, were deemed (too) 'modern' and rejected by the panel for this very reason. The former did, however, receive Pagano's support because it was 'modest, anti-rhetorical and had a moral message', while the latter was rightly seen as being in touch with European influences (Giuseppe Pagano, 1934, 'Il concorso per il Palazzo del Littorio.'[83] *Casabella* 82, no. 8 (October), in De Seta 2008, 20–29). Pagano was of course critical of monumentalism when used as a way of glorifying the regime, instead of being conceived of and used as a means both of supporting the lower classes and of facilitating the development of Fascist civilization.[84]

Terragni also entered the competition with two projects, 'soluzione A' and 'soluzione B'. Piacentini complimented him for having attempted to combine monumentalism with the pressures of social reality (Ciucci 2002 [1989], 147; Nicoloso 2008, 75–77). However, even though Terragni's works had so far been designed to accommodate the masses,[85] according to the panel, on this occasion, his two projects, especially the second one, were worryingly influenced by abstract, rationalist, foreign models, and were too elitist in conception.[86] The gruppo Foschini (Enrico del Debbio, Arnaldo Foschini, Vittorio Morpurgo) won the competition in October 1937. Theirs was a traditional project, but unlike Terragni's monovolumetric 'soluzione B', it was certainly a project which could speak to the masses by adopting a figurative, iconic and accessible language that from 1934 onwards the regime would privilege in public art (e.g. the *stile littorio*). Morality in art was now expressed through a traditional, but reconstructed syntax, which looked less towards the Mediterranean and more to the classical tradition, but which needed to embrace an accessible, figurative language. Although the competition provoked disagreement, it was a milestone insofar as it demonstrated the variety of languages spoken by Italian architects.

From 1935 onwards, Piacentini officially became the leading architect in Italy and he proceeded to sideline rationalist architecture, since its experimental drive was far too removed from the social problems, which the regime, with the decline of consensus, had to tackle. By 1936, as already mentioned, the split between the Milanese Pagano school, more attentive both to the needs of the citizens as social and personal entities and to formal experimentation, and the Rome-based school led by Piacentini, which was moving rapidly from classicism to monumentalism, became starker as the latter gradually overtook the former. The other clear emerging trend was the tension between international aspirations and about the claimed moral ascendancy of the national tradition. After 1936, with Italy's progressive isolation from the international scene after the invasion of Ethiopia, we see a change in architectural language, with a shift towards a more educational and propagandistic tone. Piacentini expressed a new understanding of the role of public architecture[87]: the restoration of Brescia's town centre, the piazza della Vittoria, showed how monumentalism could refashion classical architecture not, as before, in international terms but now as an attempt to consolidate an imperialist tradition, which resorted to clear symbols of domination and grandeur to suit a new political and institutional configuration (Cresti 2015, 17; Nicoloso 2008, 204–09).

Following the triumph of Piacentini's monumentalism over rationalist architecture, one project notable for of its use of classicism is the Sala della Vittoria[88] for the VI Triennale in 1936, designed by Edoardo Persico (1900–1936), featuring white-on-white monochrome of the *Vittoria* and the *Cavalli rampanti* by Lucio Fontana, Giuseppe Palanti and Marcello Nizzoli (Salvagnini 2000, 65–67). The Salone d'Onore is a fine expression of the guiding principles of the architectural movements we have described so far and of a brand of monumentalism which rejected bombastic rhetorical statements in favour of linearity, unity, construction and an anti-rhetorical style, creating an almost magical atmosphere. Persico on the one hand, and Fontana, Palanti and Nizzoli on the other, chose classical forms for the Salone d'Onore because they all believed that classical composition should not be bound to a specific sociopolitical configuration; rather, the universalism of the classical tradition would confer an absolute and ethical value upon rationalized and chromatically coherent forms emphasized by the parallel light beams focusing the visual perspective on the statue of Victory. Classicism thus functioned as the chief symbol of a culture, Fascist in this case, which aspired to a perfect equilibrium between art and construction with a balanced—and universal—(universal) stylistic approach: in other words, to purity and unity (Ciucci 2002 [1989], 150–51; Giò Ponti, 1936, 'La sala della Vittoria.' *Domus* 15, n. 103 (July): 3). Although the exhibition inside the Palazzo dell'Arte was about the house and its furnishings, in the pavilion in the park, Pagano and Daniel's exhibition celebrated the same quality which interested Pagano: 'the aesthetic and moral value of functionality […]. The elements of architecture must be virtually anonymous, collective, perfectible' (Ciucci 2002 [1989], 162; Danesi and Patetta 1988, 83). The 1936 Triennale, like Bontemplelli's *Scacchiera davanti allo specchio*, expressed architecture's mythical, ethereal side and the need for morality to remain quietly anchored in everyday reality.

In 1937–1938 the regime's closing era began, culminating in the planning for the never-completed complex for the E42 Exhibition.[89] This was to be the most monumental of all the projects orchestrated by the regime, with a distinctly pedagogical and propagandistic intention and led on one side by Piacentini and on the other by Pagano. All important architects (Del Debbio, Libera, Michelucci, Muzio, Terragni, the BBPR) were involved to some extent in the project, since architecture now had to work for the regime in constructing myths, based here on the Roman mythology, with very little scope for deviation. The E42 was the expression of the power of images to involve

Italians in the life of the regime, and also of the close collaboration between Piacentini and Mussolini in forging a new architectural, monumental and figurative language, which could express the link between aesthetics and power (Gentile 2009, 201; Nicoloso 2008, 196).[90] In the last major endeavour supported by the regime at the end of its life, Mussolini took the side of the classicist-monumentalists (e.g. the Palazzo della civiltà, the Palazzo dei Congressi and the Palazzo dell'Ina). Pagano was clearly uncomfortable with the project for obvious reasons, but it was Giuseppe Bottai who most forcefully condemned it, reflecting the failure of Mussolini's late artistic policies in the context of WWII. The E42 did not reflect the artistic policies he had been developing since the mid-1920s when he had started promoting artistic eclecticism over a unique style or State art. By 1942, as with his earlier defence of *Primato*'s cultural agenda of 'azione-cultura', Bottai was fully aware of the need to 'save' what could still be rescued. His dismissal of Mussolini's monumentalism was yet another expression of his effort to rescue Fascism from Mussolinism.

The value attributed to architecture throughout the *Ventennio*, however, rested on its social impact. The debate on the novel emphasized similar aspects: social significance, collective ethos, construction over fragmentation of narrative structure. To a certain extent, both were social experiments insofar as they appealed to the idea of radically changing the daily lives of Italians and in so doing become State art, erecting an overarching aesthetic and political order. Both projects called aesthetically for a return to simplicity of execution to favour the sharing of collective spaces. In both cases, a lucid, clear and direct relationship with the materiality of reality was sought—whether in writing or in public buildings, such as in the corporative cities. The spirit had to be anti-bourgeois and in contact with the real. This was to translate politically as a new rationalized dimension of the relationship between the citizen and the State. State art, up until the mid-thirties, thus favoured a pared-down aesthetic construction, which had to eliminate any excess in order to rationalize the experience of daily life for Italians, particularly in collective spaces. By the end of the regime, however, it had become a rhetorical device without resonance.

Notes

1. http://dialecticsofmodernity.manchester.ac.uk/tag/functionalist-architecture; http://dialecticsofmodernity.manchester.ac.uk/tag/fascist-architecture; http://dialecticsofmodernity.manchester.ac.uk/tag/futurist-architecture; http://dialecticsofmodernity.manchester.ac.uk/tag/monumentalism
2. The critical literature on architecture during the Fascist regime is vast and offers a thorough analysis of its historical development; for the purposes of this chapter, it is worth mentioning the works of Ciucci (2002 [1989]), Cresti (1986), Danesi and Patetta (1988), Doordan (1988), Etlin (1991), Nicoloso (2008), which present the most comprehensive and sustained analysis of the architectural field during the *Ventennio*.
3. For a detailed discussion of Wagner's use of the world and its political reverberations, see Pederson (2016, 43–46).
4. For an exploration of these intersections, with a specific view on architecture and the other arts, see Patetta, in Mozzoni and Santini (2009, 3).
5. http://dialecticsofmodernity.manchester.ac.uk/essay/499
6. http://dialecticsofmodernity.manchester.ac.uk/artefact/33; http://dialecticsofmodernity.manchester.ac.uk/artefact/34; http://dialecticsofmodernity.manchester.ac.uk/artefact/35; http://dialecticsofmodernity.manchester.ac.uk/essay/395; http://dialecticsofmodernity.manchester.ac.uk/essay/397; http://dialecticsofmodernity.manchester.ac.uk/essay/394; http://dialecticsofmodernity.manchester.ac.uk/essay/396
7. See Roberts (2011, 2) and, on Prampolini's idea of totalising architecture, Ori (2014, 26–27). On Mazzoni's Futurist architecture, see Mangione (2009, 9–45). For a detailed technical account of Mazzoni's projects for Italian train stations, see Neudecker (2007, 59–192).
8. http://dialecticsofmodernity.manchester.ac.uk/essay/436; http://dialecticsofmodernity.manchester.ac.uk/artefact/112
9. http://dialecticsofmodernity.manchester.ac.uk/artefact/241; http://dialecticsofmodernity.manchester.ac.uk/artefact/242; http://dialecticsofmodernity.manchester.ac.uk/essay/511
10. For an analysis of cultural flows between Germany and Italy in the late 1920s and early 1930s on the subject of the total work of art and total theatre, especially the BL18, see Schnapp (2012, 99–114) and Rifkind (2012, 13).

11. http://dialecticsofmodernity.manchester.ac.uk/artefact/19; http://dialecticsofmodernity.manchester.ac.uk/essay/414; http://dialecticsofmodernity.manchester.ac.uk/essay/405
12. http://dialecticsofmodernity.manchester.ac.uk/artefact/130; http://dialecticsofmodernity.manchester.ac.uk/artefact/143; http://dialecticsofmodernity.manchester.ac.uk/essay/419
13. http://dialecticsofmodernity.manchester.ac.uk/artefact/240; http://dialecticsofmodernity.manchester.ac.uk/artefact/241; http://dialecticsofmodernity.manchester.ac.uk/artefact/242; http://dialecticsofmodernity.manchester.ac.uk/artefact/244; http://dialecticsofmodernity.manchester.ac.uk/artefact/102; http://dialecticsofmodernity.manchester.ac.uk/artefact/103; http://dialecticsofmodernity.manchester.ac.uk/essay/451; http://dialecticsofmodernity.manchester.ac.uk/essay/482; http://dialecticsofmodernity.manchester.ac.uk/essay/512; http://dialecticsofmodernity.manchester.ac.uk/essay/511
14. http://dialecticsofmodernity.manchester.ac.uk/artefact/225; http://dialecticsofmodernity.manchester.ac.uk/artefact/226; http://dialecticsofmodernity.manchester.ac.uk/essay/517; http://dialecticsofmodernity.manchester.ac.uk/essay/517
15. http://dialecticsofmodernity.manchester.ac.uk/artefact/129; http://dialecticsofmodernity.manchester.ac.uk/artefact/136; http://dialecticsofmodernity.manchester.ac.uk/artefact/143; http://dialecticsofmodernity.manchester.ac.uk/essay/420; http://dialecticsofmodernity.manchester.ac.uk/essay/463; http://dialecticsofmodernity.manchester.ac.uk/essay/433; http://dialecticsofmodernity.manchester.ac.uk/essay/419
16. http://dialecticsofmodernity.manchester.ac.uk/essay/409
17. http://dialecticsofmodernity.manchester.ac.uk/artefact/137; http://dialecticsofmodernity.manchester.ac.uk/essay/427
18. http://dialecticsofmodernity.manchester.ac.uk/essay/456
19. http://dialecticsofmodernity.manchester.ac.uk/essay/464
20. http://dialecticsofmodernity.manchester.ac.uk/essay/437
21. http://dialecticsofmodernity.manchester.ac.uk/artefact/105; http://dialecticsofmodernity.manchester.ac.uk/essay/454; http://dialecticsofmodernity.manchester.ac.uk/essay/495
22. http://dialecticsofmodernity.manchester.ac.uk/artefact/116; http://dialecticsofmodernity.manchester.ac.uk/essay/436; http://dialecticsofmodernity.manchester.ac.uk/essay/407

23. Notable examples are Prampolini's cosmic experiments, especially in aero painting (Lista 2013, 211–26).
24. http://dialecticsofmodernity.manchester.ac.uk/tag/totalitarian-art
25. 'A mio giudizio la massima di tutte le arti,—disse Mussolini,—è l'architettura, perchè comprende tutto'. 1932. 'Colloqui con Mussolini sull'arte.' *L'Italia letteraria* 4, no. 27 (3 July): 1. See also the article by Bernardo Giovenale, 1933, 'Avvenire delle corporazioni.' *Quadrante* 1, no. 4 (August): 2–7, where he reinforced the point regarding Fascist doctrine being about the collective sense of life.
26. http://dialecticsofmodernity.manchester.ac.uk/essay/414
27. http://dialecticsofmodernity.manchester.ac.uk/essay/522
28. http://dialecticsofmodernity.manchester.ac.uk/artefact/41; http://dialecticsofmodernity.manchester.ac.uk/essay/497; http://dialecticsofmodernity.manchester.ac.uk/essay/494
29. http://dialecticsofmodernity.manchester.ac.uk/essay/481
30. http://dialecticsofmodernity.manchester.ac.uk/essay/518
31. http://dialecticsofmodernity.manchester.ac.uk/essay/393
32. http://dialecticsofmodernity.manchester.ac.uk/essay/418
33. These buildings have been extensively discussed in the context of the role of architecture in State art; see, for example, Storchi (2007, 237–44) and Schumacher (1991, 140–70). See also Bontempelli's praise of Terragni's use of glass, in *L'avventura novecentista*, September 1936, 336.
34. For a detailed discussion of the technical specifications of the Casa del fascio, see Federica Dal Falco, 'Caratteri costruttivi' (2002, 13–33).
35. http://dialecticsofmodernity.manchester.ac.uk/artefact/25; http://dialecticsofmodernity.manchester.ac.uk/essay/405; http://dialecticsofmodernity.manchester.ac.uk/essay/480
36. Two examples are particularly telling regarding this transition. The first was the violent polemic, published in *La Tribuna* between 2 and 26 February 1933, between Piacentini and Ugo Ojetti over the use of arches and columns, with the former accusing the latter of not being able to accept the changes required by the new society (see Piacentini 'Gli archi e le colonne e l'italianità d'oggi' and 'Archi e colonne' in Pisani 1996, 182–190). The second was Piacentini's article on the competition to design the Palazzo del Littorio. He accepts new architecture as long as it is placed in the service of the regime (1934, 'Il concorso nazionale per il progetto del Palazzo del Littorio e della Mostra della Rivoluzione

Fascista in via dell'Impero.' *Architettura* XIII: 3, cited in Pisani 1996, 191–92). Doordan sees 1936 as a watershed moment for architecture (Doordan 1988, 143).

37. http://dialecticsofmodernity.manchester.ac.uk/artefact/26; http://dialecticsofmodernity.manchester.ac.uk/essay/401; http://dialecticsofmodernity.manchester.ac.uk/essay/470
38. http://dialecticsofmodernity.manchester.ac.uk/essay/432
39. For the history of the Ca' Brutta, see Etlin (1991, 166, 180–81) and Irace (1994, 5). Equally important 'Novecento style' houses were Giuseppe de Finetti's Casa della Meridiana (1925, Milan) and Giuseppe Pagano's office-building Palazzo Gualino (Turin, 1928–1930) with their use of hyper-rationalised linear patterns and volumes combining classical linear rigour with modern functionality.
40. http://dialecticsofmodernity.manchester.ac.uk/essay/505; http://dialecticsofmodernity.manchester.ac.uk/essay/506; http://dialecticsofmodernity.manchester.ac.uk/essay/486
41. http://dialecticsofmodernity.manchester.ac.uk/essay/505
42. For a discussion of the key ideas expressed in the Manifesto, which originated from the soirées at Sarfatti's Milanese salon, and especially for the change in meaning of the word 'sintesi' (synthesis) as theorised by the Futurists first and then revised by Sarfatti and the Novecento movement, see Pontiggia (2003, 159–75). The Manifesto was written in opposition to the Valori plastici movement and De Chirico, Savinio and Carrà to call for a work of art which was synthetic, composition, construction and not fragmentation (161).
43. The artistic movement would be publicly endorsed three years later at Lino Pesaro's elegant gallery by Mussolini on 26 March 1923. Novecento stood for a return to tradition and classical tradition, combined with the need to express modern values. On this famous occasion, Mussolini dismissed the idea of State art and admitted that the artistic sphere was an integral part of the sphere of the individual, 'Alla mostra del Novecento. Parole di Mussolini sull'arte e sul Governo.' *Il Popolo d'Italia*, 27 March 1923. A similar conceptualization, only expressed in stronger terms, would be reiterated on 5 October 1926 at the Accademia delle Belle Arti di Pesaro, with the official consecration of Novecento as a movement. Mussolini now explicitly called for a new art, a Fascist art attuned to the present historical moment, but not directed by the regime (see Chap. 2).

44. For a comprehensive cultural and technical analysis of the Novecento and rationalist Milanese houses of the 1930s, see the recent volume edited by Isastia and Pierini (2017).
45. For a reading of the Ca' Brutta aesthetic premises in relation to the Valori plastici movement, see Isastia (Isastia and Pierini 2017, 468–69).
46. On Loos' influence on the Novecento movement, see Droodan's analysis of the Pizzigoni House, 1925–27, (1988, 38).
47. http://dialecticsofmodernity.manchester.ac.uk/essay/498
48. 1930, Mostra di Onoranze all'architetto futurista Antonio Sant'Elia, Como.
49. http://dialecticsofmodernity.manchester.ac.uk/artefact/20; http://dialecticsofmodernity.manchester.ac.uk/artefact/37; http://dialecticsofmodernity.manchester.ac.uk/essay/417; http://dialecticsofmodernity.manchester.ac.uk/essay/416; http://dialecticsofmodernity.manchester.ac.uk/essay/415
50. http://dialecticsofmodernity.manchester.ac.uk/artefact/30; http://dialecticsofmodernity.manchester.ac.uk/essay/492; http://dialecticsofmodernity.manchester.ac.uk/essay/491
51. Gruppo 7, 'Gli stranieri', in Cennamo (1973, 51). In 1925, returning from the Paris exhibition, Fortunato Depero introduced Le Corbusier to the Italian public (Doodran 1988, 51). See also P. M. Bardi, 1934, 'Le Corbusier a Roma.' *Quadrante* 13 (May): 5 and for a detailed account of the Swiss architect's work in relation to Italian architecture, especially the tensistruttura, see Guido Fiorni, 1933, 'L'inventore Le Corbusier poeta-archietto della presente civiltà macchinista.' *Architettura* 2, no.6 (June): 357–64.
52. Beginning in 1926, a four-part series of articles appeared in the cultural review *Rassegna italiana*, proclaiming the existence of a 'new spirit' in architecture. The principal elements of Le Corbusier's new architectural language articulated in his seminal text were: pillars, the roof as symbolic garden, open plan, ribbon windows and a free-standing façade. Gropius instead insisted on the principles of standardization and rationalization in architecture, through the use of similar designs and new materials.
53. See, for example, Alberto Sartoris, 1933, 'Surrealismo e funzionalismo.' *Quadrante* 1, no. 4 (August): 29–30 and Alberto Sartoris, 1933, 'Per un'architettura integrale.' Ibid., no. 7 (November): 8–9. Sartoris linked the lyrical element of artistic creation with individual daily necessities.

54. 'al fabbricato delle turbine, nudo, elementare, senza ombre, si innesta l'edificio quadri, a solette sovrapposte e sporgenti tutto all'intorno così da alternare ritmicamente fasce orizzaontali di luce e di ombre'.
55. http://dialecticsofmodernity.manchester.ac.uk/essay/380
56. Libera-Minucci, *Introduzione*, in *I Esposizione italiana di architettura razionale*, catalogue of the exhibition, De Alberti, Rome, 1928, now in Patetta (1972, 127–28).
57. For a clear assessment of the second MIAR exhibition and reactions to it, see Kallis (2014, 63–66) and Etlin (1991, 385).
58. http://dialecticsofmodernity.manchester.ac.uk/tag/classical-tradition
59. http://dialecticsofmodernity.manchester.ac.uk/essay/492
60. The Mostra della Rivoluzione was directed by Libera and De Renzi, supported by Piacentini and supervised by Dino Alfieri. It ran for two years, from 28 October 1932 to 28 October 1934, and enjoyed extraordinary success, with a total of 3,700,000 visitors.
61. http://dialecticsofmodernity.manchester.ac.uk/essay/466; http://dialecticsofmodernity.manchester.ac.uk/artefact/23; http://dialecticsofmodernity.manchester.ac.uk/essay/492
62. On the arguments within the rationalist front Bardi (*Quadrante*), Terragni, and Pagano, see Patetta (1972, 119–51) and Ciucci (2002 [1989], 129–51), while on those within the monumentalists front (Piacentini and Ojetti), see (Patetta 1972, 315–33).
63. P. M. Bardi, 1933, 'La Rivoluzione "Consegna" di Mussolini.' *Quadrante* 1, no. 4 (May): 1.
64. http://dialecticsofmodernity.manchester.ac.uk/essay/495
65. Vinicio Paladini, 1933, 'Imborghesimento del razionalismo.' *Quadrante* 1, no. 3 (July): 36.
66. On the relationship between architects and Mussolini and on his close scrutiny of State-commissioned projects, see Nicoloso (2008, 79–80, especially Chaps. 6 and 7).
67. http://dialecticsofmodernity.manchester.ac.uk/artefact/41; http://dialecticsofmodernity.manchester.ac.uk/essay/497; http://dialecticsofmodernity.manchester.ac.uk/essay/494
68. Giò Ponti designed the Maths building, Pagano the Physics building, and Piacentini the Rectorate.
69. http://dialecticsofmodernity.manchester.ac.uk/essay/522
70. Fillìa's 'Futurismo e Fascismo' was published in April 1929 in *La Città futurista* (Patetta 1972, 257–61). He considered Futurism and archi-

tecture to be the highest forms of artistic expression, and hence de facto as State art. Bontempelli, however, was critical of Futurist architecture, seeing it as being concerned with the aestheticization of forms rather than with the function these have to perform (January 1934, *L'avventura novecentista*, 328–39).

71. As early as the 1928 Turin Expo, the Futurist pavilion provided a dedicated space for Futurist architecture.
72. http://dialecticsofmodernity.manchester.ac.uk/essay/407
73. The theme for La Spezia was *Le vie del mare e del cielo* and the two mosaics were entitled *Le communicazioni terrestri e marittime* (Fillìa) and *Le communicazioni telegrafiche, telefoniche e aeree* (Prampolini), while in 1938 in Palermo the theme for Benedetta Cappa's frescos is the *Vie delle communicazioni di terra, di mare e d'aria, telegrafiche e radiofoniche*, and for Tato (Guglielmo Sansoni) youth and work.
74. http://dialecticsofmodernity.manchester.ac.uk/essay/396
75. http://dialecticsofmodernity.manchester.ac.uk/essay/401
76. Sironi et al. (1933), in Sironi, *Scritti*, 156. Sironi, 1934, 'Manifesto.' *L'Ambrosiano* (26 July), in *Scritti*, 173–75.
77. Anonymous, 1933, 'La casa del sabato per gli sposi.' *Casabella* 11, no. 6 (June): 10–11 in Trivellin (1996, 73, also for the attribution of the article), Arch. R. Camus, 1933, 'La casa del sabato degli sposi.' *Edilizia moderna* XI–XII, no. 10–11 (August–December): 24–27, and F. T. Marinetti, 1933, 'Premessa alla Quinta Triennale di Milano'. In *Catalogo Ufficiale* (Milan: Ceschina, 54).
78. On 6 August 1933 in *L'Italia letteraria* Edoardo Persico was fairly critical of the Casa studio, but praised the Casa del sabato for its European take on stylistic innovation, 'Alla Triennale. Gli architetti italiani.' 4, no. 32: 4.
79. On the progressive marginalization of architects from the *architettura di Stato*, see De Seta (1998, 81–91).
80. http://dialecticsofmodernity.manchester.ac.uk/essay/522
81. Giovanni Michelucci was a highly regarded professor of architecture at Florence University; for further details on the competition, see Chap 7.
82. From 1933, *Casabella* was co-directed by Persico and Pagano, who was also editor-in-chief of *Domus*.
83. http://dialecticsofmodernity.manchester.ac.uk/essay/480
84. On the nuances of the understanding of monumentalism by Piacentini, Ojetti and Pagano, see Nicoloso (2008, 61–63).
85. http://dialecticsofmodernity.manchester.ac.uk/tag/sacralization

86. For an analysis of the relationship between Terragni and Bontempelli, see Storchi (2007, 237–40), and especially Storchi (2012) on the cultural exchanges and working dynamics between Bontempelli-Bardi's *Quadrante* and the worlds of literature and architecture, and Chap. 5 for a fuller discussion.
87. http://dialecticsofmodernity.manchester.ac.uk/essay/405
88. http://dialecticsofmodernity.manchester.ac.uk/essay/427
89. http://dialecticsofmodernity.manchester.ac.uk/essay/491
90. Writing in *Casabella*, Pagano is critical of monumentalism because he deems it an unsuitable language for portraying modern society. In a later article, 'Chi si ferma è perduto', he looks back at Palazzo Gualino, thought at the time to represent an 'absurd nakedness', but now the mark of modern building (1938, *Casabella-Costruzioni*, no. 128, (August), in De Seta 2008, 45).

Open Access This chapter is licensed under the terms of the Creative Commons Attribution 4.0 International License (http://creativecommons.org/licenses/by/4.0/), which permits use, sharing, adaptation, distribution and reproduction in any medium or format, as long as you give appropriate credit to the original author(s) and the source, provide a link to the Creative Commons licence and indicate if changes were made.

The images or other third party material in this chapter are included in the chapter's Creative Commons licence, unless indicated otherwise in a credit line to the material. If material is not included in the chapter's Creative Commons licence and your intended use is not permitted by statutory regulation or exceeds the permitted use, you will need to obtain permission directly from the copyright holder.

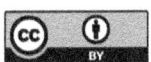

5

900 and *Quadrante*: Theorizing an Interdisciplinary Aesthetic Model

The metaphor of construction, and of the artist as constructor, enjoyed considerable currency in the Fascist period and marked many artists' and critics' vision of art and of the creative process (see Cioli 2011, 204–07; Salvagnini 2000, 30–32). Art critic Mario Tinti, for instance, had in 1927 heralded a 'new architectonic era' ('una nuova era architettonica'), calling for 'an art of the people, monumental and religious' ('un'arte del popolo, monumentale e religiosa') (cited in Salvagnini 2000, 30). The Fascist artist *par excellence*, Mario Sironi, took architecture and the figure of the architect as the subject of several of his paintings, and subsequently theorized mural painting (Sironi 1932; Sironi et al. 1933), establishing both an intellectual and a practical bond between painting and architecture. He conceived of the role of the artist in a collectivist society such as that envisioned by Fascism, as akin to that of a constructor, building on the solid cultural traditions of the nation, work and the family (Salvagnini 2000, 31; Pontiggia 1990). Our argument here, then, is that architecture and the novel intersected and developed in particularly close conjunction as intertwined aesthetic projects grounded in a set of common principles, and working to support the Fascist political project. In the journals *900* and *Quadrante*, they found two crucial platforms for expression and dissemination. The common principles they shared, as outlined in our first three chapters, were 'constructive' effort, the rationalization of aesthetic forms, the 'return to the real', the moral dimension of art, the establishment of a relationship between artists and the masses, and the collective and anti-individualistic meaning of art. The relationship between the novel and architecture under Fascism has received a certain degree of scholarly attention in relation to Bontempelli's thought (see Longatti 1969; Scarsella 1993; Tentori 1996; Storchi 2012; Sinopoli 2017). In this book, however, and in this chapter specifically, Bontempelli's crucial theoretical contribution is related to, and contextualized within, broader aesthetic projects which sought to establish structural links between the architectural and novelistic artistic fields with respect to their interaction with the Fascist regime. The chapter is divided into two sections. In the first section we will examine *900*, before moving on to analyse *Quadrante*'s programme in the second section, showing how discourses and debates on these journals constructed the novel and architecture as two deeply interconnected aesthetico-political endeavours.

Interaction between the arts was a cornerstone of Bontempelli's work and thought. Architecture and the novel held a privileged position in his interdisciplinary, inter-artistic paradigm. He saw literature as the '*substance of connection among all the superior activities of men*' ('*la sostanza di collegamento tra tutte le attività superiori dell'uomo*'), the artistic form which provided men with the means to gain and express a comprehensive vision of human experience (from a speech pronounced in 1942, reprinted in Bontempelli 1945, 217, emphasis in original). This definition should be read in light of the centrality attributed by Bontempelli to the idea of unity, not only in the arts, but in human activities more generally, as he stated in the article opening the first issue of *Quadrante*:

> The most interesting research that men can carry out by looking around themselves is the pursuit of unity. By this I mean unity of vision, and therefore of judgement. [...] Finding the centre from which one can see the movement of philosophical speculation, of artistic expression, of political action, of scientific curiosity, of the language of tradition, of everyday life—as one single harmonious fact. Unearthing its central rhythm. (Bontempelli 1933a)[1]

Crucially, this unity was also to be found in the synergy between aesthetics and politics, which Bontempelli regarded at this time as 'two facets of a unified human enterprise' (Rifkind 2012, 57).[2] As he declared on the occasion of the debate on *Critica fascista*, discussed in Chap. 2, 'by "Fascism" we mean a whole orientation of life, public and private: a total and perfect order that is practical and theoretical, intellectual and moral, application and spirit' (Bontempelli 1926a, 416).[3] He later identified this convergence of the aesthetic and political spheres as one of the defining principles of *L'avventura novecentista*: '[…] this *unforeseen book* documents a frame of mind prone to seeking harmony between the literary and the political spheres […]' (cited in Jacobbi 1974, xiv).[4]

His interest in architecture largely derived from his belief in the intertwined nature of art and politics. In one of his most famous pieces on architecture, 'Architecture as morality and politics', he asserted that the reason why he was so passionate about a subject with which he was admittedly 'unfamiliar' was that

> […] it is not a question of architecture, it is not even a question of taste or aesthetics: it is a question of morality. The polemic around architecture is a profoundly political polemic. […] An epoch reveals itself in all of its architecture. (Bontempelli 1933d, now in 1974 [1938], 334)[5]

Architecture was an art form that embodied the spirit, values and morality of an era, and as such was necessarily political. Bontempelli also used it as a metaphor for the process of artistic creation, which needed to reflect the 'constructive' spirit of the new era. Accordingly, he very often referred to processes of artistic creation using the terms 'build(ing)' and 'construction', as will be shown in this chapter.

900: Writing as Myth-Building

The first issue of *900* came out in November 1926. It was initially published in French, with the title *900. Cahiers d'Italie et d'Europe*. The title and choice of language are notable, in that they indicate an attempt at connecting and opening up Italian culture to Europe.[6] Predictably, this choice attracted criticism, particularly, but not exclusively, from hard-line Fascist milieus. In an article published in the third issue, Bontempelli acknowledged that the *900* project had been criticized in Italy for being 'a shady enterprise of Europeanist internationalism' and in Europe for being 'a vigilant critic of voracious Italian imperialism' (Bontempelli 1927b, 163).[7] Unsurprisingly, the seemingly contradictory position occupied by Bontempelli and his project—which proclaimed itself close to the regime and an advocate of a dominant and unmistakably Italian national art, but also, through its choice of language and its numerous international collaborations, clearly looked outwards to Europe—was the object of criticism from various quarters (Jewell 2008, 729; Gennaro 2010).[8] After defending his position by claiming that opposed criticisms invalidate one another, Bontempelli restated the 'principal theoretical positions' ('principales positions théoriques') of the journal (Bontempelli 1927b, 164), which up until then had been presented in a rather piecemeal fashion in the preambles and elsewhere. This list of principles is a good starting point for an analysis of the theoretical programme proposed by the journal and of how it wove architecture and the novel together in its formulation of an aesthetic project alongside the political one. These principles included: the rejection of aestheticism and psychologism, seen as the degeneration of the classical and Romantic spirit respectively; the art of writing conceived as architecture, that is, the modification of the inhabitable world, which consisted in inventing myths and fables for the new era; the rejection of lyricism, metre and style; the rejection of orientalism and the formulation of a new idea of 'imagination' and the *merveilleux* (magic—hence the name 'magical' or 'mystical realism'); the progression beyond the elitist spirit of the avant-garde in favour of a direct engagement with the masses; and the reinforcement of Italy's central position in the formation of a new Mediterranean culture.

These principles were the basis of a general effort of reconstruction and engagement with the real, particularly evident in the architectural and literary fields, which reacted against both the Romantic conception of art as an expression of personal feelings, and to the destructive spirit of the early twentieth-century avant-gardes. When applied to literature, powerful use was made of the parallel with architecture, which provided a productive metaphor and conceptual model through the idea of 'building things' and 'building stories'. The statement that opened the first issue and thus began the 'Novecento adventure'—naturally written by Bontempelli—was a declaration of the centrality of this idea to *900*'s theoretical programme: 'The most urgent and precise task of the twentieth century will be the reconstruction of time and space' (reprinted in Bontempelli 1974 [1938], 9). Bontempelli clarified that this was the task of art, and not of philosophy: the palingenetic effort pertained to the creative and irrational human sphere, rather than to the rational one (see Chap. 2, p. 25). Bontempelli discussed this further in a commentary added in January 1928 and published in *L'avventura novecentista*. The task of what he called the 'Third Era', which was about to start (Bontempelli 1974 [1938], 13), was that of recovering the belief in the objectivity of the real, in the objective existence of an external universe outside and independently of Man. The underlying idea was that something objective existed beyond human consciousness and its subjectivity, necessitating a new relationship between the subjectivity of the artist and the object, the real. Space and time, the foundations of this universe, themselves needed to be reconstructed, because the 'previous era' had undertaken to destroy them and deny their existence. The reconstruction of time and space was the essential precondition for the 'recovery of the individual' ('ritrovamento dell'individuo'), a figure possessing a definite individuality and collective identity, and an awareness of their responsibilities and absolute morality, all of which democratic relativism strove to deny (Bontempelli 1974 [1938], 9, 27–28).

These theoretical premises show how inseparable *900*'s aesthetical project was from politics, and illustrate the nature of the interrelations between the two spheres. For the new idea of art advocated by the journal was indeed a reaction to aesthetic and political tendencies of the previous period, which were perceived as decadent and leading to inexorable moral decay. In the artistic sphere, these were aestheticism, that is, the myth of beauty and of art for art's sake, which had dismissed questions of art's morality; and impressionism, which had made the artist's fleeting personal impressions into an artistic ideal, preventing proper engagement with the real. In psychology, there was Freudianism, which had led to a loss of contact with external reality. In the political sphere, there was the 'democratic spirit' ('lo spirito democratico'), which validated any idea and tendency, without acknowledging the existence of an objective reality with its 'superior laws' ('legg[i] superior[i]') that should come before personal interests and convictions (Bontempelli 1974 [1938], 27–28). The principles of *900*'s 'new art' were defined in explicit opposition to these aesthetic and political tendencies. In his first 'preamble', Bontempelli emphasized the central role of architecture and of the architectural metaphor in his aesthetic paradigm, further developing the image of art as (re) construction. As well as the necessity of reconstructing space and time, he stated the need to 'learn the art of building things again, in order to invent the fresh myths from which a new atmosphere will originate, which we need in order to breathe' (Bontempelli 1974 [1938], 10).[9]

Bontempelli's call to 'reconstruct reality' yet also 'invent myths' was only an apparent contradiction: the ultimate aim of the reconstruction of reality, of the 'solid world' ('mondo solido'), was to pace its boundaries and get to know it from the ground up in order to be able to modify it and shape it through art—again taking architecture as a conceptual model. Through this process, it would be possible to establish control over the external world, and finally 'subvert its laws' ('sconvolgerne le leggi')—achieving what Bontempelli called 'magic' ('magia'), in an aesthetic project which he duly termed 'magical realism' ('realismo magico').[10] This process would culminate in the creation of modernity, which at that time only existed as a project, an object of the imagination; modernity was 'a subject yet to come, not fully actualized' (Buonanno 2003, 241), one which needed being built. This conception of art is clearly divergent from more conventional, mimetic forms of realism in that, here, reality must be interpreted and transfigured through the artist's imagination, rather than merely documented (Micali 2002, 93). This theorization of an art that could support the regime and build its culture, while not being openly political, was in line with the complexity and heterogeneity of the nature of the relationships between the regime and the arts discussed in Chap. 2 (see also Jewell 2008, 731).[11]

The fact that Bontempelli was concerned above all with literature, despite using the more generic term 'art', was implicit given the nature of the journal, which was essentially literary, with some space devoted to interdisciplinary reflections, discussion of other artistic forms (such as theatre and cinema), and even of non-artistic activities (such as boxing and motor racing). The journal's primarily literary focus became clearer in the theoretical discussions which appeared in the first few issues. The third preamble was entitled 'Consigli' and contained suggestions for writers (Bontempelli 1974 [1938], 17–21). An article entitled 'Mendicità' published in the fourth issue, in October 1928, emphasized literature's power to embody the spirit of its time, and hence its essential value in supporting an 'imperial' political project:

> The old regime despised writers. I believe in the new regime there are a few politicians—two or three perhaps, and certainly one—who are willing to give literature the consideration it deserves. [...] By 'the consideration it deserves', I mean that literature is the highest expression of an age and at the same time its most delicate function. As such, it is the greatest ally of an epoch and of a project that wish to be called imperial. (Bontempelli 1974 [1938], 114–15)[12]

The idea of encapsulating the 'spirit' of the Fascist era was the key focus around which the whole debate about Fascist art revolved (see Chap. 2, section 'Defining Fascist Art'). Bontempelli believed literature to be an especially suitable art form to fulfil this ideal. He also believed that the regime—at least Mussolini—had understood this, and had assigned literature and writers a new, central role, which contrasted with the alienation they had suffered under the liberal state. Writers should in turn not 'ask for protection' ('chiedere protezione'), but rather 'offer collaboration' ('offrire collaborazione'), carrying out their crucial function of supporting the Fascist project and educating the masses.

The theoretical programme of *900* was articulated mainly through Bontempelli's writings. However, the contributions of other authors were also crucial to its development. The writer Corrado Alvaro, for instance, was a regular contributor, and his articles were instrumental in defining the aesthetico-political agenda promoted by the journal. Two of his articles in particular merit discussion here: 'L'età della letteratura' (1926a) and 'La prosa' (1928). As is evident from the titles, Alvaro was, like Bontempelli, an advocate of the primacy of fiction, especially in its relation with history and politics. In these two articles, he proposed an idea of literature as the national art *par excellence*, the aesthetic practice that makes a nation, and therefore *a fortiori* creates reality. He understood literature as a 'social fact' ('fatto sociale') and a 'practical instrument' ('strumento pratico'), with a stronger connection with history and eloquence than with poetry. He situated the value of literature in its social function rather than in its lyrical content: literature, and fiction in particular, was able to create myths that forged national communities, and had historically fulfilled this purpose. Alvaro cited the example of Russia where, after suffering English and French cultural domination, people 'became typically Russian after an aesthetics of the Russian character was invented by writers' (1926a, 59). Literature therefore shaped the character of the nation and of its citizens, and 'the strength of a people consists in believing in the myths that are invented for them' (57). Thus, the novelist could 'invent' the spirit, sentiments and aspirations of a new—and in this case Fascist—era, making them legible and real for all (Alvaro 1928, 70). In an article entitled 'Moralità' (1926b), also published in the fifth issue, he reiterated this idea, calling for the construction of a new Italian civilization imbued with a new 'morality', through art.

It should be noted that, like Bontempelli, Alvaro made use of architectural metaphors to describe the type of literature that Italian society needed in this phase of its history:

> Since the war, Italy has lived its first truly national life [...]. Slowly, the province becomes people, distinctive customs and characters disappear, psychological characteristics are reinforced [...]. If until yesterday the art of the Italian writer consisted in inventing social agglomerates based on foreign, and especially French models [...], today one only needs to look around to realize the immense subject matter that writers have under their noses. [...] It is natural that no poet of this transformation of classes yet exists. [...] Before the Baudelaires, we need those great builders of shared houses and castles in the air whose name is Hugo. (Alvaro 1928, 70–71)[13]

'National' novelists, who contribute to forging the spirit of a new era and building national myths, were evoked through the image of 'great builders of shared houses' which, among other things, recalled the debates and experiments being carried out in the field of social architecture at this time (see the second part of this chapter on *Quadrante*, and the section on the Olivetti factory, Chap. 7). These novelists were vital, and came before poets in the process of making a nation, just as Hugo had come before Baudelaire in France.

Architecture as a Conceptual Model

Bontempelli articulated his theorization of a new literature through the metaphor of architecture, proving how he conceived of the two artistic forms as bound together in a structural and conceptual relationship. In his aesthetic model, 'the feminine aspiration to the condition of music will make way for the virile laws of architecture' ('l'aspirazione femminile alla musica farà luogo alle leggi virili dell'architettura'), 'music' being the lyrical, Romantic, impressionist element of literature, and 'architecture' being its element of construction, connected to the 'art of narrating' ('l'arte del narrare') (Bontempelli 1974 [1938], 10).[14]

New literature would therefore be anti-lyrical and anti-Romantic. Logically, this theoretical principle led to a predilection for fiction over poetry: 'As far as literature is concerned, we will see the work of fiction come to the fore, especially fiction based on invention and storyline' (Bontempelli 1974 [1938], 16).[15] To describe this process of artistic creation, which had as its ultimate aim the creation of myths, the metaphor of the work of the architect was used:

> Once we have placed a new solid world before us, our most pressing task will be to pace around it and explore it; to carve blocks of stone from it and place them one upon the other to put up weighty constructions, relentlessly modifying the shell of the earth we have reclaimed. (Bontempelli 1974 [1938], 10)[16]

This conception of literature, grounded in the predominance of the storyline and the aspiration to 'invent myths', was opposed to the artistic ideal based on the artist's subjectivity, sensations, and the supreme value of introspection that had hitherto prevailed (see Chap. 3). Among his suggestions for writers in the third preamble, Bontempelli included the recommendation to 'learn the ropes' in a newsroom, by practising turning news snippets into stories able to engage readers (Bontempelli 1927a, reprinted in 1974 [1938], 17).

In a later article, he developed this idea into a comparison between the writer-journalist and the architect-engineer, emphasizing the primary importance of 'craft', namely the ability to tell stories for a writer, and to design functional buildings for an architect (Bontempelli 1974 [1938], 55–56). In his view, every architect first had to be an engineer, just as any writer first had to be good at crafting stories.[17] The widespread belief in a separation of such a 'technical' element, from the 'artistic' element of the work of the literary author and the architect, was what had caused the decline and failure of these arts, visible in their withdrawal from society and the public. Bontempelli called the 'new' writer a *functional* writer, establishing a connection with what at the time was called—albeit with derogatory intent—'functional architecture', following the principle of construction for utility and rejecting the idea of architecture as decoration (see the section below on *Quadrante*). The main quality of a functional writer was to 'write in order to communicate something to the public' ('scrive[re] per comunicare qualche cosa a un pubblico') (Bontempelli 1974 [1938], 56): this writer-journalist would also, therefore, bring art back to its social function.

The need to re-establish a connection with the public, in particular a mass public, was clearly a cornerstone of Bontempelli's aesthetic programme. While part of a wider reflection on the role of artists in modern society (see the section on the novel *522* in Chap. 7), the need for engagement with a mass public reflected the regime's efforts more generally towards popularization in the artistic and cultural sphere. It was also in explicit opposition to the 'non-communicative writing' ('scrivere incomunicativo') (Bontempelli 1974 [1938], 56, footnote) of the disengaged, bourgeois and Romantic man of letters. In 1936, Bontempelli wrote that the only art worthy of the name is 'communication' ('comunicazione'), which necessarily entails a political dimension; therefore, any work that has artistic value also has political value (Bontempelli 1974 [1938], 207). It is worth placing Giuseppe Pagano's words alongside Bontempelli's, in order to appreciate the extent to which these projects for the reconstruction and modernization of Italian architecture and the Italian novel converged, sharing the idea of the moral and social function of art as one of their central founding principles:

Modern architecture means, first and foremost, architecture made for men belonging to contemporary civilization. It means architecture that is morally, socially, economically, and spiritually tied to the conditions of our country. It means building in order to represent a people's civilization, to meet their needs, to 'serve' in the real sense of the word. It is essential to get it into our heads that every architectural work must submit itself to this utilitarian slavery. (Pagano 1935, reprinted in 2008 [1976], 31–32)[18]

The synergy between the two projects was acknowledged explicitly by Bontempelli in a comment presumably written when he assembled these writings in *L'avventura novecentista*, where he established a connection between the notion of '*mestierantismo*' (a term, normally used disparagingly, referring to an emphasis on craftsmanship) and that of functionalism, already embraced by architecture. He then commented that this tendency, together with other common points, inevitably led to a 'close alliance [of the new novel] with functional architecture' ('una stretta alleanza' [del romanzo nuovo] con l'architettura funzionale') (Bontempelli 1974 [1938], 63, footnote).

One of the supreme aesthetic qualities extolled by Bontempelli in his programme for the modernization of the novel was 'anonymity'; again, a quality possessed chiefly by architecture (see analysis of buildings in Chap. 7). The architectural metaphor was thus continued in the theorization of an anonymous, anti-subjective art, detached from the artist's individuality:

> The important thing is to create objects to place outside of us, detached from us: and through them, modify the world. [...] This is the spirit of architecture. Architecture rapidly becomes anonymous. Architecture reshapes the surface of the world in its own way [...]. Poetry must do the same [...]. (Bontempelli 1974 [1938], 15)[19]

Bontempelli alluded to how works of architecture naturally reveal very little of the subjectivity of their creator, of how they easily become 'common property', almost 'things of nature', and he urged writers to apply the same ideal of artistic creation to literature. An 'anonymous' art conceived in this way could perform the task that the regime expected from writers: creating artistic works that would become part of, and contribute to build, a collective heritage, thus fulfilling a social role. Bontempelli reiterated this idea in his third preamble, 'Consigli': 'The supreme ideal of all artists should be *to become anonymous*' ('L'ideale supremo di tutti gli artisti dovrebbe essere: *diventare anonimi*') (Bontempelli 1974 [1938], 19, emphasis in original). In order to clarify this statement, he recounted an anecdote about Italian writer Alessandro Manzoni, the author of the historical novel *The Betrothed* (1840–42), foundational to Italian culture and language. One day, Manzoni visited one of the towns of 'that branch of the lake of Como' that compete for the honour of having served as a model for the town in *The Betrothed*. There the author met a peasant, who offered to direct him towards the famous house of the protagonist of his own novel, Lucia. After asking him some questions, the writer realized that the man was not aware of the existence of a novel entitled *The Betrothed*, or even of a novelist called Alessandro Manzoni, despite clearly being very familiar with, and personally engaged by, the story.

Thus, Bontempelli theorized a model of fictional writing that would not have as its purpose the expression of the inner reality or the individual genius of the author, but rather the creation of a 'reservoir' of fables and myths that would educate the masses through the production of a collective imagination, with the encouragement of the regime. Again, it is worth comparing this with Pagano's parallel thoughts on 'anonymity' in the field of architecture, in which he too, interestingly, used words borrowed from the literary field to describe the creative process:

> If we want Italian architecture to proceed along a path capable of moral and aesthetic development and if we want to express our world, we need to act and think and compose poetry [*poetare*] not with an aristocratic, eccentric sensitivity, proudly enamoured of ratiocinative speculation, but rather aspire to be anonymous, to be free of rhetorical attitudes, and not imprison ourselves in an academy of forms and words. (Pagano 1937, reprinted in 2008 [1976], 150)[20]

The necessity of relinquishing individualism in favour of collective labour, realized in collaborative projects and buildings responding to social needs and functions, and in anonymous architecture, was also a tenet of the modern movement, and was included in the Manifesto of the rationalist Gruppo 7, many of whose members later became involved in the *Quadrante* project (see the section on buildings in Chap. 7).

Quadrante: A 'United Aesthetic Front' for the Modernization of Fascist Culture

The 'close alliance', as Bontempelli called it, between functional architecture and the new novel was cemented in the pages of *Quadrante*. The first issue of the journal, published on 1 May 1933, opened with two articles written by its two directors, Bontempelli and Pietro Maria Bardi. Bardi stated that

> [i]t was inevitable that I should undertake a close collaboration with Bontempelli. The decisive contribution he made to the polemic I started in favour of rational architecture is unforgettable [...]. That was how we, the new architects and I, found a common understanding with Bontempelli, exploring conditions and clarifying ideas regarding the necessity of something like a united aesthetic front. (Bardi 1933a, 2)[21]

The correspondence preceding the launch of *Quadrante*, in which the two directors discussed the contents and slant of the journal, particularly its first issue, reveals the intellectual continuity that they sought to establish between *900* and *Quadrante*.[22] From a letter of January 1933, we gather that Bontempelli's original idea was to call the journal *Quadrante '900*, and that if it was decided that it should be named simply *Quadrante*, he wanted an article in the first issue explaining why it was not called *900*. The reason was that the words '900' and 'novecentista' had been appropriated by artistic movements with which the *Quadrante* group did not wish be associated, particularly in the field of architecture, a crucial focus of the magazine (Tentori 1990, 370–71). Indeed, compared to *900*, *Quadrante* significantly shifted its focus towards architecture, specifically rational-functional architecture, which Bardi in particular aimed at establishing as the *arte di stato* of the Fascist regime (Bardi 1931a).

Quadrante played a key role in the establishment of rationalism, the Italian 'variant' of modernist architecture, and in its politicization, as shown by David Rifkind in his seminal monograph (2012). However, the journal played another crucial role in 1930s' Italian culture, namely that of establishing a platform for the creation of an interdisciplinary project of cultural renewal under the auspices of the Fascist regime. In this regard, it is useful to mention that neither Bardi nor Bontempelli were architects. One of the main principles behind the creation of *Quadrante* was the ideal of the 'unity' of the arts, as clearly stated by its directors in the first issue. Accordingly, one of its main goals was the formation of what Bardi called a 'united aesthetic front' ('un fronte unico dell'estetica'). This could be defined as a united front of aesthetic modernity, engaging not only in a 'battle for modernism', but also in a battle for modernity—understood as a specifically Fascist and interdisciplinary aesthetic modernity—which would result in the renewal of the cultural and social spheres through the arts. According to Jeffrey Schnapp,

> [*Quadrante*] set out to interpret the word 'architecture' in the broadest possible sense: as referring to the entire complex of means by which an ultramodern fascist Italy—a technologically, socially, culturally, juridically, politically, and psychologically modernized Italy—could be constructed. (Schnapp 2004, 37)

This endeavour was alluded to by Bardi in his first editorial, when he talked of *Quadrante* as a 'meeting place of unfettered, advanced, and original intelligence' ('un centro di ritrovo per un'intelligenza spregiudicata, avanzata, originale') (Bardi 1933a, 2).[23] Even the leading rationalist architect Terragni, who was involved in the preliminary discussions on the contents of the journal, as well as contributing financially to its publication (Rifkind 2012, 15), defined *Quadrante* as a 'journal of battle, which must represent and unite all the healthy and reliable forces of the *squadristi* of the new architecture, painting, sculpture, literature'.[24] The word 'squadristi' evoked two key features of *Quadrante*: the idea of 'battle' as the driving force behind the project (Rifkind 2012, 65), and its complete and militant endorsement of the regime. As Rifkind puts it, the architects, writers and intellectuals involved in the project 'enthusiastically supported the Fascist regime, and saw in Mussolini's "revolution" an analogue to the revolutionary project of modern architecture' (2012, 62). Bardi spelt this out clearly in his opening article:

> Faced with so much confusion, so many compromises, so much avoidance of a thorough and honest examination of the question, crucial to us, of an adjustment to the present and a participation of art to life (and by life we mean Mussolini's Revolution as a spiritual guideline and a synthesis of action and thought), we believe that "Quadrante" will have a useful function. [...] We are Fascists above all. (Bardi 1933a, 2)[25]

Quadrante thus set out to promote an art that was modern (adapted to the present) and directly engaged with the regime, encompassing both action and thought. The idea of reconstruction that underpinned *900*'s programme, in tandem with the political action of the regime, was reaffirmed even more forcefully as a cornerstone of *Quadrante*. In a short commentary ('Corsivo n. 1') placed prominently in the first issue, straight after the 'Principles' and a reprint of Mussolini's 1919 presentation of the journal *Ardita*, Bontempelli declared that 'In ten years, Fascism has rebuilt a politics and a morality for Italy. In ten more years, we want to rebuild its art and philosophy' (Bontempelli 1933b).[26]

Where Literature and Architecture Intersect

In his opening editorial, *Principii*, Bontempelli wrote that 'today [...] the expressive centre of our life is architecture' (Bontempelli 1933a, reprinted in Bontempelli 1974 [1938], 75), reaffirming architecture as the crux of an interdisciplinary paradigm of aesthetic modernity, and a metaphor for a necessary renewal of the processes of artistic creation, of engagement with the public, and of the place of the arts in a modern society (see Storchi 2012). He qualified the architecture 'that matters' ('che conta') with the adjectives 'rational' ('razionale') and 'functional' ('funzionale'), and gave a definition of this new interdisciplinary aesthetic modernity which was premised on the deliberate intermingling of images drawn from the fields of architecture and the novel:

The maximum of expression, the minimum of gesture, terror of the slow, decline of repose, to build without adjectives, to write with smooth walls, beauty intended as necessity, thought born as risk, the horror of the contingent. (Bontempelli 1933a, emphasis in original)[27]

This definition points to an identification of the aesthetic value of an artwork with its functionality, a mainstay of the rationalist architectural programme (De Seta 1998, 126), which, as we have seen, had been theorized in relation to the 'new novel' by Bontempelli in *900*. This principle of modern architecture and literature would be followed through the rationalization of aesthetic means in both architecture and the novel. The opening article of *Quadrante* thus put forward the ideas of rationalization and functionality as the principles of an aesthetic modernity that would build the regime's *arte di stato*, hinging in particular on an alliance between architecture and the novel.

Significantly, the subsequent pages were occupied by writings focusing on literature and architecture, thus establishing a conceptual framework grounded in the intersection between the two artistic forms. In the article 'Tradimento', writer and intellectual Marcello Gallian emphatically championed an anti-bourgeois, worthwhile art directed at the masses and close to everyday life: 'a useful literature, whose beauty lies precisely in its practical worth' ('una letteratura utile e bella appunto per quell che vale') (Gallian 1933, 4). Immediately afterwards came an article by writer Francesco Monotti, eloquently entitled 'Antiletteratura', which also strongly advocated a popular, socially meaningful and moral literature, engaging with the real and with the masses. The notion of 'anti-literature' had already been introduced by Bontempelli in *900*, where it was defined as one of the 'fixations' ('fissazioni') of the *900* movement (Bontempelli 1927c). This expression conveys the extent to which these intellectuals and artists conceived of the new literature as breaking with dominant literary traditions and conventions.[28] Monotti argued that literature in Italy had never been popular because it had always lacked contact with the masses, which constitute literature's real lifeblood. Art, and above all literature, must consist of action and exist in a direct, unmediated relationship with reality: this was its 'antitoxin' ('antitossina'), the antidote against the rampant corruption affecting literature.

Writers needed a direct relationship with reality because reality was, and had to be, the subject matter of their works. Monotti bemoaned the paradox whereby novels were full of 'common figures' like engineers, 'every sorts of maker' ('costruttori d'ogni specie') (and it is significant that he chose to mention engineers and makers drawn from all professions), but also less prestigious figures like servants and clowns, and yet these categories of people were not acquainted with literature, and if they were, they distrusted it. The fault did not lie with the public who had abandoned literature, but with the writers, who did not appeal to the wide public and therefore had lost their trust and interest.

According to Monotti, in order to correct this situation authors had to go back to the essence of life and to its 'elementarity' ('elementarietà'), a word of which Bontempelli was fond (see Bontempelli 1974 [1938], 336, for instance). In line with the journal's programme, he thus stated the need for a rationalization and simplification of literary languages and themes, a precondition for establishing the necessary relationship with the masses. This engagement with reality and the inextricable ties linking literature with life and with action would bring about moral renewal in literary works, expressed in the celebration of the essential things that mattered in life. This was an urgent message, central to the Fascist revolution, which writers had not hitherto embraced. As Monotti put it, a soldier or a *squadrista* who died fighting could teach everyone the true value of life, and novels should have the same power and moral impact. The arts under a totalitarian regime like Fascism, which aimed to shape all aspects of social life, were expected to embody and convey its values, therefore literature had to start embodying the principle of moral essentiality. A direct experience of reality was crucial to this process: the writer, like everyone else, had to be a man of action and 'get his hands dirty' ('sporcarsi le mani'), because only someone who had *done* something could have something valuable to tell (Monotti 1933).

The pieces following Monotti's article reprised the same ideas in relation to architecture. 'Un programma d'architettura', signed by most of the rationalist architects involved in the *Quadrante* project and echoing the manifesto of the Gruppo 7 (Rifkind 2012, 63), stated as its fourth principle the need for the 'moral act' ('fatto morale') and a moral consciousness to coexist alongside the 'artistic act' ('fatto artistico'), as a measure of the value of an artist.[29] The sixth principle affirmed that 'classicism' and *mediterraneità* were specific features of Italian rationalism, in contrast to 'Northist', Baroque, or Romantic tendencies. These distinctive traits were to be manifested not in the form, but rather in the spirit of new architecture, which signified an effort towards rationalization, clarity, and order.[30] Italian rationalism was identified as 'linear' and 'intransigent' ('lineare e intransigente') (Bottoni et al. 1933). The following article, 'Significato estetico del razionalismo', written by architect Giuseppe Pensabene, emphasized the need for rationalist architecture to re-establish an adherence to the real, and criticized formalism which, by focusing on the quest for perfect forms and on the 'conversation' among these forms, had lost this crucial contact with reality. His reflections echoed Bontempelli's thoughts on the primary importance of the writer's engagement with reality, first published in *900*, which theorized a new relationship between objectivity and subjectivity as a founding principle of Fascist art.

Pensabene propounded an anti-aesthetic and anti-decorative stance, stating that the value of a building could only be measured by looking at its spatiality. The monodimensional aesthetic idea of the 'façade' was anti-architectural, insofar as it was scenographic and purely ornamental, whereas architecture was '[…] an immensely more complex art which engages with the real in much more profound ways' ('[…] arte immensamente più complessa e implicante ben altrimenti il reale') (Pensabene 1933, 6). This spatial, multidimensional conception of architecture, engaging in a complex relationship with reality, was tellingly qualified as 'totalitarian' ('totalitaria'), while non-totalitarian architecture was compared to a 'stage-set' ('una scena'), a 'limited conception of life' ('una concezione ridotta della vita'), something 'fragmentary' ('frammentario') and lacking a direct relation with reality. A connection had to be established between art and life: architecture achieved this by 'superimposing itself on reality' ('sovrappone[ndosi] al reale') (Pensabene 1933, 7). We are reminded, again, of Bontempelli's invective against the idolization of the 'fragment' in literature and the 'folly of the invention of the pseudo-fragment' ('la follia dell'invenzione dello pseudoframmento') (Bontempelli 1928). The aesthetic precepts of Sartoris and Bontempelli intersected in their advocacy of the pursuit of 'totality' through art—as opposed to an aesthetic of the fragment—in the fields of architecture and literature (see section on 'The Total Work of Art', Chap. 4). Finally, Sartoris reiterated one of the central theoretical tenets proclaimed by the journal, namely, the need for the rationalization of forms coupled with functionalism, when he imagined '[...] great smooth surfaces whose beauty will lie in the revelation of their purpose' ('[...] grandi superfici liscie, la cui bellezza sarà nella rivelazione del loro scopo') (Pensabene 1933, 7). The notion that a building's aesthetic value lay in its functionality was reaffirmed as the core principle of rationalist architecture: 'only in the progression beyond the dualism between utility and beauty is it possible, today, to distinguish the principle of new architecture' (Ibid.).[31]

The second issue of *Quadrante* opened with the reproduction of a speech delivered by Mussolini at the Teatro Argentina, in Rome, on the occasion of the fiftieth anniversary of the *Società degli Autori* (Mussolini 1933). After addressing the question of theatre for the masses, Mussolini shifted his focus to the novel, defining it as 'a powerful instrument for the education of the people' ('uno strumento possente dell'educazione del Popolo') (1933, 2). He praised those contemporary Italian writers who were 'powerful, robust in form and rich in thought' ('potenti, solidi nella forma e, ricchi di pensiero'), evoking, albeit in vague terms, the type of novel theorized by the *900* group (ibid.). He also declared his complete confidence in 'the forces of the Italian spirit and intelligence' (Ibid.)[32] and acknowledged that, if the State cannot create its own literature, it can support its writers and nurture their creative endeavours, publicly stating one of the main principles of Fascist cultural policy (see Chap. 2, 17–18). In a commentary on this speech, Bontempelli expressed his belief that fiction would be the most distinctive artistic form of the twentieth century, and one in which Italians would prove their talents. He reaffirmed the centrality of the social function of art in the Fascist era, sanctioning the end of the avant-gardes, if by avant-garde one meant speaking an elitist artistic language directed at the happy few. The new avant-garde, in the sense of modernity, would have to speak to the masses and have something new to tell them, following the example set by the Fascist regime in the political sphere (Bontempelli 1933c).[33] The next article was Bardi's 'Considerazioni sulla Triennale',[34] which contained very similar ideas applied to the field of architecture. Bardi criticized the 'bourgeoisification' of the Triennial, manifested in the building and exhibition of several houses ('*villini*') destined for the urban bourgeoisie. Bardi argued that the era of the bourgeois house was over, and that the representative architecture of the Fascist era would consist of 'social houses, barracks, hospitals, *case del Fascio*, institutes of the regime' (1933b, 6).[35] In short, architecture would embody Fascist values through modern, functional buildings meant for the collective use of public space and for the articulation of the relationship between the State and the masses (see the analysis of buildings in Chap. 7). Indeed, the renewal of architecture was to be brought about through 'constructions for popular use' ('costruzioni popolari e d'uso popolare'), and therefore architectural exhibitions, too, had to '*move towards the people*' (Bardi 1933b, 6, emphasis in original).[36]

Bontempelli echoed these ideas in an article published a few months later, this time not in *Quadrante*, but in the Fascist newspaper *Gazzetta del Popolo*, in which he once again placed architecture and the novel side by side as the two artistic forms most thoroughly engaged in the construction of an art for the Fascist era—an art which should be popular, functional, rationalized and collective. Architecture was able to embody the spirit of an era, and the Fascist era could not be represented by bourgeois houses, but only by 'utilitarian' buildings ('costruzioni […] "utilitarie"') and works 'destined for the collectivity' ('opere di destinazione collettiva') (Bontempelli 1933d, reprinted in 1974 [1938], 335). While the bourgeoisie would not understand this new art, the 'common people' would, because they were used to equating beauty with simplicity, and with objects whose form followed their purpose. Literature was, according to Bontempelli, the only art that alongside architecture, had started a process of renewal based on these principles, and the best Italian literature revealed 'worthy efforts in the pursuit of a superior *simplicity* in its means, and a profound *elementarity* in its substance' (Bontempelli 1974 [1938], 336, emphasis in original).[37] The other arts should follow the example set by architecture and literature and begin 'creating […] spacious constructions for the collective life of simple souls' ('creare […] ariose costruzioni per la vita collettiva degli animi semplici') (Ibid.).

The notions of morality, essentiality and rationalization were thus tightly interrelated in the narrative woven by *900* and *Quadrante*, binding the artistic and political spheres together. These were the principles upon which the regime based the relationship between the State and the individual, in order to bring about an anthropological revolution. The arts, as we have already argued, were a crucial part of this process. Thus, these were also the principles on which the arts, in particular architecture and the novel, should be based, in order to perform a social function of educating the masses and framing them within the structures of the State. The eighth issue of *Quadrante* opened with an article written by Bottai, entitled 'Totalità, perennità, universalità della rivoluzione fascista' which significantly entered into dialogue with the aesthetic-political programme promoted by the journal. In examining the threefold nature of the Fascist revolution, Bottai observed that Fascism was a totalitarian project, as it sought to be actualized in all aspects and spheres of the national life. As a result of the actualization of the revolution, the citizen of the Fascist state would be 'totally engaged, in his faith and interests, in his consciousness and in his profession, by a superior rule of order and unity [...]' (Bottai 1933, 1).[38] This same superior law was, or should be, embodied by the new literature and the new architecture. The Fascist revolution was a revolution of the spirit, and not simply a legal or political change. It was a 'movement [...] spread across the moral atmosphere of our time, carrying out a broad revision of values and principles' (Bottai 1933, 2).[39] These same principles and values would be expressed in Fascist novels and buildings, the guiding essence of which was morality. Architecture and literature were thus conceived of not as a means for the expression of the subjectivity of the individual artist, but as spaces for the creation of a collective morality supporting the Fascist revolution, which would manifest itself aesthetically in the rationalization of languages and forms.

Notes

1. 'La ricerca più originale che l'uomo possa fare guardandosi attorno nel proprio tempo, è la ricerca dell'unità. Si vuole intendere: unità di visuale, e perciò di giudizio. [...] Trovare il centro donde si veda il muoversi della speculazione filosofica, dell'espressione artistica, dell'azione politica, della curiosità scientifica, del linguaggio, del costume della vita d'ogni giorno—come un solo fayyo armonioso. Scovarne il ritmo centrale.'

2. We are referring here to the years when *900* and *Quadrante* were published, between 1926 and 1936, a period in which the regime had the support of large sections of the Italian artistic and intellectual milieus. Bontempelli was involved with Fascism well into the 1930s. His engagement was not strictly artistic, and included being secretary of the Fascist writers' corporativist union for several years in the late 1920s. His support began wavering during the 1930s, but it was not until 1938 that he fell out with the regime, like many other artists and intellectuals. See Jewell 2008 for further details, and for a discussion of the relationship between Bontempelli's magical realism and Fascist activism.
3. '[...] per Fascismo noi indichiamo tutto un orientamento della vita, pubblica e indivuale: ordinamento compiuto e totale, cioè pratico insieme e teorico, intellettuale e morale, applicazione e spirito'. Translation by Barbara Spackman, Jennifer Roberts, and Elizabeth Macintosh (Schnapp 2000, 218).
4. '[...] questo *libro inopinato* documenta uno stato d'animo incline a cercare armonia tra il letterario e il politico [...].' *L'avventura novecentista* is a volume assembled and edited by Bontempelli in 1938, collecting writings published between 1926 and 1938, including the 'preambles' and other important articles published in *900*. As the title suggests, it reconstructs the trajectory of the Novecento movement.
5. '[...] non è una questione di architettura, non è neppure una questione di gusto e di estetica: è una questione di ordine morale. La polemica intorno all'architettura è una polemica profondamente politica. [...] Un'epoca si rivela tutta in tutta la sua architettura.'
6. On the journal's Europeanist aspirations, see Mancini 2004 and Gennaro 2010.
7. 'Des adversaires italiens ont dénoncé «900» comme étant une louche entreprise de l'internationalisme européiste. Des adversaires étrangers ont prêté serment que «900» est une redoutable patrouille du vorace impérialisme italien.'
8. Bontempelli justified this choice stating that *900* aimed at spreading 'Italian values' abroad, and in order to do that, it needed to be written in a language widely understood in Europe (Bontempelli 1926b; see also Gennaro 2010).
9. 'Occorre riimparare l'arte di costruire, per inventare i miti freschi onde possa scaturire la nuova atmosfera di cui abbiamo bisogno per respirare'.

10. For further discussion of magical realism, see the analysis of Bontempelli's novel *522* in Chap. 7.
11. Like many artists and intellectuals in this period, Bontempelli repeatedly declared that a Fascist artwork was not an artwork *about* Fascism. For instance: '[...] in a hundred years' time a purely fantastic novel could appear to be more representative of the Fascist spirit than one that stages the March on Rome' ('[...] tra cento anni un romanzo di pura fantasia potrà apparire aderente allo spirito fascista assai più di uno ove si metta in scena la Marcia su Roma') (1929, now in 1974 [1938], 213).
12. 'Il vecchio regime disprezzava il letterato. Credo che nel nuovo regime ci siano alcuni politici—due o tre forse, certamente uno—disposti a tenere la letteratura nel conto che merita. [...] Per "il conto che merita", intendo che la letteratura è la più alta espressione d'un tempo e però la sua più delicata funzione. Come tale, essa è la grande collaboratrice d'un epoca e d'una azione che vogliano chiamarsi imperiali'.
13. 'L'Italia vive dalla guerra in poi la sua prima vita veramente nazionale [...]. Lentamente la provincia diventa popolo, spariscono i costumi e i caratteri esterni, si rafforzano i caratteri psicologici [...]. Se fino a ieri l'arte dello scrittore italiano era quella di invenatre agglomerati sociali sullo stampo di quelli stranieri e generalmente francesi, [...] oggi basta guardarsi intorno per accorgersi che materia immensa ha sotto gli occhi uno scrittore. [...] È naturale che non esista un poeta di questa trasformazione di classi. [...] Prima dei Baudelaire ci vogliono quei grossi costruttori di case popolari e di castelli in aria che si chiamano Hugo.'
14. It is interesting to compare this statement with the use of a similar metaphor, albeit to support a diametrically opposed argument, by architect Marcello Piacentini, in one of his earliest attacks against rationalist architecture: 'Why then this need to make the entire essence of architecture consist of rationality alone? [....] The identification of beauty with structure does not exist. Let us leave these dry metaphysical speculations to the people of the North. Neither puritanism nor Protestantism have ever taken root under our sun. We need gesture and form; the moving word and a smile. We are essentially musical; art, for us, is always a song.' ('Perché, insomma, voler far consistere tutta l'essenza dell'architettura nella sua razionalità? [...] L'identificazione del bello con lo strutturale non esiste. Lasciamo queste speculazioni aride e metafisiche agli uomini del Nord; sotto il nostro sole non ha mai attecchito il puritanesimo, né il protestantesimo. Noi abbiamo bisogno del gesto e della forma; della parola com-

mossa e del sorriso. Noi siamo essenzialmente musicali; l'arte per noi è sempre un canto.') (Piacentini 1928, reprinted in Patetta 1972, 158).

15. 'Quanto alla letteratura, vedremo avanzarsi al primo piano l'opera narrativa, quella specialmente che si fonda sull'invenzione e sull'intreccio.'
16. 'Quando avremo collocato un nuovo solido mondo davanti a noi, la nostra più solerte occupazione sarà passeggiarlo ed. esplorarcelo; tagliarne blocchi di pietra e porli uno sopra l'altro per metter su fabbricati pesanti, e modificare senza tregua la crosta della terra riconquistata.'
17. The figure of the engineer was central to the revolutionary ideas of the avant-gardes in the first half of the twentieth century, especially, but not only, in the field of architecture (see Schnapp 2004, 1–5). The engineer was widely celebrated as the 'guarantor of an immediate linkage between art and life, as embodying the new norm to be followed by less technically proficient practitioners of thought or art, and as an ideal agent of rationalization and democratization' (Schnapp 2004, 1).
18. 'Architettura moderna significa anzitutto architettura fatta per uomini appartenenti alla civiltà contemporanea; significa architettura moralmente, socialmente, economicamente, spiritualmente legata alle condizioni del nostro paese; significa costruire per rappresentare gli ideali del popolo, per soddisfarne i bisogni, per "servire" nel vero senso della parola. È necessario mettersi bene nella testa che tutte le opere di architettura devono sottoporsi a questa schiavitù utilitaria.'
19. 'L'importante è creare oggetti, da collocare fuori di noi, bene staccato da noi; e con essi modificare il mondo. [...] È lo spirito dell'architettura. L'architettura diventa assai rapidamente anonima. L'architettura rifoggia a suo modo la superficie del mondo [...]. Lo stesso deve fare la poesia [...].'
20. 'Se vogliamo che la letteratura italiana proceda entro una strada capace di sviluppi morali ed. estetici e se vogliamo esprimere il nostro mondo, è necessario agire e pensare e poetare non con sensibilità aristocratica, eccentrica o superbamente innamorata della speculazione raziocinante, ma desiderare di essere anonimi, di essere puri da atteggiamenti retorici, di non volerci noi stessi imprigionare in un'accademia di forme e di parole.'
21. 'Era fatale che con Bontempelli dovessi realizzare una stretta collaborazione. Il decisivo ausilio che egli ha dato traverso alcuni suoi scritti alla polemica da me intrapresa in favore di una architettura razionale, è indimenticabile [...]. Fu così che noi, io e gli architetti nuovi, ci intendemmo

con Bontempelli in fraternità, scoprendo alcune circostanze e chiarendo alcune idee sulla necessità di costituire qualche cosa come un fronte unico dell'estetica.'
22. The correspondence is published in Tentori 1990, 365–77.
23. Translation by Rifkind (2012, 15).
24. '[...] una rivista di battaglia, che dovrà rappresentare e riunire tutte le forze sane e collaudate deagli squadristi della nuova architettura, pittura, scultura, letteratura'. Fondo Carlo Belli, Archivio del '900, MART. Letter from Terragni to Belli, 4 December 1931.
25. 'Tra tanta confusione, tra tanti accomodamenti, tra tanta rinuncia verso un esame pieno e franco della questione per noi cardinale d'un adeguamento ai tempi e della partecipazione dell'arte alla vita (e si intende per vita intanto la Rivoluzione Mussoliniana come direttrice spirituale e come sintesi d'azione e di pensiero) noi riteniamo che "Quadrante" avrà una funzione noninutile. [...] noi siamo fascisti prima di tutto.'
26. 'In dieci anni il Fascismo ha ricostruito all'Italia una politica e una morale. In altri dieci anni vogliamo ricostruirle un'arte e una filosofia'. Translation by David Rifkind (2012, 55).
27. *'Il massimo della espressione, il minimo di gesto, terrore del lento, disprezzo per il riposo, edificare senza aggettivi, scrivere a pareti lisce, la bellezza intesa come necessità, il pensiero nato come rischio, l'orrore del contingente'*. This well-known passage first appeared in an open letter addressed by Bontempelli to Bardi, published on *La Gazzetta del popolo* on 25 June 1932. Translation by David Rifkind (2012, 57).
28. The concept of 'anti-literature' was widespread in Fascist Italian literary culture. For instance, it was one of the tenets of the ideal of literature championed by the journal *I lupi*, where it signified the (paradoxical) 'disgust for words', and the 'esteem for the fact' and 'the concrete thing' (Napolitano 1928, quoted and translated in Ben-Ghiat 1995, 644; see also Ben-Ghiat 2001, 56).
29. The signatories were Piero Bottoni, Mario Cereghini, Luigi Figini, Guido Frette, Enrico A. Griffini, Piero Lingeri, Gino Pollini, Gian Luigi Banfi, Lodovico B. di Belgioioso, Enrico Peressutti, and Ernesto N. Rogers. Giuseppe Terragni, who had contributed to the foundation of *Quadrante*, was notably absent. According to Rifkind, this might be due to his brief disagreement with the other *Quadrante* members after they decided to exclude architect Luciano Baldessarri from the project (Rifkind 2012, 65).

30. As noted by Rifkind, 'spirit' and 'morality' were central concepts in the theories and programmes of Italian rationalists, but were never clearly defined (2012, 64). This was in line with a common tendency of Fascist discourse, which also marked the field of aesthetics (see Chap. 2, p. 24). According to Rifkind, 'the rhetoric of morality conveyed the idea of deeply held (rather than opportunistic) beliefs that were above criticism' (Ibid.), echoing the 'superior laws' governing reality in Bontempelli's thought (1974 [1938], 27).
31. 'Solo nel superamento del dualismo tra utilità e bellezza, è possibile, oggi, intravedere il principio della nuova architettura.'
32. 'Voglio dirvi che ho un'assoluta certezza nelle forze dello spirito e dell'intelligenza italiana'.
33. Articles specifically on literature became less frequent after the first few issues, because Bardi and Bontempelli had become the directors of *L'Italia Letteraria*, which targeted the same audience as *Quadrante*, but had a more specifically literary focus (Mariani 1989, 241–42).
34. The fifth Triennial Exhibition of Modern Decorative Arts, Industrial Arts and Architecture was held in Milan in 1933. It was the first one to be held in the newly built Palazzo dell'Arte, designed by Giovanni Muzio.
35. '[…] L'architettura rappresentativa della nostra epoca è l'architettura delle case economiche, delle caserme, dei sanatori, delle case del Fascio, degli Istituti del Regime'.
36. 'Anche con le esposizioni d'architettura e d'arte decorativa *bisogna andare verso il popolo*'
37. '[…] la migliore letteratura italiana sta rivelando degni sforzi nella ricerca d'una superiore *semplicità* quanto ai mezzi, d'una profonda *elementarità* quanto alla sostanza'.
38. 'Dal Fascio alla Croporazione, il cittadino dello Stato Fascista sarà totalmente impegnato, nella sua fede e nel suo interesse, nella sua coscienza e nella sua professione, da una regola superiore d'ordine e d'unità […]'.
39. '[…] un moto […] diffuso nell'atmosfera morale del nostro tempo a operarvi una vasta revisione di valori e di principi'.

Open Access This chapter is licensed under the terms of the Creative Commons Attribution 4.0 International License (http://creativecommons.org/licenses/by/4.0/), which permits use, sharing, adaptation, distribution and reproduction in any medium or format, as long as you give appropriate credit to the original author(s) and the source, provide a link to the Creative Commons licence and indicate if changes were made.

The images or other third party material in this chapter are included in the chapter's Creative Commons licence, unless indicated otherwise in a credit line to the material. If material is not included in the chapter's Creative Commons licence and your intended use is not permitted by statutory regulation or exceeds the permitted use, you will need to obtain permission directly from the copyright holder.

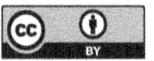

6

State Art, the Novel, and Architecture: Intersections

> *It is important for the materialist historian, in the most rigorous way possible, to differentiate the construction of a historical state of affairs from what one customarily calls its 'reconstruction'. The 'reconstruction' in empathy is one-dimensional. 'Construction' presupposes 'destruction'.*
> —Benjamin (*Arcades*, [N7, 6], 470)

Within the system of State art, the Italian novel was expected to create and to build the moral discursive space of the regime and, therefore, to contribute to the modernization of the publishing industry, just as architecture was supposed to shape the physical and symbolic spaces constructed by the anthropological revolution ignited by the regime, which aimed to accommodate the New Man, as discussed in Chap. 4. These complementary artistic projects thus worked in tandem towards the creation of a Fascist aesthetics (*arte di Stato*), a New Fascist Man and a Fascist modernity, together translating into a process of modernization of the public sphere. Their shared basis was their constructive effort, to be achieved through the rationalization of forms (a 'return to the simplicity and essentiality of expressive means'), an adherence to the real, the use of anti-subjective, anti-Romantic aesthetic codes, and an attention to the contextual reality, all of which enabled individual subjectivity to be transformed into a collective experience. What, then, is the relationship between the foundational principles of the novel and this new architectural aesthetics? A preliminary answer would be that among the many facets of the anthropological revolution for the control of the individual made collective were the reconstruction of the novel in realist tones, so that it could reach the middle and lower-middle classes, and the promotion of a rationalized spatial dimension for the arts. This topic was often discussed in cultural and literary journals and periodicals, with some notable debates taking place on the fringes of the official landscape.

Intersections

In this chapter, our focus is on the discursive intersections between realism in prose writing and the call for the renewal of architectural forms, since both projects are part of a wider discourse on modernity as a theoretical premise and on modernization as a practical intervention in the public sphere, particularly in the first half of the 1930s (see Chap. 2).[1] The key journals which engaged in a wide-ranging debate about these sets of interlocking issues are: *Il Saggiatore* (Rome, 1930–1933), *Orpheus* (Milan, 1932–1935) and *Occidente* (Rome, 1932–1935); unlike periodicals such as Berto Ricci's *L'Universale* (1931–1935), these three were not grown out of the university youth Fascist groups GUF (gruppi universitari fascisti). All three stopped their publications at the peak of the regime's popularity, and before that point they articulated an understanding of the arts from an international and interdisciplinary perspective.

However, in order to give a full picture of the wider debate on these themes, we will make references where appropriate to other journals on the cultural fringes of the avant-gardes, such as *Interplanetario* (1928) for the arts generally and *La ruota dentata* (1927) for the visual arts, and to others which promoted the mainstream cultural line at the core of the national tradition in political, cultural and literary terms, such as *L'Italia letteraria* (Rome, 1928–1936) or *Critica fascista* (Rome, 1923–1943).[2] Furthermore, aside from *L'Italia letteraria* (and its other incarnations) and *Critica fascista*, all our journals lived short lives, from 1932, from the year of the Mostra della Rivoluzione Fascista and the celebrations for the Decennale, until 1936, with the establishment of the empire and the last public appearance of the *grande dame* of the arts, Margherita Sarfatti, and the regime's progressive political isolation. As a corpus, these three journals in particular recorded the steps taken during the most important period in the history of the relationships between aesthetics and politics during the *Ventennio*, and also followed the declining curve of rationalist architecture. We have chosen journals associated with the young intelligentsia, because of the attention they paid to the European dimension of culture, to realism, and to interdisciplinary connections across the system of the arts. It was primarily within the regime's youth culture that new spaces for intellectual and cultural dialogue could be carved out and alternative theoretical positions on the arts suggested under the regime (Sechi 1984; Ben-Ghiat 2001). Unlike the Immaginist movement and the Roman underground circles, for instance, with their surrealist, anti-establishment and hyperrealist underpinnings, the journals—produced within the groupings of the regime's youth culture—provided a platform for ideas, which looked towards the international sphere to reach beyond the limits of a statist, State patronage-based approach and encourage critical, as well as self-critical, reflection on the status quo, on the future, and on modernity itself (Carpi 1981a, 117–20).

The Principles

Between 1932 and 1936, the regime reached a peak not only in terms of consensus, but also of visibility (Corner 2012, 143–45; Colarizzi 2000, 105–16). If in political terms the first half of the 1930s represented the regime's most successful years, in aesthetic terms it translated into a desire for the so-called return to realism, to 'structurally concluded forms', following the strong anti-bourgeois ideological stance the regime had assumed in the early days: in a nutshell, a decade later, this was a return to construction and no longer simply a return to order (Billiani 2013, 849–58). As outlined in Chap. 3, the Italian novel was a multifaceted phenomenon, which lacked a well-defined identity because of the still fragmented nature of the publishing industry and the still relatively low numbers of readers, especially if compared to other European nations, such as France and the United Kingdom. Because of the heterogeneous nature of the 'Italian novel' and because of the central role played by translations within the literary field, from the mid-1920s to the mid-1930s the (however present) realist-constructivist dimension ran parallel to other literary currents, such as *prosa d'arte*, intimist narrative or Modernist writing; and, moreover, it resurfaced later for instance in the visual arts, with Aligi Sassu's Gruppo Rosso and his anti-Fascist painting *La fucilazione nelle Asturie* (1935), with the second prize at the Premio Bergamo in 1942 being awarded to Renato Guttuso[3] as a sign of the importance for the younger generations that the real, articulated as coexistence of the subjective and the objective in their urge to express the tragedy of the war, and held within official State art and art more generally during the final years of the regime.[4] Or, with Ernesto Treccani's Corrente movement and *Corrente* journal, which from 1938 to 1940 brought together some of the leading intellectual lights of the generation of critics, writers and artists to survive the regime and to shape the cultural milieu of democratic Italy: Luciano Anceschi, Giulio Carlo Argan, Piero Bigongiari, Luigi Comencini, Carlo Emilio Gadda,[5] Alberto Lattuada, Eugenio Montale, Vasco Pratolini, Enzo Paci, Salvatore Quasimodo, Luigi Rognoni, Umberto Saba, Vittorio Sereni,[6] Elio Vittorini.[7] Corrente saw the cultural crisis Italy was going through as an opportunity for change, and firmly placed national culture in relation to the international scene, while promoting an understanding of the arts as an interdisciplinary practice.

Although the debate on the aesthetics of realism went in many artistic and disciplinary directions, as we have indicated so far, one of its guiding principles was the desire to represent the relationship between Man and his social dimension, between individuality and collectivity: whether taken from the point of view of the avant-garde or as an expression of anti-totality, an illustrative-documentarist form, or an indissoluble unity of the particular and the universal. On a more general level, the debate within the art world revolved around a redefinition of matter, of the real, and of the ethical and moral dimension of subjectivity.

6 State Art, the Novel, and Architecture: Intersections 129

The Debate

The Fascist system of the arts had to be constructed in the interstices between the political and the aesthetic spheres in such a way as to reconfigure the boundaries between these two realms and thus redefine the relationship between subjectivity and objectivity, between autonomous and heteronomous practices. Critics Ben-Ghiat and Sechi have noted a strong correlation between youth culture and corporativism, but for the purposes of our argument we will devote more attention to the literary side of the overall dispute (Ben-Ghiat 2001, 106–7; Sechi 1984, 63).[8] The attitude and politics of youth culture were particularly favourable to such theoretical premises because they sought to rethink the role of the arts in society from an interdisciplinary perspective. Albertina Vittoria has rightly observed how, since the mid-1920s the regime had clearly understood the role culture had to play in the construction of the totalitarian apparatus, and how this ambition became more strongly expressed in the mid-1930s with the involvement of youth culture in this long-term project (1980, 324–26, 333–34). In the first instance, as far as regime-sponsored art was concerned, this meant not only propaganda in the most general of terms, but the broader question of creating a State art of more enduring significance across the public and personal spaces of the individual.

Whereas *Orpheus* had an interdisciplinary slant, *Il Saggiatore*'s focus was more philosophical, showing a specific interest in the novel form and in the debate on realism. Alongside, a distinct disposition towards shaping the new intellectual, the two journals also shared a commitment both to the definition of a new type of art focused on the concepts of realism and the sociality of art, and to the materialist foundation of reality from a humanist perspective. *Occidente*, by contrast, concentrated mainly on literary matters and promoted the Rome-based avant-gardes as well as realist and Modernist European and American prose writing (Ben-Ghiat 2001, 104). All three embodied the denser aesthetic[9] and political discourse directed at the relationship between subjectivity and objectivity, which was seen as being necessary to fulfil a collective and/or moral function as part of a wider transformation of the individual within the fabric of society (Salvagnini 2000, 239–40, 246). *Orpheus* and *Il Saggiatore* were still concerned with a 'humanist' understanding of the relationship between subjectivity and objectivity in terms of participation of the self in the definition of the real and vice versa, while the avant-garde circles that fed the position held by *Occidente* (and earlier publications such as *Interplanetario*, *La Bilancia* and *La ruota dentata*) favoured a more technical and detached approach to the same set of issues. The thread running through all of them is the reflection on the role of the arts in society and an attempt to move away from art for art's sake: put another way, if we exclude state-sponsored propaganda art, the discussion to be had was around the boundaries of heteronomy and autonomy in the arts under a totalitarian, *dirigiste* regime.

Occidente (Rome, 1932–1935)

Occidente was published in Rome from the anniversary of the celebrations for the Decennale of the Fascist revolution in October 1932 until the eve of the Ethiopian war in 1935. Its total run of 12 3-monthly issues enjoyed only a rather limited circulation. It was directed by Armando Ghelardini, who also owned the Edizioni d'Italia. Controversial and unconventional intellectuals such as Umberto Barbaro, Vinicio Paladini and Elio Talarico, together with the omnipresent Massimo Bontempelli, worked closely with Ghelardini. *Occidente* would eventually be banned in 1935 and Ghelardini placed under virtual arrest. With issue 12 (May–June 1935), the publication was halted, with no explanation given apart from a short article by Ghelardini himself, significantly entitled 'Bilancio', which announced the end of *Occidente*. Issue thirteen was finished but was confiscated by the Fascist police at the printers, after the editor-in-chief Ghelardini had twice risked house arrest because of the journal's non-orthodox editorial line and the political orientations of some of its contributors (for instance, Umberto Barbaro).[10]

Occidente's opening article stated that the aim of the review was to offer the widest possible overview of world literature: it aspired to the transatlantic scope of journals like *Orpheus, La Ronda, Il Convegno, Lo spettatore italiano* and *Solaria*, to name but a few similar literary contemporaries and predecessors. Ghelardini described *Occidente*'s ideal reader as 'a cultivated and intelligent man' ('uomo colto ed intelligente') and that his intention was to put Italian writers in touch with foreign writers in order to 'affirm European cultural values' ('affermazione dei valori culturali europei'), although contributions on photography, cinema and photomontage were also published (1932, 'Introduzione.' *Occidente* 1, no. 1 (October–December): 2). In her analysis of the journal's position within the national cultural field, Alessandra Briganti has shown that, by welcoming the most anti-conventional and, in Fascist terms, anti-bourgeois intellectual voices of the Rome-based Second-Futurist movement, Immaginism, and by paying constant attention to the international literary and artistic scene, *Occidente* expressed a rather original vision of the shape of the novel (1988, 18).

Foreign presences were numerous and varied, and the Parisian scene was not given undue coverage. The first issue featured translations of Aldous Huxley and D. H. Lawrence; Max Beerbohm, James Cain, Hans Canossa, Jean Cocteau, Joseph Conrad, John Dos Passos, William Faulkner, Waldo Frank, Ernest Hemingway, James Joyce, Valery Labraud, Liam O'Flaherty, Franz Werfel, and Virginia Woolf would all be translated in subsequent issues. Alongside British Modernism, new French writing, American realism and German New Objectivity were found examples of the most progressive strands of Italian writing and articles by figures from the regime's centre and fringes alike in a highly eclectic mix: with contributions by Corrado Alvaro,[11] G. B. Angioletti, Umberto Barbaro, Massimo Bontempelli, Giuseppe Bottai, Anton Giulio Bragaglia, Ennio Flaiano, Francesco Jovine, F. T. Marinetti,[12] Paolo Orano, Corrado Pavolini, Mario Puccini, Salvatore Quasimodo, Enrico Rocca, Federigo Tozzi, Elio Vittorini, the debate on the novel, in terms of both form and subject matter, was particularly lively. In the first issue, stressing the impending need for aesthetic renewal, Massimo Bontempelli contributed an article in which he defined the spirit of the moment as positive and thus constructive since it was oriented towards 'work and life' ('lavoro e vita') and 'action' ('azione'), and in this 'vitalistic impulse' ('impulso vitalistico') he saw the convergence of political and aesthetic aims as also defined by the official debate on State art (1932b. 'Scuola dell'Ottimismo.' *Occidente* 1, no. 1(October–December): 9, and see Chap. 2).[13]

Throughout its brief existence, *Occidente* accorded privileged status to the novel whether it be Italian or international. *Occidente* was truly transatlantic in aspiration: in the first four issues (out of twelve) there were four substantial articles on the novel, followed by another three in subsequent issues, giving a total of seven. Every issue also contained one more or less elaborate article on the landscape (e.g. a well-informed panorama) of the European novel. Overall, however, the most sustained and wide-ranging discussion on the shape and atlas of the novel per se—and not as nationally defined—concerned the limits of realism and of realist narration.

In his 'Considerazioni sul romanzo', the former Immaginist Umberto Barbaro[14] denounced the abstract rationalism of the avant-gardes as a product of old European culture, an expression of the liberal State:

> The need was felt to reclaim technique and a return was made to the carefully constructed and well-thought-out work in its most typical from, the novel: the latter, however, like rationalist architecture and all avant-gardisms, is full of self-absorbed voracity, and now it aspires to be nothing but fantasy; nothing but technique, like in detective novels (the old anti-artistic need that Guerrazzi was already talking about long ago [...]) or nothing but sociology, morality or content, that is to say, still nothing but fantasy. (1, no. 1 (October–December): 20)[15]

Art has to reject pure rationality (or pure rationalization of forms) because true artistic expression needs to enter into dialogue with everyday reality and avoid abstraction. Rationalist architecture can help in building the metaphorical structure on which the novel relies in order to be integrated aesthetically with the characters' subjective experience: when it fuse together function with conception and design. According to Barbaro, the novel has to depicts various sides of the human experience: it needs to combine the need to tell a story with that of engaging with reality without forgetting that its primary attribute is to be a work of fiction, a journey through the imaginary. The novel, Barbaro adds, is therefore the artistic form that best embodies modernity when it rejects forms of solipsistic wandering to embrace a closer contact with objectivity, since '[t]rue morality in art consists in bringing the reader back into contact with, and constraining him within, the narrow confines of the everyday' (Ibid.:21).[16] The prose writing had to allow readers to hope for change but it could not merely be a form of escapist distraction from reality: it needed to engage productively, yet fictionally, with objectivity in all its phenomenology whether from a social or an individual point of view but never from an autonomous and de-historicized one. A similar point will emerge from the debate on the novel in *Il Saggiatore*, as will be discussed below.

The debate on the novel often returns to a common anxiety: how can one move away from 'early twentieth-century liberalism' (Sechi 1984, 67) to find a new way forward, a new utopian literary and social configuration (constructivist and corporative) in order to achieve modernity? In his 1933 article 'Coefficienti nuovi nel romanzo', Elio Talarico makes a point about Decadentism and its lack of construction, being engaged as it was in a self-referential understanding and rendering of objectivity, adding that the novel has to resist slipping into psychology and focus on building solid and composed artistic forms: 'What are we waiting for, then, why don't we begin constructing properly, right now?' (2, no. 3 (April–June): 7).[17] Talarico and Barbaro saw the new novel, the modern and contemporary novel, as being on the threshold between heteronomous and autonomous literary practices because it had to be moved by a desire both to 'build' a structure, a plot, and to tell a story, which needs to remain a fictional stance, an artefact that is different from a social experiment.

In his 'Rapporto dalla Germania' the former Novecento novelist, journalist Pietro Solari, who spent time in Berlin at the same time as Corrado Alvaro, salutes German New Objectivity because he saw it as a fictional experiment which could be the way forward in preventing further cultural impoverishment by the Italian cultural elites who had become intellectually parasitic and static in their outlook; a situation that the anti-bourgeois politics of the regime was able to rectify (1933, 2, no.5 (October–December): 41). An anonymous note 'Tramonto dell'arte borghese', published in the same issue, echoed this declaration, hailing the end of the bourgeois spirit, as a decadent, inane and damaging force (1933, 2, no.5 (October–December): 65–66). Similar points are reiterated throughout the article: Benedetto Croce, Gabriele D'Annunzio and even Oscar Wilde are dismissed without any right to appeal because they do not 'realistically portray' ('rappresentano realisticamente') the content of their novels, which they see as less important than stylistic experiments and lyricism. However, the difference between aestheticism and realism is not based exclusively on method or on content (as Barbaro put it) but also on ethical imperatives. The renewal of the novel, including the renewal of its narrative structures, needed to come from an ethical change: such a transformation fit squarely with that advocated by the regime through its *arte di Stato*. The Fascist revolution would transform the lives of its citizen because it would change their way of looking at the real, be that their objective reality or their inner one. *Occidente* was thus against 'eloquenza' and in favour of formal simplicity and directness in prose writing which could reach 'with naturalezza' to the heart of the matter. Youth culture in general and literary culture specifically sided with the regime in its interpretation of the role of the arts as conducive to action and construction, and committed to the social cause.

The novel no longer needs the heroic, solipsistic, gestures of a Julien Sorel, but rather characters who can help build reality and who are ethically convincing, as journalist, writer and translator Enrico Rocca clarified: 'So the children of this century are now called Glaeser, Körmendi, Leipmann e Kästner, Kesten and Süskind? Why is this? Moravia and Gambini, even? [...] This liberation is already a form of morality' (1933, 'Hermann Kesten, o delle ragioni del cuore' 2, no. 2 (January–March): 53).[18] Rocca is not only calling for morally sound arts but also for a more competitive national novel, which could be placed side by side with the genre's contemporary expressions. In the section on 'Europa letteraria', literary critic Giacomo Antonini in a long article titled 'Narratori italiani' a few months later concluded that new writers had to establish a 'wider contact with the public' ('largo contatto con il pubblico') since, like Körmendi's best-selling translated Hungarian novels, they needed to 'go to the people' ('andare al popolo') and to do so such novels have to bear an ethical message (1933, 3, no.7 (April–June): 26).

In his article 'Tecnica e mondo moderno', mathematician and scientist Umberto Forti went a step further in demarcating literary spaces: 'A culture which is estranged from technology and science is too much like those grand old nineteenth-century houses which had two reception rooms, plenty of grand features, but not even the tiniest of bathrooms' (1933, 3, no. 9 (October–December): 13).[19] While complaining about the still 'humanistic' attitude displayed by Italian culture, Forti added that such literature could not address the basic demands of humanity, only frivolous accessories. On this occasion, the architectural metaphor indicated a new morality but also a new configuration of the novel's thematic repertoire. The novel could and had to engage with the everyday and no longer treat it as marginal: it needed to purse a style without ornament[20] (Adolf Loos again) as well as a detached approach to the subject matter. Technique, furthermore, was now synonymous with the ordinary and not with a means of constructing alternative words (such as in surrealism, for example).[21] The reference to architecture here brings us back to the debates on the social role of architecture: Figini and Pollini's Casa elettrica was a manifesto of new technologies, markedly in the kitchen[22]; Adriano Olivetti's expansion of the Ivrea factory foresaw the integration between the daily lives of his employees and the industrial and productive apparatus within a utopian, enlightened Gropiesque vision, able to create individual spaces which could also be collective, rationalized and harmonious. La Sapienza[23] was the city and factory of knowledge production (see Chap. 7).

Occidente, then, showcased a complex cultural problem: by following the paradigm of avant-gardist rebellion against tradition while also indirectly echoing the regime's campaign for a new ethical system to support the anthropological revolution, it allowed intellectuals with various political orientations to show how they aimed to transform the arts into a set of constructivist-collective movements,[24] which could in turn contribute to building a new, aerial even, aesthetic landscape. This question is lucidly explained by critic Antonio Valenti in the mainstream publication *L'Italia letteraria* on 14 January 1934 in an article entitled 'Realtà dell'arte'. He talked about a 'realismo spirituale', which was not simply a way of dealing with everyday life but rather the outcome of a spiritual revolution, an anthropological revolution affecting the very essence of being a citizen and an individual. The novel has an ethical imperative because it executes a pedagogical function in this respect (1934, 19, no. 2 (14 January): 1). Such a function cannot be performed through a paternalistic gaze (whether Croce's or that of the avant-gardes and D'Annunzio), as this would be too technical, solipsistic and, in sum, degenerate.

Orpheus (Milan, 1932–1934)

Published in Milan from December 1932 to March 1934, *Orpheus* also had transatlantic aspirations. The journal was edited by a group of young middle-class intellectuals and writers who gravitated around the Università Statale and the Accademia di Brera, most notably Enzo Paci and Luciano Anceschi. Both born in 1911, they eventually became, respectively, a leading exponent of Italian philosophical existentialism and a noted literary critic in post-war Italy, as well as professors at Pavia-Milan and Bologna. In the 1930s at the Università Statale, Paci and Anceschi worked under the supervision of the philosopher Antonio Banfi, who in 1925 signed the Manifesto of anti-Fascist intellectuals and maintained a coherent distance from the regime. The journal's director, Pietro Torchi, was a musician who always encouraged the review to remain progressive in ethos and outlook. A medium-sized monthly review, it was sold at 2 lire per issue and a total of thirteen issues were published.[25] It devoted very little space to advertising, in favour of a modernist simplicity of line and style, with a Spartan front cover featuring only the title. It included a good selection of regular sections, containing an average of four or five long articles per issue (sometimes in the form of *appunti*, 'notes'), and a substantial section featuring longer 'Recensioni' and shorter reviews, as well as 'Cronache', 'Notiziario' and 'Notizie', often focusing on foreign works either in the original language or in translation (often into French and without the Italian translation) as well as on other Italian and foreign reviews.

Orpheus embraced multidisciplinary. But, it stood out from other comparable, non-mainstream initiatives, such as *L'Orto* (1931–1939), *Pan* (1933–1935), *Pègaso* (1929–1933) and *Solaria* (1926–1934), on account of its patently interdisciplinary scope as well as for its even stronger inclination towards the social dimension of the arts within 'Fascist mass society'—in line with *Il Saggiatore*. In a letter dated May 1933 to 'Cari amici del Saggiatore', Anceschi suggested a collaboration between the two 'movements' because of their shared interest in artistic matters and their shared desire to revise the relationship between 'art and society' (Anceschi archive, folder 'Corrispondenza *Orpheus*', b. 11). Anceschi was also keen to establish collaborations with *Quadrante* and Bardi, *Critica fascista* and the *Rivista di psicoanalisi*.[26] Amongst the key contributors to

6 State Art, the Novel, and Architecture: Intersections   137

the review we find a rather interdisciplinary set of expertise: the prominent art critic Raffaello Giolli, Riccardo Picozzi—a musician and opera teacher, the publishers Franco Formiggini and Alberto Mondadori, the academic Lorenza Maranini who was to become a leading French literature specialist, the film critic Eva Randi, Aldo Valcarenghi (son of the co-director of the Ricordi publishing house and organizer in 1931 of the pro-Toscanini manifestation), the sculptors Luigi Grosso and Giacomo Manzú,[27] the architects Isaac Saporta, Clara Valente, Federica Vecchietti, Maria and Clara Albini, Käte Bernhardt, the writer Elio Vittorini, the artist Riccardo Crippa, and the Jewish psychiatrist and academic Antonio Pesenti. The review included, unusually, eight women.

In 1932, the year of the celebrations for the Decennale of the Fascist 'revolution' and the abolition of artistic groupings in the USSR, *Orpheus* adopted a much more explicit and 'militant' position than *Occidente*, seeking to transform radically the *prosa d'arte*, the lyrical prose so fiercely championed by *La Ronda*, into a collective writing able (and thus enabling the *orfisti*) to react to the demands of a modern, Fascist society.[28] Compared to *Occidente*, *Orpheus* has a more structured approach to aesthetics and political issues: during its lifetime it carried out a systematic critique of the idea of autonomy in the arts.

In September 1933, in response to a general consultation with its readers, Paci declared that a new art 'will have to be constructed and based above all on two concepts: the concept of "collectivism" and the concept of "historical realism"' as 'transpositions onto the cultural plane of realities which are presently alive and in motion on the political and economic level' (1933, 'In margine ad un'inchiesta.' 2, no. 6–8 (July–September): 1).[29] Paci explicitly connected youth culture with economic renewal and indirectly connected the arts with an economic problem, which in the 1930s was that of the State as not only an ethical force but also a corporate one. In November 1933, discussing *Orpheus*' contribution to the survey carried out by *Il Saggiatore* on the same topic, in the opening article Anceschi reinforced the point already made a couple of months before, by claiming that the new art championed by the journal was ingrained in the principle that 'dynamic realism, [...] determined by its relationship with life [...], constitutes the meaning of our collectivist *Aufklärung*'.[30] Here the Milanese intellectual denied the value of abstract speculations since for him to theorize meant to ground one's reflections within a clear historical paradigm, a duty which needed to be performed by youth magazines. By neglecting the idea of realism as a static representation of reality, the new art therefore needed to reconfigure the relationship between individuality and collectivity. Their task would now be to 'find a new law of connection between the individual and society, between the single individual and the collectivity' (1933, 'Appunti per la definizione di un'atteggiamento.' 2, no. 9 (November): 4).[31] This 'moral and intellectual commitment' ('atteggiamento morale e intellettuale') could not tolerate indifference if it intended to forge a more profound theoretical and critical awareness of sociability in the arts, which had to translate into radically different forms of individual participation in the collective. In other words, without rejecting Fascist ideology per se, these young intellectuals wanted to 'explain' and 'clarify' ('spiegare e chiarire') further their understanding of the relationship between art and the individual as a social entity in order to produce an alternative scenario to those of art as propaganda or state-supported art. Once more, in response to the same survey in *Il Saggiatore* in December 1933, in the editorial *Orpheus* acknowledged that 'if politics is the basis of everything, then the corporative question, which expresses the most concrete revolutionary innovation of our current political configuration, is consequently the fundamental question we face' where 'social realism' ('realismo sociale') can find its 'concrete expression in a political form in movement, a synthesis and an instrument of the revolution' (1933, 'I giovani e la nuova cultura.' 2, no. 10 (December): 1–2).[32]

Thus *Orpheus*' brand of international *realismo storico*, in line with that promoted by similar reviews such as *Il Saggiatore*, was a more general expression of revolutionary humanism and less so of technological avant-gardism, which could and would bring artists and citizens—preferably collectively—back to the art of their Nation and to its social context. Moreover, by laying claim to the economic and social appeal of all artistic elements, in line with the aims of 1930s Italian corporative totalitarian art, *Orpheus* not only renounced the liberal idea of art as pure and estranged from practical existence, but also rejected its use as a form of total control of individuals through their consciousness. It is worth noting here that mural painting as the vehicle to represent the corporative totalitarian State started to emerge and gain a hegemonic position from 1933 onwards.[33]

6 State Art, the Novel, and Architecture: Intersections

In a departure from the regime's position, however, there was no mention of any State control over cultural matters; art was an autonomous field of production and moreover was ruled independently. The *rappel à l'ordre*, in this instance, took the form of a return to the logical acceptance of art as an autonomous form of collective expression, albeit one closely embedded in the social reality of its production and circulation. It was Enzo Paci who finally brought all these elements together in his long 1933 review of Benedetto Croce's influential *Poesia popolare e poesia d'arte* (1933, 2, no. 3 (April): 17–19). Discussing Croce's argument on the productive relationship between the folklore tradition and artistic poetry, he unequivocally rejected the notion of the 'autonomy of the artwork' and declared his unconditional faith in any form of literary expression, which reflected its historical context. In this important review, as elsewhere in his long, incisive articles on art and politics, Paci anticipated the post-war rejection of Croce and laid the foundations of the soon-to-be hegemonic historicist tradition of critical engagement with the arts.

Orpheus also published on cinema, photography, visual art, music and, crucially, printed three articles about international architecture. In the opening issue, the young architect Alberto Franco Schwartz wrote an article on the new architecture in France which, he argued, had the merit of providing the environment and the climate for the 'most complete and vital theoretical formulation of the problems of the new architecture in the entire world' (1933, 2, no.1 (January): 14).[34] In the May–June issue of the same year, Isaac Saporta, a student of Walter Gropius, published 'Architettura razionale' where he drew a parallel between the role of new architecture and the New Man in creating a modern society (ibid., no. 4–5: 12–13). This line of argument was also embraced by painter Pio Ponti in 'Architettura e aderanza alla realtà', in the same issue but this time dealing with Italy (ibid.:14–15). In Italy, as in the rest of Europe, he identified clear similarities between the ways in which architecture, society and aesthetic rationalization participated in the process of social modernization. The writing on contemporary aesthetics published in *Orpheus* thus clearly shows how the novel, the literary field and the other arts must be read as dynamic and historicized manifestations of the real, while presenting a modern view of society as a site which can be shaped, transformed and modernized by the arts.

Whether or not it is in a state of flux, of constant evolution and crisis, art can never be extricated from its historicity. By establishing such an unbreakable connection between text and context, *Orpheus* moved away from Benedetto Croce's aesthetic reflection and Decadentism's lack of any moral concern or historical awareness, instead drawing closer to European experiments, such as German New Objectivity, transatlantic modernism and rationalist architecture, and crucially closer to a deeper understanding of the role played by the arts in moulding the social sphere.

Il Saggiatore (Rome, 1930–1933)

As already mentioned, in 1933 *Il Saggiatore* launched an '*inchiesta*' ('survey') of the new Fascist culture and its generational divides, thereby bringing to an ideal closure our analysis of the arts and Fascist culture under the banner of realism. Amongst the many responses to the *inchiesta* (including contributions from Bragaglia, Marinetti and Sarfatti), the consensus yet again seemed to gravitate around the idea that the new intellectual generation had to embrace an idea of culture, which took into account the arts' practical role in society, thereby rejecting any form of idealism in favour of pragmatism (Carpi 1981, 78–81). European realism in particular played an important role as an example of the arts' social mission, since it represented just such a rejection of idealism (Voza 1981, 65–105; Tarquini 2011, 175–76; Ben-Ghiat 2001, 102–22; Sechi 1984, 63–108).

Il Saggiatore was very similar in its stance to the journals we have discussed so far: short-lived, rich in debates, and attuned to the latest artistic developments worldwide. After the Florentine *Leonardo* (1903–1907), *Il Saggiatore* was the most philosophical journal published in Italy in the first half of the twentieth century. And, just like its illustrious predecessor, it welcomed pragmatism as the main philosophical prism through which to evaluate every other artistic current, thus clearly rejecting Croce and Gentile's brand of idealism. Its editor was Luigi de Crecchio Parladore, a lawyer and a State functionary, assisted by intellectuals of the standing of Domenico Carella and Giorgio Granata, at the time still university students, Nicola Perrotti, a medical doctor who would also practise as a psychiatrist and, Attilio Riccio, a writer close to *900* and Bontempelli. The relationship between artistic creation and psychoanalysis was discussed extensively, thereby creating a more varied intellectual landscape within the journal. Several other intellectual figures of note drawn from *Occidente* and *Orpheus* as well as avant-garde circles, contributed, including: Corrado Alvaro, Luciano Anceschi, Umberto Barbaro, P. M. Bardi, Massimo Bontempelli, Corrado Pavolini, Mario Puccini, Emilio Radius, Elio Vittorini, Bonaventura Tecchi and Dino Terra. All these names played key roles both at the fringes and at the centre of the cultural apparatus of the dictatorship, and they found these sorts of cultural venues to be especially useful arenas for debate.

Although not explicitly focused on the arts, *Il Saggiatore* contributed to the philosophical discussion underpinning the idea of culture itself during the regime. In less than three years, it conducted two major surveys, the first dedicated to the new generation of intellectuals, from March to June 1932, and the second examining the 'new culture' in October 1933. From 1933 onwards, one can simultaneously note a sharp intensification in the regime's anti-bourgeois campaign, which was intrinsically associated with a stronger role for corporativism in directing the regime's cultural campaign (Parlato 2000, 112; Santomassimo 2006, 102–03). Thus, to a certain extent, it is safe to assume that the more experimental and militant cultural debates followed—albeit indirectly—top-down instructions to promote collectivity, the new aesthetics and realism.

In *Il Saggiatore*, the debate on realism was unambiguously conducted in parallel to that on the new culture and the philosophical debate regarding the limits of individual and collective agency. The main difference introduced by this debate on the relationship between the political and aesthetic spheres was the existential-humanistic element, described as the distinctive trait of the generation of men and women living under the Fascist regime but often imbued with rather mystical and spiritual connotations. Sechi has studied the journal extensively and drawn some definitive conclusions on the role of pragmatism as a counterpoint to the Croce-Gentile axis and on the 'materialist refounding' of both reality and the new literature for the 'present moment' (Sechi 1984, 84; see, e.g. Domenico Carella and Attilio Riccio, 1931, 'Morte dell'idealismo.'

Il Saggiatore 2, no. 3 (May): 101–05).[35] We will, therefore, concentrate here on the importance of realism for prose writing, and also on its limits. From a strictly philosophical—as opposed to literary—point of view, *Il Saggiatore* was against bourgeois prose writing and in favour of art forms connected with their social context, since it insisted that the 'novel' had to reflect lived experience (Giorgio Granata, 1930, 'Dei giovani.' 1, no. 1 (March): 14). As artists, writers had the moral responsibility to address the naked reality before them, and as in all the fields we have analysed thus far, the issue of realism and morality was discussed with some regularity. However, the debate which unfolded in the Rome-based journal introduced a new element: the relationship between subjectivity and objectivity in building a new brand of realism, a question raised in Mario Pannunzio's two interventions specifically addressing the debate on the novel. In his 'Del romanzo', he described the act of writing as an 'X-ray' of reality and its contradictions.[36,37] 1930s realism, he argued, could not simply reflect the surface of reality but had to use its techniques to dig into the depths and intricacies of the world and provide a more nuanced picture (1932, 2, no. 11 (January): 432–38).

This said, it was important not to lose sight of the pursuit for complete factual anonymity, as Attilio Riccio had already pointed out in his reading of Borgese's *Tempo di edificare* and, we could add, as Bontempelli had called for as foundational to the act of writing (see Chap. 5). Riccio objected to Borgese's apparent side-stepping of the psychological dimension of artistic creation in his call to build a new architecture for the novel since 'the artwork has to be at the same time real and constructed, the architectural idea needs to lose its transcendental nature and transform itself into a ductile figure, ready to welcome the emotions produce by the real' (1931, 'In margine all'ultimo Borgese.' 2, no. 9 (November): 337–38).[38] In June 1932, meanwhile, Giorgio Prosperi published an article entitled 'Realismo e impersonalità'. He argued that realism is based on a process of selection and construction and not on that of developing a close association between art and life, citing to this effect playwright Luigi[39] Pirandello's *Sei personaggi in cerca d'autore* as an example of realist narration on account of the play's metanarrative construction, abolition of the fourth wall and its open-endedness. For, he explained 'In place of analytical fragmentism ever greater preference is being given to construction, to content, to sentiment, in other words to works which have a voice' (1932, 2, no.12: 486).[40] The type of realism theorized in *Il Saggiatore*, then, was not a form of pure objectivity offering a direct representation of the real (not even of the collective real) but rather a speculative type of objectivity filtered through individual experience to create a new naturalism (Mario Pannunzio, 'Necessità del romanzo.' 3, no. 4 (June): 154–62; see Moravia,[41] Chap. 7). In Pannunzio's words, novelists have to interpret and deform reality through their own technical language. This language has to abolish punctuation, favour interior monologue, and create surprising syntactical connections in order to be analytical and 'radiographic' rather than descriptive. Dialogues play a crucial role in this since they can prismatically reveal subjective positions and they can do so simultaneously. Moreover, the journal published reviews of John Dos Passos, Aldous Huxley, D. H. Lawrence, Virginia Woolf and the novelists of the German New Objectivity, thus offering its readers both a plethora of narrative and theoretical choices, and giving an idea of the spectrum of alternatives available in Italy and elsewhere. Other interventions on realism included Domenico Carella's forceful claim that culture as a whole cannot be detached from life if it wants to be meaningful and gain social relevance, and De Crecchio's call a few months later for committed artists who are not confined within a solipsistic understanding of the real, like Michele in *Gli indifferenti* or Filippo Rubè[42] in the eponymous novel by Borgese, but are active participants in the construction and modernization of the social sphere (1932, 'Questa realtà.' 3, no. 9 (November): 337–42, and 1933, 'Funzionalità dell'Arte.' 4, no. 2 (April): 59–63, and see Chap. 3).

Despite its philosophical orientation and its lack of a dedicated debate on the novel per se in order to focus more on theories of realism, *Il Saggiatore* reiterated some of the key principles we have discussed regarding the novel and architecture: construction, social context, morality and stylistic simplification. Its originality lay in how it raised these questions to a higher theoretical level than ever before, while reintroducing the importance of subjectivity as a cardinal point in the definition of the artistic sphere and of the aesthetic experience (from a psychoanalytical and philosophical perspective). The themes of morality, reality, construction, context and tradition recur constantly in the debates analysed here, whether these notions are explicitly connected to architecture or to the novel, or used more generally to address the regime's cultural policies on the arts, collectivism and corporativism. In both the aesthetic and political spheres, this constant revisiting of the same topics is indicative of a concerted effort and a distinct programmatic intention, which, as we will see in the final chapter, were put into practice by writers and architects alike throughout the Ventennio, following a trajectory delineated by the broader contextual debates.

Notes

1. See Giò Ponti's article on 17 September 1933 about architecture and the other arts 'Il "momento" dell'architettura in Italia.' *Quadrivio* 1, no. 7: 1.
2. For a systematic analysis of the Roman underground movements, and for a detailed scrutiny of the Futurist, communist, anarchist and Fascist journals, which populated it, see Mondello (1990).
3. http://dialecticsofmodernity.manchester.ac.uk/essay/490
4. Fagone discusses extensively the relationship between Sassu, *Corrente* and the idea of expressionistic realism, fused with that of heroic mythology, as together seen as an antidote to the Fascist regime's brutality and progressive closure. Sassu was arrested in 1937 and released from prison in 1938 due to Marinetti's mediation (2001, 189–96).
5. http://dialecticsofmodernity.manchester.ac.uk/essay/488
6. http://dialecticsofmodernity.manchester.ac.uk/essay/488
7. On the policies about State art, the 2% law, and the role played by Bottai in the 1940s as indirect patron of the arts, see Vivarelli (1993, 24–38), and the volume edited by Alessandro Masi (1992).
8. On regime policies of youth culture patronage, Ruth Ben-Ghiat points out that contributors to journals such as *Il Saggiatore* and *L'Universale* and rationalist architects alike received subsidies from the regime, and much more regularly after 1933 (2001, 108–09).
9. http://dialecticsofmodernity.manchester.ac.uk/tag/aesthetic-theorization
10. Paolo Flores, Vinicio Paladini and Dino Terra were all closely associated with anarcho-communist circles (Mondello 1990, 67–70). Ghelardini was spared house arrest thanks to personal interventions by Ministers Giuseppe Bottai and Galeazzo Ciano. Bottai published an article on

literature and corporativism in 1935 entitled 'Appunti sulla letteratura corporativa.' 4, n. 12 (August): 11–16. Nevertheless, the journal had to be closed indefinitely.
11. http://dialecticsofmodernity.manchester.ac.uk/essay/437
12. http://dialecticsofmodernity.manchester.ac.uk/essay/455
13. Bontempelli is an admirer of Verga and in n. 10 there are some unpublished letters by the Sicilian writer.
14. http://dialecticsofmodernity.manchester.ac.uk/essay/454
15. 'Si è sentito il bisogno di recuperare la tecnica e si è tornati all'opera costruita e pensata, nella sua forma tipica, il romanzo: ma esso, come l'architettura razionalista, e come gli avanguardismi, è pieno di eautonotimerumena voracità, oggi aspira ad essere tutta fantasia; tutta tecnica, come nei romanzi gialli (vecchio bisogno antiartistico di cui parlava già Guerrazzi [...]) o tutta sociologia e morale o contenuto, cioè ancora tutta fantasia.'
16. 'La vera moralità dell'arte sta nel ricongiungere, riconstringere nelle angustie della quotidianità il lettore.'
17. 'Che cosa si aspetta dunque, perché non costruire davvero, subito?'
18. 'I figli del secolo oggi si chiamano, Glaeser, Körmendi, Leipmann e Kästner, Kester? e perché? anche Moravia e Gambini? [...] Questa liberazione è già moralità.'
19. 'Una cultura estraniata dalla tecnica e dalla scienza somiglia troppo alla vecchie case umbertine, che avevano due salotti, molte cose di pretesa, ma nemmeno una stanzetta da bagno.'
20. http://dialecticsofmodernity.manchester.ac.uk/tag/architectural-principle.
21. See Sartoris' article (1933) on surrealism and new architecture in *Quadrante*, cit.
22. http://dialecticsofmodernity.manchester.ac.uk/artefact/28
23. http://dialecticsofmodernity.manchester.ac.uk/artefact/41; http://dialecticsofmodernity.manchester.ac.uk/essay/497; http://dialecticsofmodernity.manchester.ac.uk/essay/497
24. http://dialecticsofmodernity.manchester.ac.uk/tag/collectivity
25. From 1 November 1933 the price increased to 3 lire because of a format change, which meant a larger size and more illustrations. *Orpheus* had 50 subscribers but was distributed in batches of a hundred copies in bookstores.
26. A note in the folder 'Corrispondenza *Orpheus*' lists 42 journals for *Orpheus* to be in contact with: most notably, *Camminare*, *Domus*, *Frontespizio*, *Il Saggiatore*, *L'Italia letteraria*, *L'Orto*, *L'Universale*, the

Nouvelle Revue Françoise, Occidente, Il Milione, Quandrante, Oggi, La rassegna musicale, Scenario, Il Convegno, L'Italia che scrive, Arti plastiche, Solaria, Circoli, L'Italiano, Il selvaggio, Nuova Antologia, Il secolo fascista, Tempo nostro, Critica fascista. The list includes also 46 subscribers (Anceschi archive, 'Corrispondenza *Orpheus*', b. 11).

27. http://dialecticsofmodernity.manchester.ac.uk/essay/430
28. A profound dislike for Croce and the prosa d'arte i salso expressed privately by Pietro Tronchi in a letter dated 12 September 1933 to Luciano Anceschi (Anceschi, folder 'Corrdispondenza *Orpheus*', b. 11).
29. 'si dovrà costruire e basare sopra tutto su due concetti: il concetto di "collettivismo" e il concetto di "realismo storico"' as 'trasposizioni sul piano culturale di realtà ormai viventi ed in moto su quello politico e su quello economico.'
30. 'realismo dinamico, [...] determinato dai rapporti con la vita. [...], costituisce il senso della nostra *Aufklärung* collettivista.'
31. 'trovare una nuova legge di connesione tra l'individuo e la società, tra il singolo e la collettivià.'
32. 'se la politica è il fondamento di tutto, il problema corporativo, che esprime l'innovazione rivoluzionaria più concreta della nostra attuale politica, è conseguentemente il problema fondamentale' 'espressione concreta in una forma politica in moto, sintesi e strumento della Rivoluzione.'
33. On this point, see Fagone (2001, 19–23, 26–46).
34. 'formulazione teorica più complete e vive dei problemi della nuova architettura in tutto il mondo'. For instance, Schwartz also wrote articles on Frankfurt-based popular architecture and housing for the *Rassegna dell'architettura*.
35. Other significant contributions on the debate on realism are: Nicola Carella, 1931, 'Omaggio al realismo.' 1, no. 11 (January): 351–65; and Francesca Bruno, 1931, 'Realismo germanico.' 2, no. 4 (June): 160–65 with a specific reference to the practice of 'lucid realism' in prose writing championed by the German New Objectivity movement, ibid.:164.
36. http://dialecticsofmodernity.manchester.ac.uk/essay/449
37. In 1932 Enrico Emanuelli published a newly realist novel entitled precisely *Radiografia di una notte* and in 1934 Mario Soldati the cinéroman *24 ore in uno studio cinematografico*, both with the Milanese publisher Ceschina. On the critical reception of the novel, especially by his contemporaries and on Emanuelli's borrowing from European Modernist and contemporary novels, see Ben-Ghiat (2001: 59–61).

38. 'L'opera d'arte deve essere allo stesso tempo reale e costruita, l'architettura deve perdere la sua natura trascendentale e trasformarsi in una figura duttile, pronta ad accogliere i dati emozionali della realtà.'
39. http://dialecticsofmodernity.manchester.ac.uk/essay/459
40. 'Al frammentismo analitico si preferisce sempre di più la costruzione, il contenuto, il sentimento, cioè l'opera che abbia una voce.'
41. http://dialecticsofmodernity.manchester.ac.uk/essay/456
42. http://dialecticsofmodernity.manchester.ac.uk/essay/440

Open Access This chapter is licensed under the terms of the Creative Commons Attribution 4.0 International License (http://creativecommons.org/licenses/by/4.0/), which permits use, sharing, adaptation, distribution and reproduction in any medium or format, as long as you give appropriate credit to the original author(s) and the source, provide a link to the Creative Commons licence and indicate if changes were made.

The images or other third party material in this chapter are included in the chapter's Creative Commons licence, unless indicated otherwise in a credit line to the material. If material is not included in the chapter's Creative Commons licence and your intended use is not permitted by statutory regulation or exceeds the permitted use, you will need to obtain permission directly from the copyright holder.

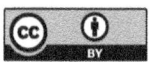

7

Novels and Buildings

Novels

Gli indifferenti: The Reconstruction of the Novel

When it appeared in 1929, *Gli indifferenti* was hailed as an example of the new realism that was at the centre of debates in literary and cultural journals (see Chaps. 3, 5 and 6; see also Ben-Ghiat 1995, 641; 2001, 57; Buchignani 2012, 68). Moravia started publishing short stories in *900* in 1927, which suggests that the young writer shared, or at least felt close to, the journal's programme (see Chap. 5).[1] In 1928 he also published several short stories in the Fascist avant-garde magazines *I lupi* and *Interplanetario*.[2] These writings anticipated *Gli indifferenti* with their narrative strategies, specifically the restoration of the function of characters, and the attempt at striking a balance between action and psychological analysis (see Carpi 1981b). Moravia theorized these aesthetic strategies as the necessary response to a perceived 'crisis of the novel', in an article he wrote in 1927 for the magazine *La fiera letteraria*, entitled 'C'è una crisi del romanzo?'[3] In this article, like many other authors and critics at this time, Moravia blamed the crisis of the novel on its excessive psychologism, which caused concrete reality to dissolve into pure thoughts and introspection—what he called the novel's 'psychoanalytic dead weight' ('zavorra psicoanalitica'). Moravia located the problem in an imbalance between plot and psychological introspection, which needed to be redressed. He did not suggest returning to 'pure' action or pure description, which would imply a regression towards a traditional, naturalistic structure. Rather, novelists should seek to strike a balance between the dimension of action and that of consciousness. One way to do this was rehabilitating the mediating role of characters, who would no longer be reduced to mere sequences of thoughts and consciousness (see Voza 1997, 12–13). Moravia complained that too many Italian authors were far from producing 'a true and convincing representation of life' ('una rappresentazione vera, e soprattutto convincente della vita') (Moravia 1927, reprinted in Voza 1982, 211).

In *Gli indifferenti*, Moravia achieved this on a formal level through his recourse to a third-person, partially omniscient narrator, in what has been defined by critics and by the author himself as a 'theatrical novel' (Schettino 1974). The effect of this type of narration is to underscore the autonomy of the characters and the distance that exists between them and the narrator. Commenting on *Gli indifferenti* many years later, Moravia said that he had intended to write a novel that would simultaneously possess the qualities of a work of fiction and those of a play—thus, a novel with a rationalized narrative structure, in which the characters would emerge as strong and independent, and the author would practically disappear:

> A novel with few characters, with very few settings, with its action unfolding over a short time. A novel with nothing but dialogues and background details, in which all the commentaries, analysis and interventions of the author would be carefully abolished to create a perfect objectivity. [...] Besides, I had convinced myself that it was not worth writing if the author did not compete with the Creator in the invention of independent characters, living a life of their own. (Moravia 1964, 63–64)[4]

Moravia explains here how the mutual interferences between the genres of fiction and drama have an important role in the work's gestation. However, his comments also relate to his involvement in the project of reconstructing the novel, already discussed in his abovementioned article, which was based on some of the principles that we have discussed in previous chapters. These principles were what united the novel and architecture in their efforts to effect aesthetic renewal under the Fascist regime: the rationalization of forms, an adherence to reality, and the construction of 'objects' which were detached and independent from the subjectivity of the author. A drive for positive reconstruction underpinned these artistic undertakings, which reflected, and often actively supported, the regime's anthropological enterprise of forging a new culture and a new civilization. In his article, Moravia stated his commitment to this constructive effort—which defined the spirit of that era—by denouncing a 'pathology' affecting the novel (by implication, something that can be cured, and is reversible), and identifying ways to take 'restorative' action (Moravia 1927, reprinted in Voza 1982, 210–12).

The first reviewer of *Gli indifferenti* was the writer and literary critic Giuseppe Antonio Borgese, who in 1923 had written an article with the revealing title of *Tempo di edificare* (*Time to build*). In this important essay, he called for a new, constructive literature removed from the dominant 'fragmentism' famously championed by the early twentieth-century literary journal *La Voce*, and a return to long, well-structured and fully developed novels, which would contribute to the building of new values for a modern society (see Chap. 3). Unsurprisingly, Borgese wrote a positive review of *Gli indifferenti*, published in *Il corriere della sera* on 21 July 1929 (reprinted in Borgese 1962, 214–20), in which he lauded the qualities of a novel which was contributing to the reconstructive effort which he had himself called for a few years earlier. Borgese praised the novel's broad and 'solid' structure, the rationalized narration, the vigorous and 'healthy' prose (which he compared to strong, vigorous brush strokes in painting), and its simplified, sparse style. The language used, he claimed, was 'beautiful, because it is purged of any embellishment' ('un'arte di scrittura molto bella, perché depurata di ogni belluria [...]'). It exemplified a much-needed clean break with the excessively ornate and flowery style of those writers that Borgese himself had called 'calligraphic', a tendency which according to him and many other critics had ruined Italian prose and poetry. In *Gli indifferenti*, Borgese argued, the writer's concern was not for the elegance of single words or fragments, but rather for a large-scale, natural and cohesive narration, whose overarching effect was one of 'soundness and vigour' ('sanità', [...] vigore'). Accordingly, the plot was stripped down to material facts and reduced to what read like a news story. This comment, in particular, is reminiscent of Bontempelli's advice for writers (see Chap. 5, pp. 101–102).

Borgese's comments highlighted and praised an extreme rationalization and simplification of both the contents and the form of the novel, matched by an almost disturbing adhesion to reality, only made bearable for the reader by the writer's talent. In the book, Moravia portrays a cross section of the empty, deceitful and miserable life of a Roman bourgeois family in decline. The family is composed of Mariagrazia, a shallow widow who inherited the large Villa Ardengo, in which the story is mostly set; and her two children, Carla and Michele, both in their 20s, who are unhappy and alienated, but unable to change their lives. The other characters are Leo Merumeci, Mariagrazia's lover, a wealthy, unscrupulous investor who has lent her money and plans to appropriate the family's villa; and Lisa, a divorcée who is Mariagrazia's friend, but also Leo's former lover. As the plot unfolds, Leo seduces Carla, and Lisa seduces Michele. Carla and Michele have a painful awareness that giving in to Leo and Lisa's propositions is morally wrong and against their true desires, but are unable to resist. In the end, Leo decides to marry Carla. As Borgese wrote, Moravia was merciless and unsparing in his depiction, and did nothing to embellish his 'decaying' subject matter, an approach which matched his unadorned style. His perspective was not one of 'perverse complicity' ('complicità perverse') or, on the contrary, of overblown moralism; rather, he cultivated a detached disgust that was all the more effective in highlighting the bleakness of the story and the moral decay of an entire social class.

This grim depiction of an amoral, hypocritical bourgeoisie fills the novel with ethical tension and foregrounds a desire for moral change, expressed mainly through the (unfulfilled) yearnings of the younger characters. While Mariagrazia, Leo and Lisa seem unaware of this and mostly at ease in their world, the general lack of transparency and moral principles distresses Carla and Michele, who feel alienated and desperately crave a new, different life. They long for a world in which behaviour, relationships and discussions 'adhere to reality', in which people are honest and act upon their feelings, rather than being governed by indifference and paralysis. However, this desire alone is not sufficient to give them the new way of life to which they aspire; they are powerless and ultimately find themselves stuck in their numb and unhappy lives— Carla's obsession with a 'new life' even leads her to sleep with Leo and arguably leaves her worse off. While some post-war critics saw this ethical tension as a sign of the antifascist nature of the novel, many Fascist critics, on the contrary, hailed it as a banner of a new Fascist morality grounded in the need for honesty, transparency, and the value of action, which the new realist novel was expected to embody (see Ben-Ghiat 1995, 643–45; see also Talbot 2006, 129–30).[5] The novel was understood by many critics as a condemnation of the apathy, hypocrisy, and amorality of the liberal bourgeoisie, which in their view was completely at odds with the Fascist moral code and would be swept away by the regime. Several exponents of Fascist culture, in particular those of the so-called 'sinistra fascista' (Fascist left wing), praised it as a 'significant manifestation of a "constructive" and "moral" literature, immersed in contemporary life' (Buchignani 2012, 68). The most illustrious of these critics was Giuseppe Bottai, who praised *Gli indifferenti* in the pages of *Critica fascista* (Bottai 1931, 1932; see also Ben-Ghiat 2001, 61). Certainly, as Moravia stated in his abovementioned 1927 article in *La fiera letteraria*, *Gli indifferenti* responded to the need for a reconnection of the novel with reality, in order to restore its crucial documentary and ethical-cognitive value, and thus fulfil a new ethical commitment that was expected from the modern writer (Voza 1982, 209). The novel was thus highly representative of the constructive and ethical spirit of this era.

Luce fredda: The Morality of the Novel

Umberto Barbaro was an eclectic and extremely dynamic figure in the twentieth-century Italian cultural and artistic landscape. He was a tireless innovator in different artistic fields (mainly literature, theatre and cinema) during the Fascist and post-war periods, and he frequently engaged in theoretical reflection on the arts. His 1927 article on expressionist playwright Ernst Toller offered a critique of the dominant literary approaches of Crocean philosophy, *dannunzianesimo*,[6] and Futurism, highlighting their shared aesthetic principles in order to move beyond them (Barbaro 1927b). He identified these as a disengagement with content on the one hand, and stylistic fragmentism on the other. According to Barbaro, these artistic tendencies were not equal to the task of representing modern reality and fulfilling the role that art had to play in a modern, mass society. His artistic ideal, set out in a large number of writings, was opposed to the idealist tradition and upheld a close relationship between art and life, seen as crucial in allowing art first to exceed the individual dimension, and then act upon and transform reality.[7] Clearly, the type of art that Barbaro envisioned had a profound political meaning and potential, which would be fully realized in the post-war period, through Barbaro's activity as a film critic and theorist of socialist Neorealism (see Brunetta 1976; Briganti 1984; Di Giovanna 1992, 185–91). Although Barbaro was a Communist, his anti-individualist, anti-Romantic, and socially oriented conception of art, as well as his revolutionary and 'populist' language, were perfectly compatible with the type of engaged aesthetics promoted by the regime and endorsed by Fascist intellectuals which, focusing on the construction of a new morality, was eagerly embraced by Barbaro (see Brunetta 1976, 21–22; Andreazza 2008, 324–25; Ben-Ghiat 2001, 63). In the late 1920s and early 1930s, then, revolutionary right-wing and left-wing writers worked together towards the construction of a new art, and specifically a new literature (Buchignani 2012, 68).

The affinities of Barbaro's artistic views with those upheld by the Fascist cultural 'programme' manifested themselves in the various connections and relationships he built with intellectual figures and groups openly endorsing the regime (Andreazza 2008, 322). His aesthetics overlapped significantly with the theories championed by the journal *900* (see Chap. 5), and indeed Barbaro, like Moravia, gravitated towards the Novecento movement, contributing several articles to this and other journals (see Buchignani 1987, 728). His aesthetic ideas fed into a distinct movement called *Immaginismo*, made up of a group of artists and writers (including Vinicio Paladini, Dino Terra, Bonaventura Grassi, Paolo Flores, Ivo Pannaggi, and others) which grew out of the Rome avant-garde scene of the late 1920s (see Carpi 1981a; Buchignani 1987). Barbaro, who proclaimed himself the 'theorist' of the movement, founded the journal *La ruota dentata* in February 1927, in order to provide the group with an artistic and theoretical platform. Due to a lack of funds, however, the journal was discontinued after the first issue. The journal, and the movement behind it, aimed to bring together all the avant-gardes, as the first page of the only issue of *La ruota dentata* reveals: 'Futurists, suprematists, cubists, expressionists, constructivists, avant-gardists, realists, everyone with the Immaginist movement!'.[8] Elsewhere, Barbaro claimed that the aesthetic programme gathering the avant-gardes under the banner of the Immaginist movement was the only possible way forward, through 'a common way of seeing reality and trying to make this reality creative, and modify it through art' (Barbaro 1927c).[9] He thus privileged the subversive and 'political' function of avant-garde art, rather than shared formal features, in this Immaginist attempt at rallying the avant-gardes (Andreazza 2008, 320).

Barbaro also upheld the idea of art as a means of shaping reality in his crucial article in *La ruota dentata*, 'Una nuova estetica per un'arte nuova', which occupied almost half of the journal's sole entire issue (Barbaro 1927a, reprinted in Barbaro 1976, 75–84). This article offers a critique of Croce's aesthetic theory, which was based on the process of intuitive expression, denying any relationship between art and reality and thus underpinning the bourgeois ideal of 'pure' art, which Barbaro rejected. He proposed an alternative model of the creative process comprising two moments: a 'destructive' one, governed by fantasy, and a 'constructive' one, governed by imagination. Through this two-phase process, the subject is taken out of the self to undergo change, before re-entering the self and restoring harmony (Barbaro 1976, 75). Barbaro saw this detachment of the subject from the self and its subsequent recomposition as constituting the heuristic essence and universal value of art, ensuring its relationship with life, as opposed to the sterile knowledge and expression of the self offered by Crocean aesthetics (Ibid., 78). He concluded that the empty formula 'art for art's sake' should be replaced by 'art for life's sake' ('arte per la vita') (Ibid., 84).

Barbaro discussed similar ideas, this time specifically in relation to the novel, in an article from 1932, the year following the publication of his novel *Luce fredda*, which, as will be shown below, constituted a key artistic actualization of his theoretical reflections. In this article, entitled 'Considerazioni sul romanzo' (Barbaro 1932, reprinted in 1976, 132–38), he reaffirmed the power of art to create reality and shape every other human activity, extolling its 'efficient morality' ('moralità efficiente') (1976, 133). The novel, in particular, was an artistic genre that tended to minimize the more lyrical and Romantic elements of art, constituting the archetypal form of the 'well-conceived and well-built artwork' (l'opera costruita e pensata') (Ibid., 135), to which artists felt the need to return, following not only the excesses of 'pure art' but also 'the over-indulgence with either pure technique or straightforward realism' (Billiani 2016, 490). For this reason, the novel had been disparaged by advocates of 'pure art', who feared the moment when art and life would be so close as to correspond completely, and 'pure' artworks would disappear (Barbaro 1976, 136).

Crucially, Barbaro stressed the artist's urgent moral duty to effect a renewal of reality and society through a renewal of art itself (Ibid., 137). This strong moral, and hence social function of the novel would be realized by shocking its readers' consciences and thus encouraging them to make their reality better, to transform their world, thereby turning art into a driving force of social change:

> The real morality of art lies in reconnecting readers to, and forcing them into, the hardships of everyday life, to provoke their anxious desire to escape, to do better, to transform themselves and the world [...]. (Barbaro 1976, 138)[10]

With this article (and others), Barbaro announced and clarified his contribution to the project of the renewal and 'reconstruction' of the novel, grounded in the principles of the return to realism and 'well-built' artworks, the morality of art, and the artist's relationship with the masses. His artistic and intellectual endeavours can thus be seen as a 'constructive' evolution of the avant-garde culture that had developed in the early decades of the twentieth century (Buchignani 2012, 67), dismissing the latter's obsession with technique, but preserving the ethical value of art. We will now discuss these principles, which formed the intersection of the literary and architectural fields, in relation to the novel *Luce fredda*.

Luce fredda was published in 1931 and has significant points in common with Moravia's *Gli indifferenti*, beginning with a shared cultural milieu in terms both of its subject matter—the Roman bourgeoisie—and its origins in Roman avant-garde circles. Furthermore, the two novels share a fierce anti-bourgeois sentiment, ethical tension, the rejection of lyricism and fragmentism (*'prosa d'arte'*) in favour of a well-built narrative, and realist aesthetics, albeit interpreted and applied in different ways (see Carpi 1981a, 141–45; Andreazza 2008, 325). However, the two books differ in other respects. Barbaro's realist intentions and social concerns coexist with a thoroughgoing narrative, stylistic, and linguistic experimentalism that differs from Moravia's more traditional narrative choices. Like *Gli indifferenti*, the book portrays some young members of the bourgeoisie who, like Carla and Michele Ardengo, are alienated by the hypocrisy and lack of value they perceive in their world. Similarly, the older, pre-Fascist generation (represented, for instance, by Maria's parents, father Roggi, and the lawyer Falerno) is at ease with the status quo, whereas the younger generation (represented by Sergio, Maria, Leone, Tilde, Lorenzo, and Vincenzo) is uncomfortable with bourgeois codes of conduct, and feels suffocated by the apathy and immobilism that dominate their world. However, they are generally too immersed in, and influenced by this culture, and the attitudes and behaviour it engenders, to be able to break free, embrace a new morality and change their lives.

Compared to *Gli indifferenti*, however, there are more positive examples of action and change. Maria decides to renounce her privileges and seek financial independence, so she leaves her parents' house and moves to Rome to look for a job (131–32).[11] This happens shortly after she visits a factory owned by her father, and meets working women who are exploited and physically debilitated by their work, yet energetic and dignified (153–55). The youngest character, 17-year-old Ruggero, represents an even younger generation which has grown up under Fascism and is thus less influenced by bourgeois liberal norms and behaviour; this generation will go one step further and transform this realization into action. Indeed, Ruggero takes moral obligation to the extreme committing suicide to redeem himself for a misdeed (forging his father's signature in order to obtain a loan from the bank). Despite the tragic nature of this action, it is taken as an example of righteousness by other characters, in particular Sergio. He sees Ruggero's uncompromising behaviour as 'proof of the possibility of salvation on earth' and of the 'categorical existence of morals, independent of norms and external sanctions' (224). This gesture is a spur for him to 'throw himself into action' too, but he is immediately gripped by fear and insecurities which, once again, paralyse him, and he falls asleep. He is thus unable to effect the necessary change in his life, reminding us of Michele Ardengo's failed attempts to challenge events and behaviour he perceives as wrong.

In a 1933 article, tellingly entitled 'La mia fede' ('My faith'), Barbaro wrote that 'if we wanted to reduce it to its essence, my aesthetics would concern the relationship between art and life' (Barbaro 1933, reprinted in 1976, 139).[12] For this reason, he advocated a 'demanding, problematic, and content-focused' type of production ('impegnativa, problematica e contenutistica') (Ibid.), marked by a constant ethical tension and a strong rejection of individualism. He claimed that this conception of art and life was strongly reflected in *Luce fredda*. The book indeed represents a complex specimen of a modern novel that thematically, but also narratively, rejects and defies individualism. Through his narrative choices, Barbaro distanced himself not only from the shallowness of *prosa d'arte*, but also from a naturalistic type of realism, based on a simplistic and outdated relationship between the subject and the object (Salaris 1990, 238; Billiani 2016, 490). Instead, *Luce fredda* could be defined as a 'polyphonic' or a 'choral' novel: although the character of Sergio is slightly more prominent than the others, it is difficult to identify a protagonist figure in the traditional sense of the term. The novel is rather about a *group* of people, representing the Roman petit-bourgeois intellectual or pseudo-intellectual class. The text is thus marked by an extensive, almost structural, use of free indirect speech and inner monologues. The narrative is not linear, but comes across rather as an assembly of narrative sections and fragments of 'reality' (like letters and excerpts of journal), reminiscent of the cinematographic technique of montage (Durante 2000, 125).

Luce fredda was thus an experimental model for Barbaro's new concept of Neorealism, departing from naturalism and rooted in the experiences of the avant-gardes, but progressing beyond the latter by embracing the need for the constructive engagement of literature and the arts in modern society. As he explained in a review of Sejfullina's novel *Virineja*, progressing beyond avant-gardism would mean that 'formal and technical values, whose sphere almost all modernists have limited themselves to, are [...] balanced with a rich and elevated content' (Barbaro 1928, reprinted in 1976, 88–89).[13] The novel's choral perspective, giving voice to a multitude of characters whose subjectivities, through the use of free indirect speech, are mixed and almost melded into one another,[14] can be related to the notion of the 'collective novel', which was popular under Fascism. For many critics and writers, this was the literary equivalent of Fascist collectivism, and a response to the need for an anti-individualistic art that would sublimate individual experiences into collective ones, making art modern and relevant for a mass society:

> The attempt at reconciling, including in the artistic sphere, the individual with society, the singular with the multiple, finds a solution in a literature that adheres to reality and goes beyond the traditional, biographical and psychological novel, in order to become the narration of collective facts or the projection of individual facts onto the masses. The collective novel should thus be a social or choral novel. (Busoni 1934, cited in Buchignani 1987, 740)[15]

The same concern was central to the field of architecture, as architects belonging to the Modern Movement in particular believed that the Fascist revolution would be expressed and brought about through buildings destined for the collectivity (see analysis of buildings in the second part of this chapter).

The *Romanzo Fiat* and the Creation of Modern Myths: *522* and *La strada e il volante*

The novels *522: Racconto di una giornata* and *La strada e il volante*, written by Massimo Bontempelli and Pietro Maria Bardi, respectively, grew out of a unique partnership between literature and industry (specifically the Fiat company). As such, they exemplify the new modalities of the writing 'profession' ('*mestiere*'), in Bontempelli's definition, and the new place and function of writers in modern mass society, which Bontempelli had addressed in his theoretical reflections on modern artistic production (see Chap. 5, pp. 101–102). This partnership was the result of the initiative of Gino Pestelli, hired by Fiat in 1928 to direct their press office. Before that, Pestelli had been the co-director of the Turin newspaper *La stampa* (Tongiorgi 1994b, 399). Pestelli had revolutionized Fiat's advertising strategy, adapting it to the changing conditions of modern mass society, and to the new market that Fiat was seeking to create and expand.[16] Fiat needed a different promotional approach to target potential buyers for the new range of popular, mass-market models which it was launching in this period. Pestelli developed an innovative promotional strategy, in which literature featured prominently. Fiat employees and workmen were encouraged to try their hand at writing, and their texts were published in the company magazine *Il rosso e il nero*, founded in 1932 to replace the more refined and elitist *Rivista Fiat* that had been discontinued in 1927 (Tongiorgi 1994b, 401). Pestelli also intended to get 'established' writers involved and start a programme of commissioned literary pieces, in order to raise the company's cultural and intellectual profile. In a programmatic document produced in 1929 to explain Fiat's new advertising strategy to Mussolini, he described his intention to 'create a veritable Fiat literature' ('creare una vera e propria letteratura Fiat'), comprising different genres: 'the Fiat *novel*, the Fiat *short story*, the Fiat *tale*, and so on' ('il *romanzo* Fiat, la *novella* Fiat, la *storia* Fiat, ecc.') (cited in Tongiorgi 1994b, 405, emphasis in original; see also Galateria 1997, 708). Pestelli's strategy was not limited to the production of alluring imagery around single products, but rather set out to create a veritable 'moral culture' associated with Fiat.

This is the background to the significant (and unique, in the context of interwar Italy) collaboration between Fiat and the established duo of Bontempelli and Bardi. Pestelli got his friend Bontempelli, who had a notorious passion for cars involved first. Bontempelli was commissioned a novel that would 'advertise' a Fiat model. The contract was signed in 1930 and the writer was remunerated with a Fiat 514, establishing a seemingly rather rudimentary relationship between artists and industrial patrons. A year later, he swapped the 514 for a 522, the car which was the protagonist of his novel, written in 1931 and published by Mondadori in 1932 with the title *522: racconto di una giornata* (Bontempelli 1932a; see Galateria 1997, 708–10). It may have been Bontempelli who put forward Bardi, his friend and collaborator, as the next 'Fiat author'. Bardi wrote a novel on the following model, the Fiat 1500, which he published in 1936, with the title *La strada e il volante*. He was also paid in kind—with a Fiat 1500. Bontempelli and Bardi worked together on various cultural projects, mainly magazines, which developed the theoretical encounter between architecture and the novel. As shown in Chap. 5, the most important of these was *Quadrante*, which constituted the most significant platform for the identification and development of the theoretical-aesthetic principles that linked architecture and the novel. The fact that they were involved in the 'Fiat novel' writing programme is thus very significant, because it places this literary endeavour in the context of the aesthetico-political projects articulating the theoretical and aesthetic connection between the two artistic forms. Furthermore, Bardi's *La strada e il volante* was published by Edizioni Quadrante, a publishing initiative that emerged out of the magazine, making the link between the two experiences even stronger. As we argue below, the two short novels displayed and developed some of the principles that were shared by architecture and the novel as aesthetico-political projects directed at the cultural and political modernization of Fascist Italy; namely, the anti-subjective and anonymous spirit, the creation of myths for the modern era, and the fulfilment of art's social function in modern mass society.

The establishment of a partnership between literature and industry provided a way of actualizing an idea of art that moves towards reality and finds a suitable role within mass society, a notion central to Bontempelli's thought. The attempt at producing an 'advertising' artwork enabled the artist, specifically the writer, to fit into the structures of modern society, giving rise to new modalities of the production and enjoyment of art. The modern writer was, according to Bontempelli's vision, a well-integrated, constructive and dynamic member of a society of which technological and industrial development was a constitutive part; no longer was he a subversive, alienated figure. In this paradigm of literature in modern society, writers were first and foremost creators of myths for the modern age. Through this mythopoeic process they were to perform their social function and establish a connection with the masses. As discussed in Chap. 5, in order to produce literature which possessed this social utility, writers needed to detach themselves from their subjectivity and build stories, create 'objects', in the same way as architects, achieving the ideal of anonymity. These stories would help readers make sense of reality—especially modern reality. There was no scope for the expression of the inner self that had been the prerogative of Romantic and early twentieth-century literature.

522 and *La strada e il volante* are emblematic examples of this idea of literature and of the role of the writer in modern society. *522*, in particular, achieves the mythologization of modern reality through Bontempelli's favoured aesthetic mode, 'magical realism', which he considered the best aesthetic strategy for realizing this artistic ideal. It consisted in transforming everyday reality through literature by attributing new, unexpected, 'magical' elements to it, shaped by the writer's imagination. This aesthetic strategy allowed everyday reality to be turned into myth, creating stories that would be immediately comprehensible, engaging and foundational for the collectivity, thus fulfilling art's social function. This was achieved in *522* through the skilful anthropomorphization of the automobile, which becomes the novel's real protagonist. 522 is attributed both a physical and a psychological dimension that makes 'her' ('car' is feminine in Italian, and 522 is not only humanized, but also feminized) feel physical sensations and psychological emotions that challenge the image of the car as a cold and insensitive machine. The narration of anthropomorphized impressions and feelings is intensified by the idea of the freshness and purity of emotions experienced for the first time. Indeed, Bontempelli did not choose to narrate just any day in the life of 522, but rather her first 24 hours outside the factory—her first day of 'life'. This narrative choice affords the story a typically 'magical realist' perspective that comes across as new, primordial and unspoiled. 522 sees and perceives everything with a 'lucid wonder' that epitomizes the sentiment underlying the reconstruction of the world according to the principles of magical realism, and allows her—and the readers—to experience everyday reality as new and extraordinary (Galateria 1997, 714). The novel is infused with a sense of recreation and a new beginning that evokes the palingenetic spirit of the Fascist era. Bontempelli crafted a story that turned an ordinary episode into a magical adventure and a myth for the modern era, which would help readers familiarize themselves with an object that was still perceived with some hostility and/or awe by common people, but was destined to become a mass consumer product, and a symbol of modern society.

7 Novels and Buildings 163

The novel addresses the theme of the relationship between man and machine, and between nature and machine, representing it not in terms of conflict, but rather of cooperation and harmony. As previously mentioned, Bontempelli saw the writer, and himself, as a modern man, integrated in modern society and looking favourably rather than problematically, upon technological and industrial development as an inevitable and indisputable fact of the society of which he wanted to be a part. The writer was no longer an outcast, and his myths were a positive response to modernity, not in conflict with it. At the same time, both *522* and *La strada e il volante* are removed from the 'aesthetic mythologization of the machine' that was typical of early twentieth-century avant-gardes (Tongiorgi 1994b, 406). Instead, they aimed to promote the familiarization and popularization of the automobile as a consumer product and a reliable instrument of modern life, accessible to all—Bardi even included a list of twelve rules to be followed by car drivers in the novel's penultimate chapter. The two writers progressed beyond an ideal of speed as a risky pursuit carried out for its own sake and without any practical purpose. Their Fiat novels instead represent and exalt a 'controlled, reasonable, reassuring' idea of speed (Galateria 1997, 716), which frames the car in terms not of a formidable and dangerous technological object for the elites, but rather a new, loyal and dependable companion for common people in their everyday lives. This new 'tame' image of the automobile is expressed clearly in Bontempelli's preface to Bardi's *La strada e il volante*, which establishes a clear continuity between the two books:

> We are a long way, here, from the emphatic discovery of speed to which past literature—from Carducci's beautiful and horrible monster to the prewar speed-centred avant-gardes—accustomed us. Here you do not even feel speed anymore: this is the aesthetic, intimate and truly important discovery of Filiberto's simple adventures. [...] This is how the rhetorical absurdity of speed as an absolute fact is dismantled. (Bontempelli 1936, 8)[17]

This shift in the representation and mythologization of the car is part of the writers' effort to popularize their literary products and connect with the masses, which coincided with Fiat's advertising purposes in commissioning these novels. These were directed at changing the perception of the automobile in order to reach new categories of consumers for the new 'low-cost' models and expand their market base. In this paradigm of art for the modern mass society, technology and machines had to find their place in the life of the everyday man, and thus needed to be humanized and made familiar.

As seen in Chap. 5, Bardi was not primarily a writer, but a critic of art and architecture, and the high priest of rationalist architecture. His trying his hand at writing a novel in itself constitutes a concrete encounter between architecture and literature. In his preface to *La strada e il volante*, Bontempelli commented upon and elucidated this encounter by stating that movement was the origin, and a constitutive part, of the new rationalist city:

> all the movement found in new architecture sprang from the fact that the city started being seen not as a series of still contemplations [...], but as the product of the movement that men carry out in its streets. (Bontempelli 1936, 7)[18]

Driving an automobile, he argued, was the most 'characteristic' of these forms of urban movement. The car, he continued, contributed with its rectilinear trajectories to modern 'smooth-walled' urban aesthetics. This explained how Bardi, the 'missionary' of rationalist (or rather 'natural') architecture, as Bontempelli called him ('missionario dell'architettura "naturale"'), had embarked upon writing a novel centred on Filiberto, a novice driver. Bontempelli's preface established a connection between literature and architecture through the myth of the automobile, which also, crucially, comes to embody Fascist morals here. Conveying a more radical and 'revolutionary' message compared to Bontempelli's *522*, *La strada e il volante* narrates Filiberto's journey through Italy, from Rome to Turin, which functions as an anti-bourgeois path to personal growth (Tongiorgi 1994a, 22). It thus shares *522*'s emphasis on a new beginning, the joy of discovery, and a fresh, unspoiled perspective on reality, as Filiberto is a 'neophyte', whose decision to embrace motoring changes his life. However, the new beginning here assumes a less 'magical' and more explicitly political meaning, as becoming a motorist is the means for Filiberto to achieve a personal transformation that turns him into the perfect Fascist: anti-bourgeois, collectivist, disdainful of risk and of any form of immobilism. Here, then, technological progress is not only framed as an aspect of the grandiloquent but undefined Fascist morality, but also Fascist ideology is effectively translated into the myth of the automobile, through Filiberto's unfolding psychological development. In this image of a new beginning can be discerned the primordial and palingenetic spirit that marked the Fascist era in all areas of public and private life, and the novel functions as an emblematic representation on an individual level of the anthropological revolution that the regime aimed to impose on the Italian population.

Filiberto is a lawyer—a bourgeois professional *par excellence*. What prompts him to seek a change is his self-perception as insecure, overcautious, boring, and afraid to take risks—in sum, the prototypical bourgeois that 'revolutionary' Fascists like Bardi so despised. In the change that leads him to embrace motoring, Filiberto 'went from the consideration of his own laziness to the consideration of the renewed life that surrounded him' (15).[19] Here, Bardi celebrates aspects of the social life promoted by the regime. Not by chance, the list begins with a novelty that was a mainstay of Fascist architecture and of the rationalist movement, the construction of stadia, evoking the contribution of modernist architects to the new life created by the regime for Italians. He then exalts sport, *dopolavoro* ('after-work activities'), and the value of these practices in establishing a collective life. Speed as an ideal embodied by the car (provided that it is a 'reasonable' and 'functional' speed) is opposed to bourgeois immobilism, and represents the essential virtues of the Fascist man: dynamism, promptness, spontaneity, vigour, and bravery. Through the experience of movement and speed granted by the automobile, Filiberto undergoes a mental and psychological transformation that typifies the Fascist anthropological revolution:

> With the new joy of the automobile, he reviewed his mental positions. He had got it into his head that behind the wheel, alone, speeding along the roads, conquering distances and freedom of movement, he would be able to think [...]. (26)[20]

He develops an anti-democratic attitude, prone to action, functional to the streamlining and fast-tracking of mental and practical processes:

Filiberto no longer reasoned like he used to, following the judicious principle of respecting the ideas and interests of the majority [...]. His reasoning had become streamlined; it moved forward, terse, swift and conclusive. The wheel gave him a new personality compared to other people. (36)[21]

The novel also depicts wider transformations in the life of Italians, moving towards a motorized modernity which is similarly connected to the Fascist regime. For instance, Filiberto exalts the physical transformation of the peninsula, which the Fascists are covering with roads (Bardi 1936, 40, 95) and describes the increase in the Italians' use of cars, which provides new ways of spending free time, such as going out for short Sunday trips in the car (95). Among the most significant themes of the book is the celebration of Fascist corporativism and of the collectivist spirit it generates as an essential part of Fascist ideology and the anthropological revolution, and of the social cohesion it has created. The most remarkable section of the novel in this respect is the chapter depicting work in a factory (Chap. 9, 79–86), in which technological industrial production is portrayed as a collective process, which erases the individuality of single workers and class differences in the interest of the collectivity (Tongiorgi 1994a, 28–29). Filiberto would like to know who is the engineer who designed the car that is being assembled before his eyes, but nobody can tell him: '[...] it was all the engineers, it was all the technicians, it was all the workers sharing ideas, work discipline, and an everyday aspiration to achieve the best result [...]' (86).[22] Clearly, this section also functions as a celebration of Fiat and of the supportive and collegial work environment it promoted, contributing to the new Fiat promotional programme's objective of creating a 'Fiat morality', and strongly connecting it with Fascist ethics.

The Symbolic Function of Architecture in *Luce fredda*, *La strada e il volante*, and *Gli indifferenti*

The close connections and intersections between architecture and the novel that existed during the Fascist period are also manifested explicitly in the content of the novels. Most of the works analysed feature architecture, and reflections on architecture, as an important presence, generally with a central symbolic function. This reflects the well-established presence of architecture in the intellectual and artistic horizon of these novelists.

Luce fredda opens with Sergio, the pseudo-protagonist, looking for a new accommodation—the theme of the house, as in *Gli indifferenti*, is from the very beginning given prominence and placed in a hyper-central position in the narrative construction. Even more remarkably, Sergio's indignant reflections on houses and living spaces, which follow the visit of the first room he is considering, are an almost too precise and rigorous presentation of rationalist polemic against 'old' architecture, and of the main principles of the programme through which the rationalist movement was fighting its cultural battle. Sergio complains about the small and overcrowded spaces in which most people live—including himself— as he believes that the quality of the environment in which one lives influences one's ideas, behaviours and morality:

> Absurd shambles, overloaded with spoilt furnishings and useless, tacky baubles ... What kind of ideas can develop in similar environments, what kind of souls can be formed? The house should be made entirely of concrete, glass, porcelain—clear, clean, transparent, so as to provoke in those who live in it the love for order, organisation, swiftness, determination, balance; all the indispensable requisites for a dignified life. (Barbaro 1990 [1931], 9)[23]

In his tirade, which for its contents and its caustic language could be an article in *Quadrante*, Sergio even mentions the new construction materials, which for their simplicity, lightness and functionality had been enthusiastically adopted by modernist architects, in particular concrete and glass (see the section on the Fabbrica Olivetti below). Sergio then goes on to uphold some of the cornerstones of the modernist architectural revolution: the rejection of the 'artistic' element of architecture, modular buildings, standardization, and Taylorization, which in Italy had been theorized and championed by the likes of Giuseppe Pagano, Alberto Sartoris, Adriano Olivetti, Luigi Figini, Gino Pollini, Enrico Griffini, and others.[24] Finally, he reiterates that architecture is a 'social art' because it has an impact on society, people's life and social behaviours:

Build in series and to hell with art! Standardize, Taylorize ... Smash the pots, the knick-knacks, the paintings and all the rest ... Or at least scrape these dusty, damned hovels to the bone, so that they are not repulsive from the outside, and that inside one can work, rest, be content, and conceive the idea of a healthier, cleaner future!

It really is true that architecture is a social art! ... But go say that to those charlatan architects! (Ibid.)[25]

Architecture and the remaking of houses and living spaces is cast as a fundamental part of the 'moral change' that Sergio and other characters of *Luce fredda* dream of, but cannot achieve. Indeed, Sergio's outraged reflections about architecture, and about his accommodation, are thwarted by self-doubt and apathy, and ultimately come to nothing, like all other instances in which he desires change:

> But the heat and the animosity betrayed his own convictions, distorting them. In the end, Sergio smiled at his usual outburst. At the end of the day, you adapt yourself [...] and this is the most hideous thing. You end up adapting yourself, and this intolerance is temporary, fleeting. (Ibid., 10)[26]

Unlike Sergio, Filiberto, the protagonist of Bardi's Fiat novel *La strada e il volante*, has acted upon his dissatisfaction and transformed his life, thanks to the radical change brought about by his adoption of motoring as a lifestyle and almost a 'religion'. In a symbolic moment of this transformation, when he is preparing for his life-changing driving trip to Turin, and has started behaving according to the impulses of his new self, he suddenly decides that upon his return he is going to get rid of what he now perceives as obsolete and stifling furnishing in his office:

> Upon his return from his trip, he would change his office: he would jettison the 16th century-style furniture, tear up the curtains, sweep away the neoclassical inkpot. Away with the smell of mould, staleness, and bureaucracy. (Bardi 1936, 34)[27]

Old-fashioned furniture represents Filiberto's former bourgeois self, which he has disowned. The renovation of his working space is thus a consequence of the moral change that has invested his life—he is not a boring, insecure, shy lawyer anymore, and feels uncomfortable in a working space that does not reflect his new identity. In the case of *La strada e il volante*, the inclusion of an, albeit brief, allusion to architectural and design innovation as an element of the formation of a Fascist, anti-bourgeois identity is even less surprising. As we have seen, Bardi, despite not being an architect, was a staunch supporter of the rationalist movement and the spearhead of their cultural battle.

Finally, the theme of the house, and therefore indirectly that of architecture, is central to Moravia's *Gli indifferenti*. The entire narrative revolves around Villa Ardengo, which is also where a large part of the action is set. As Esposito has argued, '*Gli Indifferenti* is nothing but the story of the house and of the bundle of conflicting relationships that its possession [...] provokes in the protagonists' (Esposito 1978, 9). The house and its ownership are the main prerogative and the emblem of that amoral and corrupted bourgeoisie, which is the subject of the novel and the target of the book's condemnation. According to Voza, it is in the house, and in the relationship the characters establish with it, that the evil of indifference is outlined. Villa Ardengo, its rooms and its objects 'become emblematic of a bourgeois universe, deprived of values and inhabited by an elementary and paralysing logic of inauthenticity' (Voza 2007, 152). The connection between decadent, outdated architectural forms and the amorality and irreversible crisis of the bourgeoisie is more explicit in one of the short stories which Moravia published before *Gli indifferenti*, 'Villa Mercedes'. Its relevance to the novel itself is that, as has been established by scholars, it constitutes an antecedent, or even 'preparatory work', for *Gli indifferenti* (the expression has been used by Carpi [1981b, 699]). The short story concerns a neighbourhood of recent construction, whose houses are described, towards the end, as 'the secret villas of the false architectures' ('le ville segrete dalle false architetture)' (reprinted in Carpi 1981b, 705). Despite the 'modern comforts' with which all houses are equipped, it is evident from the language, the images and the metaphors used to describe the neighbourhood that we are worlds apart, here, from the rationalist model and its connotations: Villa Mercedes, and the neighbourhood, are associated with death, disease, decadence, social and cultural crisis, and especially falsehood, inauthenticity and artificiality. It is worth mentioning that *Interplanetario*, the journal in which the short story was published, was an early advocate of rationalist architecture, and championed it specifically as an anti-bourgeois endeavour (Carpi 1981b, 700).

Conclusion

The novels analysed in this chapter are illustrative of various aspects of the synergies between architecture and the novel as intersecting aesthetico-political endeavours, and in different ways worked towards the construction of an 'arte di stato' envisaged by the regime. *Gli indifferenti* is a significant example of new realism and represents a crucial step in the reconstruction of the novel form, through the rationalization of style and the ethical tension that runs through the novel. *Luce fredda* also exemplifies the advent of a new realism that incorporates the achievements of the avant-gardes, but is grounded in a powerful engagement with the real and the construction of a new morality, as well as the anti-individualism and the collectivist ambition that marked both the novel and architecture. *522* and *La strada e il volante* embody a new conception of literature as a productive activity integrated within the structures of modern society and supporting its development. They illustrate the social function of literature as a means of creating myths for the modern world and at the same time building a Fascist morality. Besides examining these works in the light of theoretical and structural principles they share with architecture and coeval projects in the architectural field, we have analysed intersections between architecture and the novel as they manifest in the contents of most of the novels in question, in the importance and the symbolic function attributed to architecture in the texts. Architecture, houses, offices and their design are emblematic of the morality of characters and even of entire social classes or milieus, and form an integral part of their moral change, or lack thereof.

Architecture

During the Fascist period, the Italian rationalist movement placed particular emphasis on the development of modern building types and forms, broadly falling under the categories of infrastructural and industrial architecture, supported by advances in construction technology and modern materials.[28] While these 'utilitarian' and 'ordinary' building types had traditionally been shunned by architects in favour of more prestigious commissions, but they fully embodied the principles and values of the rationalist architectural 'revolution': the social function that constituted architecture's moral dimension, an anti-rhetorical and anti-bourgeois spirit, modernity, anonymity, functionalism, and aesthetic rationality. Rationalist architects and supporters of rationalist architecture rejected the idea that there was a hierarchy of building types (see, e.g. Piacentini 1928). In his article 'L'architettura come morale e come politica', Bontempelli dismissed and subverted the disdainful 'division of labour' practised by 'conservative' architects, who wanted to keep for themselves the design of 'manor houses and villas' ('le case padronali, le ville'), and leave to young (modernist) architects those 'utilitarian buildings' ('edifici utilitari') which they disregarded as 'ephemeral architecture' ('architettura effimera'), 'things for engineers and not for architects' ('cose non da architetti ma da ingegneri'). The constructions that traditionalists disdainfully called 'utilitarian' were in fact, Bontempelli argued, 'representative, or rather "expressive", constructions *par excellence*' ('le costruzioni rappresentative, anzi "espressive" per eccellenza'), and had the noblest function, as they were destined for the collectivity (Bontempelli 1933d, reprinted in 1974 [1938], 335; see also De Seta 1998, 165).

In an article in *Casabella*, Pagano stated that the profile of a city and ultimately of a nation is not shaped by 'exceptional' works of architecture ('opere di eccezione'), but rather by what critics and historians would call 'minor architecture' ('architettura minore'): buildings for everyday use, without any pretensions to monumentality, and subject to functional and financial limitations (Pagano 1935, reprinted in 2008 [1976], 32). This 'modest and solid' architecture ('architettura modesta e soda') constituted the 'standard' production and embodied the principles of modern architecture. Pagano echoed contemporaneous theorizations of the novel when he stated that 'the closer Italian architecture moves towards the people, the more national it will be' (Ibid., 35),[29] and identified the fundamental principles of modern architecture as brutal clarity, exemplary simplicity and modesty, all of which were shared by projects to rejuvenate the novel. These 'ethical principles' ('principi etici') on which Fascist architecture and literature needed to be based, were ideally a reflection of Fascist values, namely '[…] those moral concepts which make of the new corporativist Italy a nation of soldiers who do not like the softness of luxury, nor the flattery of adulations' (Ibid., 35).[30] As Bardi had claimed in his key contributions *Architettura arte di stato* and *Rapporto sull'architettura (per Mussolini)*, the Fascist style was not merely an aesthetic matter; it was the '[…] use of a language as the expression of precise political content' ('[…] uso di un linguaggio come espressione di un derminato contenuto politico') (Ciucci 2002, 110). Works of architecture, and also of literature, would thus be judged in relation to their effectiveness in embodying Fascist values. Following this principle, Fascist architecture had to be 'serene and lively, sober and even martial, mirroring the qualities of strength and order that are favoured by the Italians of Mussolini' (Bardi 1931b, reprinted in Patetta 1972, 187).[31]

Pagano, Bontempelli, Bardi, and others were thus convinced that infrastructure, industrial architecture and public buildings were crucial to the development of Fascist architecture (see Chap. 5, pp. 111–112). It was through these works that the social modernization of the country would be brought about, realizing one of the primary goals of the Fascist regime (see Ghirardo 67–68). Many of these architectural forms were also seen by rationalist architects and Fascist officials as a means of configuring public space for collective use, to enable the inclusion of the masses in the life of the State, and their regimentation. They were therefore instrumental not only in the process of social modernization, but also in the fascistization of the masses, and the accomplishment of the anthropological revolution. These new building types are thus particularly representative of an understanding of architecture as a constructive, social, modernizing endeavour, a collective enterprise meant for the collectivity, which in the 1920s and especially in the 1930s converged with literary projects of 'reconstructing' the novel, based on identical principles.

As we saw in Chap. 5, in 1933 Bontempelli praised the efforts of architects and writers, who had set an example for the other arts in embracing these principles, undertaking the creation of 'spacious constructions for the collective life of simple souls' ('ariose costruzioni per la vita collettiva degli animi semplici') (1974 [1938], 336). We will therefore analyse some significant examples of these building types, identifying the principles that connect them to the contemporaneous works that we have singled out in the field of literature. These are Santa Maria Novella railway station in Florence, a symbol of social modernization coupled with architectural modernity, and the extension to the Olivetti factory in Ivrea, which involved the rationalization and modernization of a crucial collective space, as well as the 'morality' of architecture. We will conclude the chapter, and our book, with the examination of the Danteum project, which constituted an ideal encounter between architecture and literature in a public building meant for the creation of powerful myths rooted in the national artistic tradition.

Florence Railway Station: Social Modernization and Architectural Modernity

Florence railway station, built between 1933 and 1935, is one of the most significant and iconic achievements of the Italian Rationalist movement, and epitomizes architectural modernity in a building which was in turn a symbol of the modernizing mission of Fascism. The 'problem' of the railway station in Florence arose in the context of a development programme for the city launched by Alessandro Pavolini, secretary of the Florentine PNF (Fascist National Party) between 1926 and 1934, aiming to enhance the network of transport links and other infrastructure in order to facilitate trade and access to the city (Conforti et al. 2016, 11). However, it was also part of a broader national programme of modernization of the railway network—including the introduction of electrification—implemented by the Fascist regime (see Giuntini 2003), which demanded a corresponding modernization of railway architecture. Infrastructure, as already noted, constituted social and modernizing architecture *par excellence*. Railways, in particular, were the primary collective system of transport, and the regime therefore invested heavily in them. They represented the possibility of mobility and the promise of modernity made by the regime to all Italians, including the lower classes (see Ghirardo 2013, 67–68). The most prolific architect and engineer of railway stations under Fascism was Angiolo Mazzoni, an employee at for the Ministry of Communications. As such, he designed projects for the station in Florence, but after a heated debate, they were discarded owing to their 'ambiguous' style: not modern enough, but not really traditional either (Conforti et al. 2016, 13; Mariani 1989, 212).[32] The design by the Gruppo Toscano, led by Giovanni Michelucci, was favoured. The group constituted the Tuscan regional unit of the MIAR (Movimento italiano per l'architettura razionale), and had been formed during the third national exhibition of rationalist architecture, organized by Michelucci himself in Florence, in March 1932. The group included Italo Gamberini, a final-year student at Florence school of architecture, who had been working for a year on a thesis developing a new design for the railway station (Etlin 1991, 308) (Fig. 7.1).

The construction of Florence railway station, and the polemic surrounding it, was one of the key moments of the architectural debate and

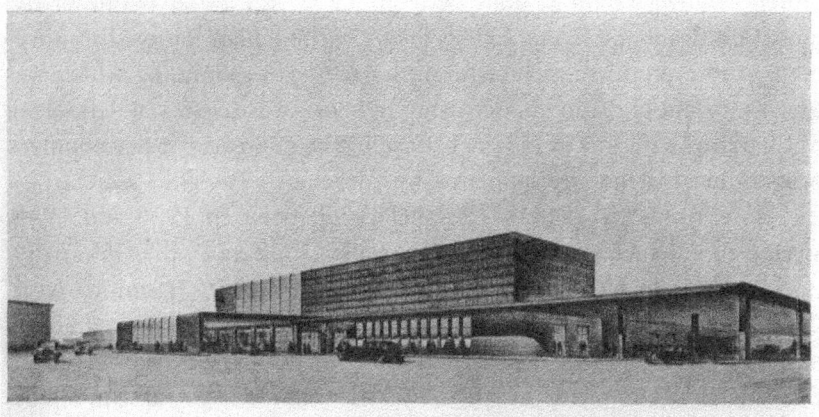

Fig. 7.1 Drawing of Florence railway station, Gruppo Toscano project. *Architettura* 13, no. 4 (April), 1933: 201

the wider struggles for hegemony between antagonistic movements in Fascist Italy (see Chap. 4). It marked the peak of the rationalist front's success, as Pagano's article 'Mussolini salva l'architettura italiana', published in June 1934, demonstrates. Pagano triumphantly declared: 'Now modern architecture is *arte di Stato*' ('Ora l'architettura moderna è arte di stato') (Pagano 1934, reprinted in 2008 [1976], 9). The project had initially been given to Angiolo Mazzoni, but his proposal was the object of heavy criticism from various quarters; not just the modernist front, with Bardi of course leading the attack, but several journalists, artists and critics, and ultimately 'large sections of Italian culture' (De Seta 1998, 165).[33] The polemics started with two letters from sculptor Romano Romanelli (who was not known for his modernist leanings), published on the newspaper *La Nazione* in 1932. In these, Romanelli questioned the validity of Mazzoni's project, arguing that the railway station of a city like Florence, rich in history and artworks, should not be monumental but on the contrary, functional and self-effacing, like a lift in a beautiful palace (Romanelli 1932a, 1932b; see also Etlin 1991, 308). The controversy developed and intensified in 1932 and 1933. As a result Costanzo Ciano, the director of the Ministry of Communications, decided to announce a public competition on 28 July 1932, despite personally approving of Mazzoni's project (Giacomelli 2003, 158, 164). The judging committee consisted of architects Cesare Bazzani, Armando Brasini, and Marcello Piacentini, sculptor Romano Romanelli, art critic Ugo Ojetti, and Futurist artist Filippo Tommaso Marinetti. The argument continued to rage and the debate over the station's construction received unprecedented public coverage, becoming the object of popular interest on a local and later a national level (Mariani 1989, 215; De Seta 1998, 165). On 12 March 1933 an exhibition was opened at the Palazzo Vecchio, in Florence, displaying the 102 projects submitted for the competition. In just one day, 40,000 people visited the exhibition, a truly extraordinary number (Mariani 1989, 217) (Fig. 7.2).

Despite his well-known conservative positions, Piacentini opportunistically lent his support to the modernist front in the competition, thus isolating Ojetti, and determining its outcome. He thereby implemented what Mariani has called the 'subtle strategy' of discarding his reputation as a conservative academic, instead legitimizing himself as a champion of

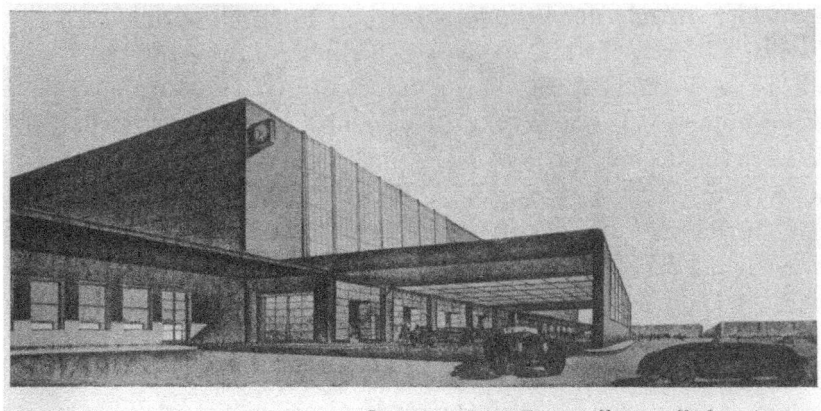

Fig. 7.2 Drawing of Florence railway station, Gruppo Toscano project. *Architettura* 13, no. 4 (April), 1933: 203

modernity, and rising to a position of 'ideological, academic and professional control over Italian architecture' (Conforti et al. 2016, 14). In so doing, he also gained power over Bardi, who had until then been his staunch opponent, and the leading champion of modern architecture (Mariani 1989, 218–19; De Seta 165). It was Mussolini himself, however, who gave the Gruppo Toscano's project his seal of approval, after seeing the models of the station (see Pagano 1934, reprinted in 2008 [1976], 9). The *Duce* received the architects at the Palazzo Venezia and pronounced a famous speech in defence of modern architecture:

> I wish to unequivocally clarify that I am in favour of modern Architecture […] It would be absurd to not want a rational and functional architecture for our time. Every epoch has produced its own functional architecture.[34]

As well as stating that the Florence railway station was 'very beautiful' ('la stazione di Firenze è bellissima'), Mussolini upheld functionalist principles when he said that 'a station is a station and cannot be anything but a station' ('la stazione è una stazione e altro non può essere che una stazione'), and that 'not everything has to be monumental' ('non tutto deve essere monumentale'). He conveyed the idea that Fascist architecture had to be modern, clearly distinct from styles of the past, and that the style and form of buildings should reflect their function. Despite this endorsement, he would soon change his tune and increasingly favour monumentalist architecture (see Chap. 4).

The leading supporters of the rationalist front participated in the debate, almost unanimously praising the Gruppo Toscano's project for its modernity and for applying the precepts of rationalist architecture. In 1933, Bardi devoted considerable space to the discussion in his column in the journal *L'Ambrosiano*, also including contributions from other commentators.[35] On 29 July he published a letter from the painter and theorist of abstract art Carlo Belli, one of the most tenacious opponents of Mazzoni's project, in which he asserted that young Fascist architects wanted an 'asbolutely *rationalist*' station ('assolutamente *razionalista*') (cited in Mariani 1989, 213, emphasis in original). He argued that rational architecture synthetized the spirit of the Fascist era, because like Fascism, it was 'courageously bare, genuine, and practical' ('coraggiosamente nuda, schietta e pratica') (Ibid.). He later praised the winning project, indicating that he saw these qualities in it. Bontempelli defended the Gruppo Toscano's design in various articles (reprinted in Bontempelli 1974 [1938], 322–27), locating the main principle of modern architecture, exemplified by the new station, in functionalism and a close connection with engineering, involving the 'construction of simple relationships and the pursuit of a plain naturalness' ('[…] la costruzione di rapporti semplici e la ricerca di una piana naturalezza') (Ibid., 326). Pagano also weighed into the polemic in the pages of *Casabella*, the journal he had directed since 1933, and strongly supported the project of the Gruppo Toscano, despite having submitted his own project for the competition (De Seta 2008, lvi). In the aforementioned article *Mussolini salva l'architettura italiana*, Pagano saluted the new station as an avant-garde work, and the decision of the committee as a brave and responsible choice for which Italian architects had long been waiting (Pagano 2008 [1976], 136). However, the project's extreme linearity and rationality was also referred to by its detractors. Ardengo Soffici, for instance, argued that the Gruppo Toscano had not designed a station, but its 'packing crate' (cited in Mariani 1989, 217) (Fig. 7.3).

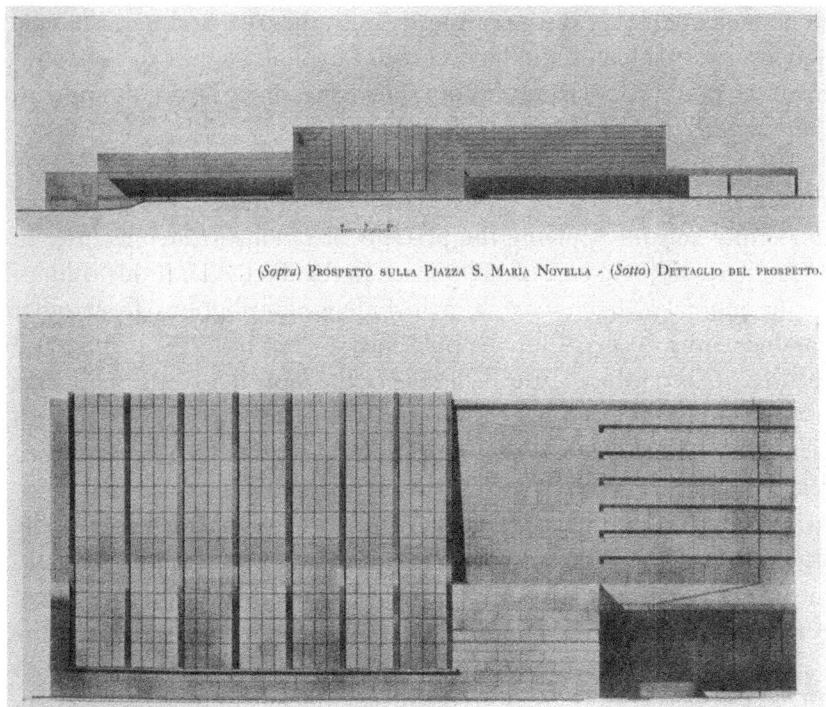

Fig. 7.3 Drawing of Florence railway station (with detail), Gruppo Toscano project. *Architettura* 13, no. 4 (April), 1933: 203

The building presents a low horizontal mass, bare and compact. It was conceived as a modern equivalent of Florence's city walls, which Michelucci had celebrated less than a year earlier for their simple, pure surfaces (Etlin 1991, 310). In both design and materials—it employs unpolished *pietra forte*, the typical stone used for Florentine civil architecture since the Middle Ages—the new station harmonized with its context, despite its undisputable modernity. Michelucci also explained in a letter that the building created a balance of masses in the square, because through its horizontal movement it emphasized the vertical movement of the adjacent church of Santa Maria Novella (Conforti et al. 2016, 26). The only element that interrupts the uniformity of the façade is the glass window composed of seven sections, the so-called waterfall of glass, which 'flows' over the building from one side to the other. The glass window marks the entrance to the station and lights the large foyer containing the ticket office. The façade is free of any decorative elements, exemplifying the rationalist tenets of functional aesthetics. Three monumental *fasci littori*, emblem of the regime, placed on the Eastern corner of the façade and removed after the fall of the regime were the only exceptions to this rule. Inside, the building is also marked by an anti-monumental and anti-rhetorical style, visible, for instance, in the elegant lettering of the signs indicating the different parts of the station. The space inside the station was rationalized and designed to cater for travellers' different needs, including facilities such as a left-luggage office, several waiting rooms, a restaurant, a bar and also a 'daytime underground hotel', which was later dismantled, featuring facilities for 'passengers' rest and hygiene' (Conforti et al. 2016, 20). The station was also, like so many Fascist public buildings enriched with artworks, realizing the Fascist ideal of the constant involvement and education of citizens through the enjoyment of art. Two panels painted by Ottone Rosai, depicting Tuscan landscapes, were placed in the bar. Another artwork by Fortunato Depero was to decorate the restaurant, but was never installed (Ibid.) (Fig. 7.4).

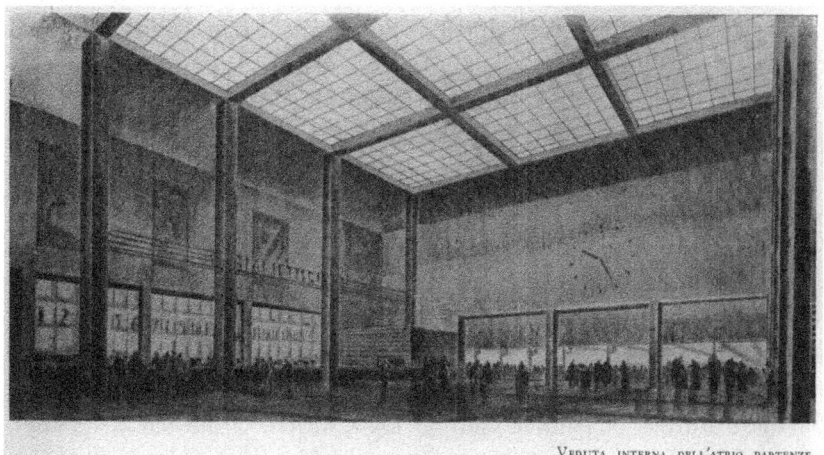

Fig. 7.4 Drawing of Florence railway station (foyer), Gruppo Toscano project. *Architettura* 13, no. 4 (April), 1933: 205

As an exemplary functionalist building, the station's linear and rational form mirrored its function, and reflected the shift in meanings and dominant perceptions associated with the idea of travel. The grand, monumental model of railway architecture that prevailed in the 19th and early twentieth century—exemplified by New York's Grand Central Terminal, but also by Milan's central station, which had attracted much criticism—corresponded to an idea of travelling as something exceptional and glorious. The qualities of plainness and constructive rationality which distinguished the new Florentine station, by contrast, embodied modernity in that they suggested a more humble, trivial, everyday idea of travel that was emerging in the 1920s and 1930s, and which the regime certainly encouraged (Conforti et al. 2016, 12). This process clearly mirrored the popularization and domestication of the image of the car pursued through the Fiat novels (see previous section). Yet this rationalization of architectural style also paralleled the rationalization and simplification of language and narrative construction in the novels analysed in the previous section, in particular *Gli indifferenti*. Being the result of a collective project, Florence railway station also embodied the rationalist ideal of the anonymous and collective nature of cultural production, which also marked the attempts, both theoretical and practical, to reconstruct the novel in the same period, as discussed in the previous section on novels, and in Chap. 5. Indeed, Bontempelli had explicitly argued that novelists should take inspiration from architects in order to achieve anonymity in their works and escape the influence of subjectivity in the process of artistic creation. This artistic quality was fully expressed in collective artworks, in which the co-authors necessarily had to renounce their individualism in favour of the pursuit of collective construction. Collective artistic production and anonymity also embraced Fascist anti-individualist and collectivist totalitarian rhetoric, and translated it into artistic production. This rhetoric was a cornerstone of the Gruppo 7 Manifesto (Rifkind 2012, 24), and of theorizations of modern architecture and the new novel more generally (see Chap. 5). As the writer Alberto Savinio, brother of painter Giorgio De Chirico, wrote ten years later, Florence railway station was anonymous and invisible, which allowed it to blend in perfectly with its surroundings. Echoing Romanelli's call for a discreet and unobtrusive station, Savinio argued that 'the most beautiful ornament of utilitarian buildings is discretion' (il più bell'ornamento degli edifici utilitari è la discrezione') (Savinio 1984 [1944], 352; translation by Etlin, 310). Anonymity was thus a key concept, both in the sense of anti-subjectivism, chiefly achieved through collective creation, and anti-monumentalism: a building, particularly if it is 'utilitarian', should not be conspicuous.

The Extension to the Olivetti Factory in Ivrea: The Morality of Industrial Architecture

These principles of anonymity and collective production can be identified in another project from the same period, the extension to the Olivetti factory in Ivrea, which patron of modern architecture Adriano Olivetti commissioned from architects Luigi Figini and Gino Pollini in 1934 (Pollini 1988; Astarita 2012 [2000], 105). In this case, the principle of collective creation assumes a new dimension, as it involves an active collaboration not only between two architects, but also between the architects and the client (Pollini 1988; De Seta 2012 [2000], 13–14). We will analyse it here as a notable example of industrial architecture, which in the 1920s and 1930s became increasingly central to the concerns of modernist architects and in particular the rationalist movement.[36] As De Seta has argued, industrial architecture was crucial to the development of modern architecture in the twentieth century, and the buildings commissioned, and co-designed, by Olivetti from 1934 onwards were among the most significant examples of this genre (De Seta 2012 [2000], 11).[37] Adriano Olivetti was an engineer and entrepreneur, who saw architecture and urban planning as central aspects of the project of modernization which he had initiated on taking over the family business, a factory producing typewriters, in 1932 (Astarita 2012 [2000], 43).[38] His modern and enlightened idea of entrepreneurship involved putting the 'financial power and the refined technique' of the enterprise 'at the disinterested service of the social and cultural progress of the territory in which it operates' (Olivetti 1960, 44–45).[39]

In 1926, engineer and architect Gaetano Minnucci authored a long article entitled 'L'architettura e l'estetica degli edifici industriali' in

Architettura e arti decorative. He celebrated industrial architecture as the most sincere expression of an age in which architecture's task was more and more 'utilitarian' and 'human' ('[…] un compito sempre più utilitario, sempre più umano'). It was, firstly, a form of architecture to which strict rationality 'naturally' applied, involving the suppression of any form of decoration; and secondly, it had a strong social vocation, in that its ultimate goal was improving peoples' working conditions, especially among the working classes (Minnucci 1926). These reasons made industrial architecture central to the concerns of the rationalist movement, and they converged with Adriano Olivetti's ideas. It is therefore not surprising that Olivetti turned to rationalist architects to realize the changes he had in mind. The construction of two new buildings to extend the factory plant—which consisted of a redbrick construction built by Camillo Olivetti, Adriano's father—began in 1934 and lasted around eight years, during which a series of extensions were added (Pollini 1988, 155). The main principle that guided the design of modern industrial buildings was the rationalization of the productive space, accompanied by the need for order and transparency; functional values which, nevertheless, also assumed symbolic meanings. As Walter Gropius, who had designed one of the twentieth century's most emblematic industrial buildings (the Fagus Factory, in Alfeld-an-der-Leine) stated, the architect needed to consider the aesthetic, as well as the technical and practical aspects of designing such buildings. A modern, ultra-rational industrial aesthetic created by architects would not only provide factory workers with light, air, and cleanliness, but also offer them 'a great common ideal' (cited in Astarita 2012 [2000], 35). The purpose was dignifying work and workers, and making them feel part of a great collective project, conferring greater meaning upon a mechanical type of work that risked being monotonous and dehumanizing. A rational, aesthetically pleasing environment would besides materially improving their working conditions, also satisfy an innate aesthetic sense among the workforce (Ibid., 37) (Fig. 7.5).

Figini, Pollini and Olivetti himself applied these principles in designing the extension to the Olivetti factory. Scientific management theories influenced the layout of the working space, which followed the production line according to functionalist principles (Astarita 2012 [2000], 36).[40]

7 Novels and Buildings 183

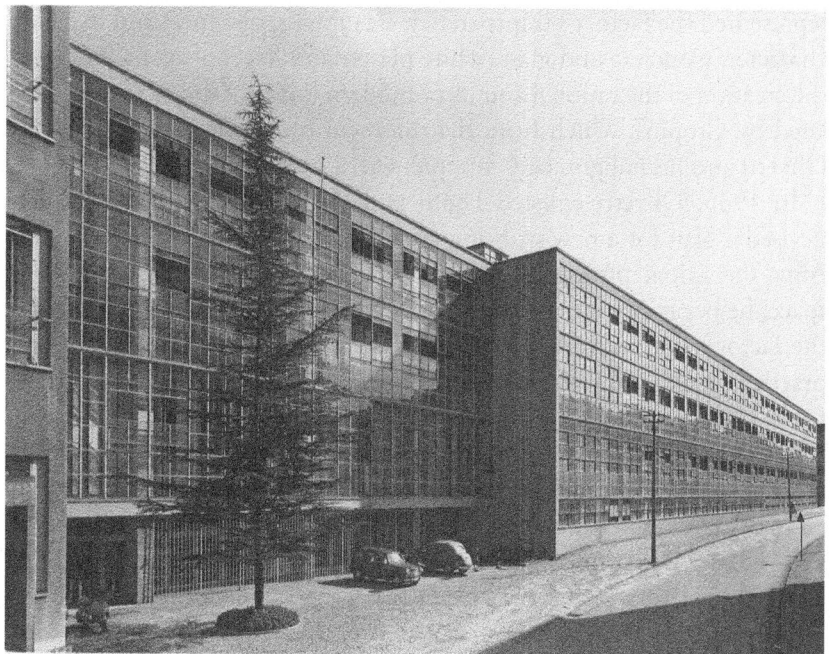

Fig. 7.5 Luigi Figini e Gino Pollini, Ampliamento delle Officine Olivetti a Ivrea, fronte lungo via Jervis, 1939–1940

As far as the structure was concerned, the architects rejected 'the typology of the workshop enclosed by walls' ('la tipologia dell'officina chiusa da muri') creating a barrier between the inside and the outside (Pollini 1988, 156). Simple reinforced concrete or steel frames were used, applying a rationalist aesthetic based on pure functionality and the visibility of the construction methods employed, bestowing aesthetic value upon the very materials and structural elements used in the building. The use of steel frames was also instrumental to the inclusion of a key element of modern architecture, large windows, which became the symbol of the Olivetti factory. The architects, encouraged by Olivetti himself, opted for a fully glazed façade, never before built in Italy (Pollini 1988, 156; Astarita 2012 [2000], 107). Large windows enabled functional lighting and were essential in the model of the 'daylight factory', which exploited enhanced natural lighting throughout the working day, and symbolically represented the factory's transparency, cleanliness, openness and hygienic character. Concrete and glass, white plaster and flat roofs contributed to the creation of the rational and ultra-modern image of the factory formulated by Gropius, which from that moment on became a trademark of Olivetti and his enlightened entrepreneurial model.

In 1935, Olivetti enlisted Figini and Pollini again, and with them devised a plan for a new working-class district near the factory, in Ivrea. After the initial project of modernizing and rationalizing the factory space, he began planning building projects and infrastructure centred on the factory, but reaching outwards to shape the surrounding area. This practice ensued from his belief that the presence of a factory should positively impact upon its context, and generate social and cultural change. This enlightened agenda marked all of Olivetti's subsequent endeavours, creating classic examples of the virtuous synergy of industrial and social-cultural development, up until his death in 1960 (see Ghirardo 2013, 155–58). Olivetti intended to promote and create a 'qualitative social architecture that was initially private, but was naturally projected into the public dimension' (Pampaloni 1980, 24). We find, therefore, in his understanding of industrial and social architecture, and chiefly in the building analysed here, an embodiment of the crucial artistic ideal of the morality of architecture and its social function, achieved through the rationalization of aesthetic languages. This was one of the main principles that formed the intersection between developments in architecture and the novel in the Fascist period, and characterized the novels analysed in the previous section, in particular *Luce fredda* and the Fiat novels.

Olivetti's enlightened ambitions converged with the rationalist belief not only in the social function of architecture, but in its power to act upon reality and change it radically, wherein lay its moral potential. The goal of these projects was not only to provide factory workers with a modern and healthy work environment, but also improve their living conditions more generally. Olivetti also believed that these improvements should not only concern factory workers, but also spill over to benefit the surrounding areas and communities, so that the factory could become a factor of positive change beyond itself and its workforce. This was a 'total' conception of architecture as an intervention upon reality, which included producing urban plans and building innovative industrial architecture, but also blocks of housing and infrastructure (such as kindergartens or primary schools). The meanings and functions of 'architecture' associated with the factory thus expanded to include processes of the formation and shaping of collective spaces, and the veritable creation of 'moral' communities. Through the rationalization and enhancement of the working space and the living environment, rational architecture could stimulate the adoption of healthy, virtuous lifestyles and a new morality, fostering collective welfare and social improvement.

This understanding of architecture as an instrument of social engineering and community creation through the management of the collective space was of course, in the 1930s, very much aligned with the social goals of the regime and the accomplishment of the Fascist 'revolution'. Olivetti embraced some aspects of the regime's economic and artistic policies, in particular in the field of urban planning, where he saw the regime as a strong central power which could directly implement the necessary transformations in urban areas, following the model of 'corporativist urbanism'.[41] In 1935 he wrote an article entitled 'Razionalizzazione e corporazioni' which was published in *Il lavoro fascista* and *Quadrante* (Olivetti 1935), in which he stated the need to establish a centralized institute for construction and urban planning. He claimed that since 'new urban planning must be the most obvious expression of the Fascist revolution', the centralization and standardization of directives would be instrumental in the creation of a 'style, an architecture and urban planning of the Fascist era, in their material expression' (Olivetti 1935, 6).[42] In 1936 Olivetti met with Mussolini to discuss the aforementioned project for a working-class district in Ivrea. Gino Pollini, one of the project's designers, mentioned the project and the meeting in a letter to Bardi: '[...] houses for about 3000 people near the Olivetti factory [...] an organic complex of a functional and corporativist city that Olivetti wants to take to [Mussolini], because the project cannot be realized without financial assistance' (cited in Tentori 1990, 129).[43] The project was presented in *Casabella* in 1936, in an article entitled 'Architettura al servizio sociale' (no. 101: 4–5). Pagano, as well as reviewing it very positively, inserted a special card in the copies of this issue after printing, which announced that the project had pleased the *Duce* (Astarita 2012 [2000], 48). The Olivetti factory complex thus realized the Fascist ambition of an art that could shape socially modernized and rationalized communities, an ambition which was projected onto both architecture and the novel.

The Danteum: The Construction of Imperial Myth

In 1938, architects Giuseppe Terragni and Pietro Lingeri received a commission to design the 'Danteum', a 'temple' to Dante Alighieri to be erected in Rome, which would function as a 'National Organization' including a library and a museum (from Valdameri's 1938 Statute of the Danteum, reprinted in Schumacher 1983, 145–146, and Schumacher 2004, 153). The initiative came from Rino Valdameri, the Director of the Royal Brera Academy in Milan, who was a great lover of Dante and a convinced Fascist since the March on Rome (Schumacher 2004, 36). He proposed this idea to Mussolini and obtained financial support from industrialist Alessandro Poss, who offered to contribute 2 million lire.[44] The site designated for the building, on Via dell'Impero, and apparently chosen by Mussolini himself (Marazzi 2015, 65), had a high symbolic value, having originally been selected for the Palazzo del Littorio in the 1934 competition, which Terragni and Lingeri had entered (see Chap. 4). The two architects prepared a set of drawings of the Danteum and presented them to Mussolini in November 1938, during an audience to which Valdameri and Poss were also invited (Schumacher 2004, 36). Mussolini approved of the project, and decided it should be built in time for the Exposition of 1942 (E42). However, the Danteum suffered the same fate as many other E42 buildings, and never saw the light of day, owing to the outbreak of war. Giuseppe Terragni drafted a *Relazione sul Danteum* to accompany the drawings, which is key to reconstructing the design of the building as well as the intentions and meanings attached to it (reprinted in Schumacher 1983, 135–144, and translated in Schumacher 2004, 127–50).[45] Terragni envisioned the Danteum as a 'translation' into architectonic terms of the *Divine Comedy*. Unlike the other buildings analysed here, the Danteum, rather than exemplifying a convergence between Fascist architecture and the novel in terms of theoretical, conceptual and structural principles, instead constitutes a unique formal, spiritual and symbolic 'encounter' between literature and architecture, glorifying the Fascist imperial ideal. For this reason, and also on account of its time frame, which covered the regime's final phase, we have chosen to conclude our book with it.

Within the modern movement, Terragni was the chief exponent of a strand that believed architecture should be the expression of ideals, proportions, and pure forms:

> Architecture is not simply construction, or even satisfaction of material needs; it must be something more [...]. Only when a harmony of proportions is reached, inducing the observer to pause in contemplation or emotion—only then will the constructive scheme have become a work of architecture. (Terragni 1931)[46]

For Pagano, however, architecture was strictly functional and constituted the primary means through which the social and cultural revolution of the Fascist regime would be accomplished. It embodied the morality of the Fascist ideal and of the Fascist revolution, and was strictly anti-rhetorical. For Terragni, architecture ought to represent the order, purity, and rationality of the Fascist ideal (exemplified by the famous statement 'Fascism is a house of glass', referring to Como's Casa del Fascio), which corresponded to the supreme harmony of pure art and to the superior laws of architecture, and thus had an educational function, helping the masses to recognize, receive, and internalize this ideal. The difference here was between an understanding of modern architecture as the style of a modern state as opposed to the image of a spiritual regime; architecture as a moral form versus an ideal form (Ciucci 2002 [1989], 144–49; see also Chap. 4). However, the two models shared the principle of aesthetic rationalization, and of the collective function and objectives of architecture (Fig. 7.6).

The Danteum is an emblematic expression of the conception of architecture upheld by Terragni. The project was not grounded in the same principles of adherence to reality, functionality, utilitarianism, and modesty identified in the previous buildings analysed here, although its architectural language is distinctly rationalist. In the *Relazione*, Terragni stated

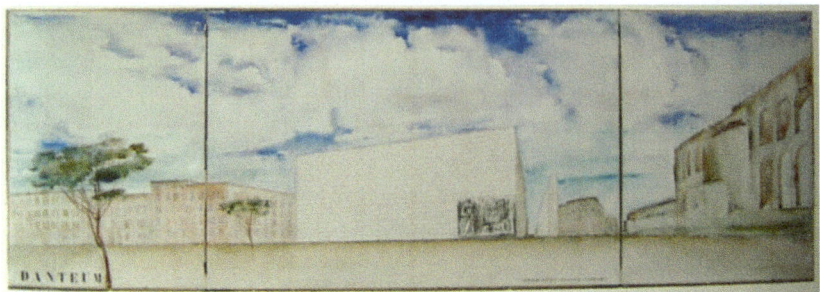

Fig. 7.6 Progetto per il Danteum, view towards the Colosseum, 1938, Archivio Pietro Lingeri

that the project sought to confront and explore universal 'aspects of spiritual life' that modern architecture had hitherto avoided. These were defined by the words 'monumentalism', 'symbolism', and 'solemnity' ('monumentalità', 'simbolismo' e 'aulicità'), and were seen as particularly relevant to the Danteum because they defined the architectural environment in which it would be built, with the ruins of the Imperial Fora, the Basilica of Maxentius, and the Colosseum unequivocally conveying the legacy of Imperial Rome. These were indeed concepts that were largely alien to the architectonic language and ideas embraced by the rationalists, and were 'laden with dangers and equivocations'. According to Terragni, only a 'synthesis' of—and not a compromise between—modern architecture (seen as functional, spontaneous and pure) and these 'universals' of architecture could resolve this confrontation (Schumacher 2004, 128). The correspondence that he established between the *Divine Comedy* and the Danteum was symbolic, formal and spiritual. The Danteum was conceived as a celebration of the most illustrious Italian poet, taken as a symbol of the nation's literary genius, of the imperial ideology that the regime had revived and appropriated, and of Italy's unification and the construction of its national identity, to which Dante's artistic endeavours had made a fundamental contribution. However, Dante's poem itself was seen as a *construction* based on a well-defined composition relying on rhythmic patterns, symbolic numbers, geometry and proportions, which could be recreated as spatial and architectural factors determining the relationships between dimensions, spaces, and volumes in a building. As

Terragni wrote in the *Relazione*, the Danteum's purpose was to 'express through architectural harmony the marvellous philosophical and poetic "construction" of the most important spiritual declaration that humanity can claim', namely the *Divine Comedy* (*Relazione*, Schumacher 2004, 127) (Fig. 7.7).⁴⁷

Terragni's starting point for the project was the golden rectangle, which he considered to be a symmetrical structuring principle analogous to that governing the structure of the *Divine Comedy* (based on the numbers 1, 3, 7, 10), as well as the 'value of "Absolute" geometric beauty' ('valore di "Assoluta" bellezza geometrica') (*Relazione*, Schumacher 2004, 130; 1983, 135), thus inextricably linking his project to classical architecture and to the surrounding ruins. Indeed, the long side of this rectangle forming the floor plan of the Danteum was equal to the short side of the adjacent Basilica of Maxentius, establishing a direct relationship with the temple's illustrious surroundings. Over the golden rectangle were superimposed two partially overlapping squares. The internal divisions and proportions of the building's rooms were also derived from the decomposition of the golden rectangle, bringing the idea of the 'infinite' into the project, as well as the numbers one and three: the golden rectangle

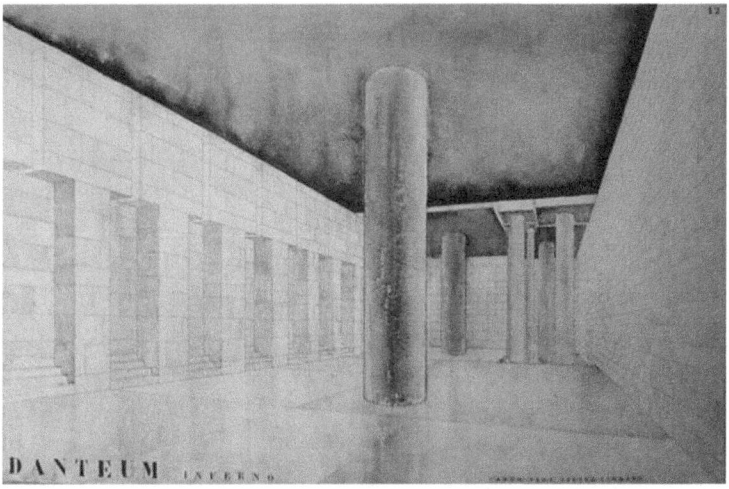

Fig. 7.7 Progetto per il Danteum, Inferno, 1938, Archivio Pietro Lingeri

'expresses the harmonic law of unity in trinity' because 'one is the rectangle, three are the segments that determine the golden ratio' (*Relazione*, Schumacher 2004, 131).[48] The building was divided into three main rectangular rooms, representing Inferno, Purgatory, and Paradise, preceded by two square areas: an open court, and an area with a hundred marble columns. The courtyard was intentionally 'wasted' from a planning point of view, alluding to the perdition of Dante's worldly life, while the following space represented the 'forest' where Dante's journey starts.[49] In the rooms representing the three canticles, Terragni aimed to establish a spiritual and 'emotional' correspondence with the poem through spatial and plastic elements, recreating 'mythical' atmospheres that would cause visitors to feel the emotions evoked by Dante, rather than mimetically reproducing elements recalling the plot, characters or settings (which also enabled Terragni to observe a strict anti-decorativism). Thus, for instance, in the Inferno room, the

> fractured ceiling and the floor, which is decomposed into diminishing squares, the scanty light that filters through the cracks in the blocks in the ceiling, all will give the catastrophic sensation of pain and useless aspiration to gain the sun and light. (*Relazione*, in Schumacher 2004, 146–47)[50]

Paradise, by contrast, was an ethereal and luminous space filled with 33 glass columns supporting a transparent frame, giving a view of the sky and conveying a sensation of otherworldly peace. It was this recreation of spiritual atmospheres and the emotional response that Terragni sought to elicit in visitors which 'endow[ed] the building with mythical values and ma[de] it a temple rather than a museum, palace or theatre' (Lu 2010, 240) (Fig. 7.8).

This conception of the building as a creation and an embodiment of myths, the 'primordal' emotions that it should elicit in the audience, as well as the intersection of architecture and literature constructed through two overlapping and intercommunicating artistic forms, are clearly reminiscent of Bontempelli's theories of modern art and magical realism (see Chap. 5). In the second paragraph of the *Relazione*, Terragni included a sentence which was virtually a quotation from Bontempelli's well-known programmatic statement on rationalist and anti-rhetorical art:

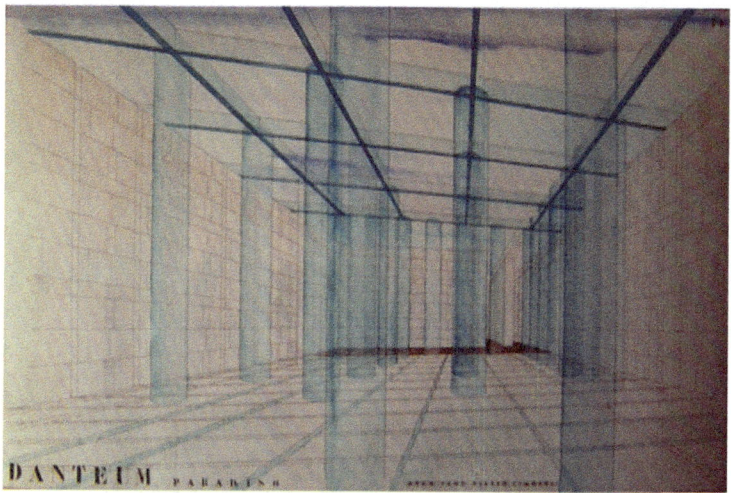

Fig. 7.8 Progetto per il Danteum, Paradiso, 1938, Archivio Pietro Lingeri

> Glorifying a great man by honoring that work of his which was called Divine [...] means that the maximum of expression is to be obtained with the minimum of rhetoric, the maximum of emotion with the minimum of decorative or symbolic adjectives. It means to create a great symphony with elemental means. (*Relazione*, in Schumacher 2004, 127)[51]

Bontempelli, who was Terragni's friend, certainly had an influence on the architect's reflections on literature and architecture as two intercommunicating aesthetic languages, and had a role in the events surrounding the design of the Danteum. He was the first person to read the *Relazione*, given to him by Lingeri, and which he passed on to to Marino Lazzari, general director of Antiquities and Fine Arts, who in turn discussed it with Bottai (Marazzi 2015, 72). Some scholars have even speculated that he made changes or interventions to the draft of the *Relazione* (Milelli 1996, 571). As has already been argued, this solemn crystallization of myths realized the building's political function, which consisted in rooting Mussolini's imperial project in the ideas and endeavours of one of the most eminent Italian poets and political thinkers, building a veritable foundational myth (Fig. 7.9).

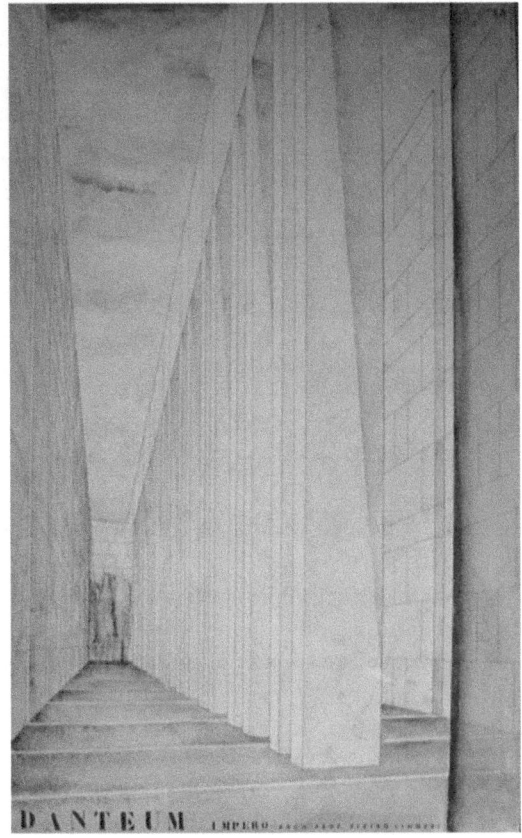

Fig. 7.9 Progetto per il Danteum, Impero, 1938, Archivio Pietro Lingeri

This mythopoeic function found a powerful expression in the Empire room, a long corridor-like room that was supposed to end the visitor's itinerary. Terragni defined this space 'of fundamental spiritual importance' ('di fondamentale importanza spirituale') because 'it comes to represent the germ of the architectural whole' ('viene [...] a rappresentare il nocciolo dell'organismo costruttivo'), and was equivalent to the 'central nave of a temple' ('la navata centrale del tempio). The room was a tribute to the 'universal Roman Empire that was envisaged and forecast by Dante as the ultimate purpose and the only remedy for saving humanity and the Church from disorder and corruption' (*Relazione*, Schumacher 2004,

138–39).⁵² At the end of this space loomed the image of an eagle, the perfect symbol encapsulating the meanings, concepts and figures that the building sought to glorify and perpetuate. The eagle is the symbol of imperial justice, and in Canto XVIII of Paradise it appears as a transformation of the last letter of the phrase *Diligite Justitiam Qui Judicatis Terram* (He who rules the earth must administer justice); it is also, of course, the first letter of the name Mussolini, which the Duce often used as a signature (Schumacher 2004, 121). It thus fulfilled the project's overall purpose of giving a plastic-architectonic form to myths and symbols drawn from the repertoire of the national literary tradition in order to bolster Fascist imperial ideology. From the foundational literary work of the national canon, Terragni drew a principle of order and symmetry which, when turned into an architectonic principle, could embody the ideal of geometric harmony based on pure forms which he wished to express in his rationalist architecture, and at the same time function as the symbol of the illustrious roots of the Fascist imperial myth.

Conclusion

Like the novels analysed in the first section of this chapter, the buildings examined here embody the principles that constitute structural links between architecture and the novel taken as two aesthetico-political endeavours working towards the construction of a Fascist culture and the cultural and social modernization of the nation. Florence railway station is an emblem of modernity in a utilitarian building, which represents both the modernizing mission of the regime and the anti-rhetorical revolution of the modern movement. At the same time, it marked the high-water mark for the Rationalist front in their ultimately vain battle for hegemony within the Fascist aesthetic system. The station had been built according to principles of functionality and anonymity that were central to both new architecture and the new novel. The expansion of the Olivetti factory also exemplifies the principles of anonymity and collective production, as well as epitomizing the morality of modern, specifically industrial and social architecture, which was achieved through the rationalization of space, both public and private. Finally, the Danteum constitutes a unique example of interconversion between architecture and literature, on the basis of symbolic, formal, and spiritual principles, which ultimately serves the purpose of contributing to the creation of national myths for the regime, and glorifying Fascism's imperial ideology.

Notes

1. *900* published the short stories *La cortigiana stanca*, translated into French as *Lassitude de courtisane*, in 1927 (2, no. 3 [Spring], pp. 134–45); *Caverne: doppio uso*; *Delitto al circolo del tennis*; and *Caverne* in 1928 (respectively 3, no. 1 n.s. [July]: 44–45; 3, no. 3 n.s. [September]: 125–31; and 3, no. 6 n.s. [December]: 284–85); *Il ladro curioso* and *Apparizione* in 1929 (4, no. 1 [January]: 18–26 and 4, no. 5 [May]: 215–22).
2. *I lupi* published *Dialogo tra Amleto e il principe di Danimarca* in 1928 (1, no. 3 [29 February]: 3). *Interplanetario* published *Cinque sogni*, *Assunzione in cielo di Maria Luisa*, *Albergo di terz'ordine*, and *Villa Mercedes*, all in 1928 (respectively 1, no. 2 [15 February]: 3; 1, no. 4 [15 March]: 2; 1, no. 5 [1 April]: 3; 1, no. 7–8 [1 June]: 4).
3. This is the only article that Moravia signed using his real name, Alberto Pincherle. It was reprinted in Voza 1982, 210–12.
4. '[…] mi ero messo in mente di scrivere un romanzo che avesse al tempo stesso le qualità di un'opera narrative e quelle di un drama. Un romanzo con pochi personaggi, con pochissimi luoghi, con un'azione svolta in poco tempo. Un romanzo in cui non ci fossero che il dialogo e gli sfondi e nel quale tutti i commenti, le analisi e gli interventi dell'autore fossero accuratamente aboliti in una perfetta oggettività. […] D'altra parte mi ero convinto che non mettesse conto di scrivere se lo scrittore non rivaleggiava col. Creatore nell'invenzione di personaggi indipendenti, dotati di vita autonoma.'
5. Mussolini's own appraisal of the novel, revealed to Mussolini's biographer Yvon De Begnac, was rather ambiguous: 'a novel that is obscenely bourgeois and antibourgeois at the same time, written by the nephew of a union official friend of mine, De Marsanich, the son of a sister married to a Jewish engineer, Pincherle. That book, the debut novel of a young author, written in mediocre Italian but powerful in describing a Roman environment which I would not have suspected could still survive,

disclosed to me the presence of real antifascism, an antifascism that does not speak, does not reveal its presence.' '[...] Un romanzo oscenamente borghese e antiborghese al medesimo tempo, dovuto al nipote di un mio amico sindacalista, De Marsanich, figlio di una sorella maritata a un ingegnere ebreo, Pincherle. Quel libro, opera prima di un giovanissimo, scritta in mediocre italiano, ma potente nel raccontare un ambiente romano del quale mai avrei sospettato la sopravvivenza, mi aveva svelato la presenza del vero mondo dell'antifascismo, dell'antifascismo che non parla, che non rivela la propria presenza.' (De Begnac 1990, 483–84).
6. An artistic, and specifically literary, tendency inspired by the life and works of Gabriele D'Annunzio, marked by aestheticism, decadentism, and a flamboyant and flowery style.
7. See for instance the articles 'Un'estetica nuova per un'arte nuova' (1927a), 'Considerazioni sul romanzo' (1932), and 'La mia fede' (1933), reprinted in Barbaro 1976, 75–84; 132–38; and 139–41.
8. 'Futuristi, suprematisti, cubisti, espressionisti, surrealisti, costruttivisti, realisti, avanguardisti, tutti con il MOVIMENTO IMMAGINISTA!'.
9. '[...] per un comune modo di vedere la realtà e per volere rendere creativa e modificare con l'arte questa realtà'.
10. 'La vera moralità dell'arte sta nel ricongiungere, ricostringere nelle angustie della quotidianità il lettore, per dargli l'ansia insopprimibile di uscire, di farsi migliore, di trasformare sé stesso e il mondo [...].'
11. All quotations refer to the 1990 edition of *Luce fredda* (Montepulciano: Editori del Grifo).
12. 'A volerla in nuce la mia estetica si riduce a un problema di rapporti tra arte e vita.'
13. '[...] I valori formali e tecnici, nella cui sfera sono rimasti fin ora quasi tutti i modernisti, sono [...] in armonia con un ricco ed. elevato contenuto.'
14. See, for instance, p. 197, where the characters' thoughts and actions are mixed up and it is not clear even to them whose point of view they are expressing.
15. 'Il tentativo di conciliare anche nell'arte i due termini, individuo e società, e quindi il singolare e il molteplice, vuol trovare una soluzione in una letteratura aderente alla vita e che superi il romanzo tradizionale, biografico e psicologico, per divenire il racconto di fatti collettivi oppure proiezione sulla massa di fatti individuali: il romanzo collettivo dovrebbe quindi essere romanzo sociale o corale.'

16. See, for example, the article 'E io ti dico che non è più un genere di lusso' ('And I tell you it is no longer a luxury product') from a 1924 issue of *Rivista Fiat*. This text represents the new popular image of the car as a consumer product, which Fiat sought to establish in this period (reprinted in Tongiorgi 1994b, 423–26).
17. 'Qui siamo ben lungi dalla enfatica scoperta della velocità cui la letteratura andata—dal bello e orribile mostro carducciano alle avanguardie velociste d'anteguerra—ci aveva abituati. Anzi, qui dentro la velocità non la senti più: questa è la scoperta estetica, intima e veramente importante, delle avventure semplici di Filiberto. [...] Così si smantella l'assurdo retorico della velocità come fatto assoluto.'
18. 'Perché tutto il movimento dell'architettura nuova è nato dal fatto che s'è cominciata a vedere la città non come una serie di contemplazioni ferme [...], ma quale il prodotto del movimento che gli uomini compiono nelle sue vie.'
19. '[...] passò dalla considerazione della sua pigrizia alla considerazione della vita rinnovata che lo circondava'.
20. 'Con la gioia nuova dell'automobile rivedeva le sue posizioni mentali. S'era fissato che al volante, solo, correndo per le strade, conquistando distanze e libertà di movimento, avrebbe potuto pensare [...]'.
21. 'Filiberto non ragionava più come una volta all'insegna del giudizioso principio di rispettare le idee e gli interessi della maggioranza [...]. Il suo ragionamento s'era sveltito, procedeva sincopato, veloce e conclusivo. Il volante gli dava una personalità nuova al confronto con gli altri'.
22. '[...] Erano tutti gli ingegneri, erano tutti i tecnici, erano tutti gli operai in comunione di idee, in disciplina di lavoro, in quotidiana aspirazione di raggiungere il meglio [...]'.
23. 'Cafarnai assurdi, stracarichi di suppellettili avariate e di carabattole inutili e di pessimo gusto... Che idee possono nascere in simili ambienti, che anime ci si possono formare? La casa dovrebbe essere tutta di cemento, vetro, di porcellana: limpida, pulita, trasparente: in modo da provocare in chi l'abita l'amore per l'ordine, l'organizzazione, la rapidità, la decisione, l'equilibrio; per tutti quelli che sono requisiti indispensabili di una vita dignitosa.'
24. See, for instance, Alberto Sartoris, 1929, 'Architettura standard'. *La Casa Bella* 23 (November): 10; Enrico A. Griffini, 1932. *Costruzione razionale della casa*. Milan: Hoepli; and Giuseppe Pagano, 'Le costruzioni in serie'. *Casabella-Costruzioni* 144 (December): 2.

25. 'Costruite a serie e mandate l'arte al diavolo! Standardizzate, taylorizzate... frantumate i vasetti, i ninnoli, i quadri e tutte le altre porcherie ... O per lo meno raschiate fino allo scheletro questi abituri polverosi e maledetti! Che non facciano schifo di fuori e che dentro ci si possa lavorare, riposare, godere; ci si possa concepire l'idea di un futuro più sano, più pulito! È proprio vero che l'architettura è un'arte sociale!... Ma vallo un po' a dire a questi ciarlatani di architetti!'
26. 'Ma il caldo e l'animosità tradivano le sue stesse convinzioni deformandole. Alla fine Sergio sorrise della sua solita sfuriata. In fin dei conti ci si adatta [...] e questo è l'atroce. Che ci si adatta, che questa insofferenza è momentanea, passeggera...'
27. 'Quando sarebbe ritornato dal suo viaggio, avrebbe cambiato lo studio: gettato a mare i mobili stile Cinquecento, strappate le tendine a punto Verona, spazzato il calamaio neo-classico: via l'odor di muffa, di stantio, di notarile.'
28. See, for example, the Gruppo 7 Manifesto, published across several articles in *La rassegna Italiana* between December 1926 and May 1927, partially reprinted in Patetta 1972, 119–32; 'L'architettura e l'estetica degli edifici industriali' by Gaetano Minnucci (1926); and 'Architettura industriale in Italia' by Giuseppe Pagano (1939). See also Rifkind (2012, 24) and Antonucci (2014, 44–45).
29. 'L'architettura italiana sarà tanto più nazionale quanto più andrà verso il popolo.'
30. '[...] quei concetti morali che fanno della nuova Italia corporativa una nazione di soldati che non amano le mollezze del fasto né le lusinghe delle adulazioni.'
31. '[...] serena e colorita, sobria e persino militare, rispecchiante i caratteri di robustezza e d'ordine che sono le preferenze precipue degli Italiani [sic] di Mussolini [...]'.
32. For a detailed analysis of Mazzoni's projects, see Giacomelli 2003. Although his project for the station was rejected, Mazzoni did design the heating plant and main control cabin, recognized as a masterpiece of Futurist architecture (see Pieri 2003).
33. Reconstructions of the controversy can be found in De Seta 1998, 165; Mariani 1989, 212–19; Conforti et al. 2016, 11–19.
34. '[...] tengo a precisare in maniera inequivocabile che io sono per l'Architettura moderna [...] è assurdo non volere un'architettura Razionale e Funzionale del nostro tempo. Ogni epoca ha prodotto la sua

architettura funzionale.' The speech, entitled 'Non avere paura di avere coraggio', has been reprinted in Carli 1980, 95–96. Translation by David Rifkind (2012, 161).
35. For a detailed account of the debate around Florence railway station on *L'Ambrosiano*, see Tentori (1990, 284–350).
36. For an exhaustive examination of the development of industrial architecture in Italy, see Parisi 2011.
37. Another emblematic building which predates this period is the Fiat Lingotto factory (1914–1926). It became legendary among modernist architects of the Fascist period, and was even, famously, celebrated by Le Corbusier (De Seta 1998, 122–24; Astarita 2012 [2000], 26–27; see also Pozzetto 1975; Olmo 1994).
38. On Adriano Olivetti and his crucial role in Italian culture see Astarita (2012 [2000], 42–64), Pampaloni (1980), and Fabbri and Greco (1988).
39. '[...] la sua potenza finanziaria e la sua raffinata tecnica al servizio disinteressato del progresso sociale e culturale del territorio in cui opera'.
40. Olivetti significantly contributed to the circulation of Frederick Taylor's scientific management theories, and their application in Henry Ford's factories, in Italy, publishing them in his journal *Tecnica e organizzazione*. For Olivetti, however, these represented a starting point of his 'modern project', and not a goal in themselves, as his real aspiration was the eradication of the dehumanizing aspects of factory work and the assembly line (Astarita 2012 [2000], 62).
41. Corporativist urbanism was mainly theorized in *Quadrante* as an attempt to synthesize rationalist planning principles with the economic organization of the corporativist state (Rifkind 2012, 264). See, for example, Gaetano Ciocca and Ernesto N. Rogers, 1934, 'La città corporativa'. *Quadrante* 2, no. 10 (February): 25; Ludovico B. Belgioioso and Gian Luigi Banfi, 1934, 'Urbanistica corporativa'. *Quadrante* 2, no. 16–17 (August–September): 40; Gian Luigi Banfi, Ludovico B. di Belgioioso, Enrico Peressutti, and Ernesto N. Rogers, 1935, 'Urbanistica corporativa'. *Quadrante* 3, no. 23 (March): 20.
42. 'L'urbanistica nuova dev'essere l'espressione più evidente della Rivoluzione fascista. Una progressiva centralizzazione di direttive in materia potrebbero realizzare l'armonia e la coordinazione degli sforzi latenti enormi fatti oggi troppo individualmente e spesso con insufficiente coscienza artistica e tecnica per creare nella sua espressione materiale uno stile, un'architettura, un'urbanistica del tempo fascista.'

43. '[...] abitazioni per circa 3000 persone, nei pressi della fabbrica Olivetti [...] un complesso organico di città funzionale e corporativa [con il quale] Olivetti vuole andare dal Capo del Governo [...] perché la cosa non potrà essere realizzata senza un contributo [...]'.
44. For a close analysis of the network of relationships and connections underlying the project, see Marazzi (2015, 25–35).
45. The version of the Relazione reprinted and translated in Schumacher 2004 includes a part, at the beginning, which was missing from the previous Italian version, published in Schumacher 1983. This part (the so-called *giustificazione teorica*) was only found in 1986 by Giorgio Ciucci and Silvio Pasquarelli in a document conserved at Rome's Archivio Capitolino, and first published in *Casabella* 522 (March 1986), pp. 40–41.
46. 'L'architettura non è costruzione e neppure soddisfazione di bisogni d'ordine materiale; è qualcosa di più [...]. Quando si sarà raggiunta quella "armonia" di proporzioni che induca l'animo dell'osservatore a sostare in una contemplazione, o in una commozione, solo allora allo schema costruttivo si sarà sovrapposta un'opera di architettura'. Translation by Rifkind (2012, 27).
47. '[...] esprimere in una armonia architettonica la meravigliosa "costruzione" filosofica e poetica della più importante manifestazione dello spirito che l'umanità può vantare [...]' (Ciucci and Pasquarelli 1986, 40).
48. '*Uno* è il rettangolo *tre* sono i segmenti che determinano il rapporto aureo' (*Relazione*, Schumacher 1983, 136).
49. For a detailed description and analysis of the building layout see Terragni's *Relazione* (Schumacher 2004, 127–50, 31–59); and Milelli (1996).
50. '[...] questo soffitto fratturato e il pavimento pure scomposto in riquadri digradanti, la scarsa luce che filtra attraverso le fenditure dei blocchi di copertura daranno quella sensazione di catastrofe di pena e di inutile aspirazione verso il sole e la luce [...]' (*Relazione*, Schumacher 1983, 143).
51. 'Glorificare un grande valendosi dell'esaltazione di una sua opera che fu definita divina [...]. Si tratta di ottenere il massimo di espressione col. minimo di retorica, il massimo di commozione col. minimo di aggetivazione decorativistica o simbolistica. E una grande sinfonia da realizzare con gl strumenti primordiali (Ciucci and Pasquarelli 1986, 40).
52. 'L'Impero Universale e Romano quale fu intravisto e preconizzato da Dante è lo scopo ultimo e l'unico rimedio per salvare dal disordine e dalla corruzione l'umanità e la Chiesa' (Relazione, Schumacher 183, 139).

Open Access This chapter is licensed under the terms of the Creative Commons Attribution 4.0 International License (http://creativecommons.org/licenses/by/4.0/), which permits use, sharing, adaptation, distribution and reproduction in any medium or format, as long as you give appropriate credit to the original author(s) and the source, provide a link to the Creative Commons licence and indicate if changes were made.

The images or other third party material in this chapter are included in the chapter's Creative Commons licence, unless indicated otherwise in a credit line to the material. If material is not included in the chapter's Creative Commons licence and your intended use is not permitted by statutory regulation or exceeds the permitted use, you will need to obtain permission directly from the copyright holder.

8

Conclusion

It is good to give materialist investigations a truncated end.
—Benjamin (*Arcades*, [N9a, 2], 473)

Throughout this book we have analysed structural, practical and conceptual intersections between the fields of architecture and the novel during the Fascist regime, as these emerged in literary and cultural debates. In other words, we have analysed how the field of architecture impacted on that of the novel and vice versa, by looking at them both from a theoretical and a practical point of view. This book responds to the need to identify and theorize underlying points of contact between different artistic forms and their development during the Ventennio, to demonstrate their significance not simply as discrete artistic phenomena, but rather as part of a system of the arts, which was integral to the dictatorship and to its legitimation as a totalitarian apparatus.

Our argument was that the aesthetic urgency of reconstituting the novel converged with that of rebuilding a new architecture to create an *arte di Stato*, which could sustain the anthropological revolution initiated by the Fascist regime. Such convergence was guided by some key principles which could give coherence and consistency to the whole project. In this respect, one central point we wish to draw attention to, by way of conclusion, is how similar discursive patterns and programmatic claims were consistently reiterated across different, frequently disconnected, fields. These concerned the need to reconstruct the Italian novel and to reconfigure the aesthetic practices of architecture by rationalizing its structures and languages in order to represent the nation, and more particularly the Fascist nation. Politically, the arts could sustain the regime when they created artworks which announced precisely this rationalized, anonymous and unmediated relationship between the individual and the State. The novel and architecture, by following such a political and aesthetic trajectory, had a particularly important role to play in supporting the regime in its creation of collective spaces where the new relationship between subjectivity and objectivity could be articulated. Moreover, both projects were driven not only by a constructive and rationalizing effort, but also by a moral imperative. The call for a new morality and ethics in the arts was directed at writing a national literature and constructing buildings, which were in contact with the everyday reality of the Italian citizen and of the Fascist New Man.

If the regime allowed a certain degree of 'pluralism or eclecticism', it nonetheless wanted to fashion an *arte di Stato*, which systematically called for contributions by artists working in every field, with virtually no exclusions; and most artists accepted to embark on such a messianic mission. As a result, a definition of Fascist art was never properly formulated, although ample space was given to—often inconclusive—debates about it. One of the few firm points in these debates was the call for 'art as action' by Bottai. This action, as we have argued, translated into support for the new novel and the national publishing industry, and for the new architecture.

As demonstrated in Chap. 3, the book market was growing in response to an increase in the reading public. There was, however, a gap in the publishing field since Italian novels were not really addressing readers' aesthetic demands. Translations of captivating foreign novels were instead. While the national literary field remained quite fragmentary yet driven by the desire to build a new novel, translations were, in fact, the leading phenomenon in this respect because of their modern topics and clear

8 Conclusion   203

prose. The theoretical debate on the novel revolved around the definition of realism and how to write in such a way that enabled the novelist to communicate with the reader. As we have seen, realism assumed different meanings, from Bontempelli's theorization of magical realism to the idea of social realism upheld by the youth culture generated within fringes of the regime. But the common denominator was the need to 'build' a national novel, which was perceived not only as still lacking within the national paradigm, but also as lagging behind to other major European countries, such as France, Germany and England, which could champion a long novelistic tradition.

This constructive desire, again driven by a social mission, resurfaced in the architectural world, where young architects strove to produce a theoretical map to reshape and rejuvenate the discipline. For the most part, they conceived of their mission as a social one, in the sense that they wanted to use their skills to transform the social sphere through the design of buildings, which could perform the specific function of directing the collective ethos of the citizens. This is why architecture often aspired to become the official *arte di Stato*: architects believed that they could create new spaces for the individual made collective, and shape new communities. The Fascist project of moulding the New Man, the ultimate result of its anthropological revolution, and a process to which the arts had to contribute linked all these endeavours.

The second part of the book examined the manifestations and realities of these cultural developments. The journals *900* and *Quadrante*, to which an entire chapter was dedicated, were foundational in constructing a theoretical paradigm intersecting the novel and architecture in the conception of a State art that could support the regime and its modernizing mission. Their initiators and directors, Bontempelli and Bardi, were key figures in these crucial attempts at building a Fascist modernity in which the arts would feature prominently, and would be a foundational part of a new, rationalized and collectivist society. The debate on realism was vivid in many quarters of the Fascist intelligentsia, but more so on its cultural fringes and in its youth culture. Realism was a wide-ranging concept, which was applied to various phenomena, often with the aim of finding a new paradigm for a new culture, in a not dissimilar fashion to what the new architecture was trying to achieve. When referred to in the context of the novel, however, realism meant a rationalized prose style, an adherence to everyday reality and a collective ethos. The realist novel no longer had to focus on the subject but on subjectivity made collective. Finally, the last chapter sheds light on how these shared constructive principles worked out in practice, in the conception of novels and buildings between the late 1920s and the late 1930s. Novelists and architects worked to apply the principles of reconstruction, aesthetic rationalization, morality, functionalism and engagement with an envisioned mass public, achieving different results in their respective fields, but largely pursuing shared goals and ideals.

To expand the reach of our argument, we have linked this book to another project entitled *The Dialectics of Modernity*, which comprises a website-database where other relevant data written up both as theoretical, interpretative hypotheses and as short essays, which analysed individual artefacts are stored. The book might, or might not, be read in conjunction with the website-database, but in both scenarios readers can access information in nonlinear fashions. From the book chapters, readers can move to the artefacts explicitly linked to the book, or alternatively they can decide to navigate the other artistic fields visualized in the website-database to provide further information on the Fascist system of the arts.

This slim book has covered quite a lot of ground and with its direct links to a website-database has multiplied its access points in a labyrinthine fashion. It has nonetheless reached a fairly straightforward main conclusion as far as two key areas of Italian culture of the time are concerned: the arts made a crucial contribution to supporting the Fascist regime in building its totalitarian apparatus, and they did do so not by acting in isolation, but by moving according to a set of principles regulating what one can legitimately define as a system of the arts. Finally, we can desume that the arts were fundamental to paving the Italian way to totalitarianism because they contributed substantially to its very 'definition' as an anthropological revolution to create a New Man. And, crucially, the arts have done so in fields as diverse in their theory and in their practice as the novel and architecture, for they operated both according to the logics of State art but also according to a distinctive drive towards experimentalism.

Open Access This chapter is licensed under the terms of the Creative Commons Attribution 4.0 International License (http://creativecommons.org/licenses/by/4.0/), which permits use, sharing, adaptation, distribution and reproduction in any medium or format, as long as you give appropriate credit to the original author(s) and the source, provide a link to the Creative Commons licence and indicate if changes were made.

The images or other third party material in this chapter are included in the chapter's Creative Commons licence, unless indicated otherwise in a credit line to the material. If material is not included in the chapter's Creative Commons licence and your intended use is not permitted by statutory regulation or exceeds the permitted use, you will need to obtain permission directly from the copyright holder.

Bibliography

Adamson, Walter L. 1993. *Avant-Garde Florence: From Modernism to Fascism.* Cambridge, MA: Harvard University Press.
———. 2001. Avant-Garde Modernism and Italian Fascism: Cultural Politics in the Era of Mussolini. *Journal of Modern Italian Studies* 6 (2): 230–248.
Affron, Matthew, and Mark Antliff, eds. 1997. *Fascist Visions: Art and Ideology in France and Italy.* Princeton: Princeton University Press.
Alberti, Leon Battista. 1443–1445. *De re aedificatoria.*
Alvaro, Corrado. 1927a. L'età della letteratura. *900* 2 (5): 50–61.
———. 1927b. Moralità. *900* 2 (5): 139–142.
———. 1928. La prosa. *900* 3 (2) n.s. (August): 68–71.
Anceschi, Luciano. 1933. Appunti per la definizione di un atteggiamento. *Orpheus* 2 (9): 1–5.
Andreazza, Fabio. 2008. Prima della specializzazione. La traiettoria di Umberto Barbaro dalla letteratura al cinema. In *Figure della modernità nel cinema italiano (1900–1940)*, ed. Raffaele De Berti and Massimo Locatelli, 315–331. Pisa: ETS.
Andreotti, Libero. 2005. Architecture as Media Event: Mario Sironi and the Exhibition of the Fascist Revolution. *Built Environment* 31 (1): 9–20.
Aniante, Antonio. 1927. Arte di Stato. *Critica fascista* 5 (2): 23.
Annitrenta, arte e cultura in Italia. 1982. Milan: Mazzotta.
Anonymous. 1933. Tramonto dell'arte borghese. *Occidente* 2 (5): 65–66.

Antliff, Mark. 2002. Fascism, Modernism, and Modernity. *Art Bulletin* 84 (1): 148–169.
Antonini, Giacomo. 1934. Europa letteraria. Narratori italiani. *Occidente* 3 (7): 25–32.
Antonucci, Micaela. 2014. Pier Luigi Nervi / Louis I. Kahn. Estetica dell'ingegneria e monumentalità architettonica. In *Pier Luigi Nervi: gli stadi per il calcio*, ed. Micaela Antonucci, Annalisa Trentin, and Tomaso Trombetti, 43–55. Bologna: Bononia University Press.
Astarita, Rossano. 2012 [2000]. *Gli architetti di Olivetti: una storia di committenza industriale*. Milan: Franco Angeli.
Barbaro, Umberto. 1927a. Una nuova estetica per un'arte nuova. *La ruota dentata* 1 (1): 2–3.
———. 1927b. Noi, l'espressionismo e Toller. *Lo Spettacolo d'Italia* 1 (5): 3.
———. 1927c. Capisaldi dell'immaginismo. *Lo Spettacolo d'Italia* 1 (9): 3.
———. 1928. Lidija Sejfullina. *Rivista di letterature slave* 3 (4–6): 508–514.
———. 1931. *Luce fredda*. Lanciano: Carabba.
———. 1932. Considerazioni sul romanzo. *Occidente* 1 (1): 18–22.
———. 1933. La mia fede. *Il Giornale d'Italia* (3 February).
———. 1976. *Neorealismo e realismo*, vol. 2. Ed. Gian Piero Brunetta. Rome: Editori Riuniti.
Barberi-Squarotti, Giorgio. 1982. 'Realtà' e lingua di Carlo Emilio Gadda. In *Novecento. Gli scrittori e la cultura letteraria nella società italiana*, ed. Gianni Grana, vol. 6, 4926–4967. Milan: Marzorati editore.
Bardi, Pietro Maria. 1931a. Architettura arte di stato. *L'Ambrosiano* (31 January).
———. 1931b. *Rapporto sull'architettura (per Mussolini)*. Rome: Critica Fascista.
———. 1933a. Principii. *Quadrante* 1 (1): 1–2.
———. 1933b. Considerazioni sulla V Triennale. *Quadrante* 1 (2): 3–6.
———. 1936. *La strada e il volante*. Rome: Edizioni di Quadrante.
Ben-Ghiat, Ruth. 1995. The Realist Aesthetic in Italy, 1930–1950. *The Journal of Modern History* 67 (3): 627–665.
———. 2001. *Fascist Modernities: Italy, 1922–1945*. Berkeley: University of California Press.
Benjamin, Walter. 2003 [1939]. The Work of Art in the Age of Its Technological Reproducibility: Third Version. In *Selected Writings*, ed. Michael W. Jennings, Marcus Bullock, Howard Eiland, and Gary Smith, 259–283. Cambridge, MA: Belknap Press.
Biasin, Gian Paolo. 1979. Il rosso o il nero: testo e ideologia in *Rubè*. *Italica* 56 (2): 172–197.

Bignamini, Mauro. 2012. Sull'espressionismo visionario del primo Gallian. In *L'avanguardia radicale di Marcello Gallian*, ed. Renzo Cremate, 133–152. Bologna: Clueb.

Billiani, Francesca. 2007. *Culture nazionali e narrazioni straniere: Italia 1903–1943*. Florence: Le Lettere.

———. 2013. Return to Order as Return to Realism in Two Italian Elite Literary Magazines of the 1920s and the 1930s: *La Ronda* and *Orpheus*. *The Modern Language Review* 108 (3): 839–862.

———. 2016. Documenting the Real Across Modernity in the 1930s: Political and Aesthetic Debates Around and About the Novel in Fascist Italy. *Italian Studies* 71 (4): 477–495.

———. 2018. Il romanzo: tra arte di stato e arti visive. In *Post zang tumb tuuum: Art Life Politics: Italia 1918–1943*, ed. Celant Germano, 380–387. Milan: Fondazione Prada.

Bo, Carlo. 1982 [1958]. Unità poetica di Palazzeschi. In *Novecento. Gli scrittori e la cultura letteraria nella società italiana*, ed. Gianni Grana, vol. 6, 5251–5262. Milan: Marzorati editore.

Bontempelli, Massimo. 1926a. Arte fascista. *Critica fascista* 4 (22): 416–417.

———. 1926b. Perché *900* sarà scritto in francese. *Il Tevere* (18 May).

———. 1927. Dichiarazione. *900* 2 (5) (Autumn): 129.

———. 1927a. Conseils. *900* 2, no. 3 (Spring): 7–13.

———. 1927b. Déclarations. *900* 2, no. 3 (Spring): 163–164.

———. 1927c. Dichiarazione. 900 2, no. 5 (Autumn): 129.

———. 1928. Indole del poeta italiano. *900* 3 (1) n.s. (July): 7.

———. 1929. Canzone all'Italia. *La Gazzetta del Popolo* (18 August).

———. 1932a. *522: racconto di una giornata*. Milano: Mondadori.

———. 1932b. Scuola dell'Ottimismo. *Occidente* 1 (1): 9–11.

———. 1933a. Principii. *Quadrante* 1 (1): 1.

———. 1933b. Corsivo n.1. *Quadrante* 1 (1): 3.

———. 1933c. Untitled. *Quadrante* 1 (2): 2–3.

———. 1933d. L'architettura come morale e politica. *Gazzetta del Popolo* (26 August).

———. 1936. Presentazione. In *La strada e il volante*, ed. Pietro Maria Bardi, 7–9. Rome: Edizioni Quadrante.

———. 1945. *Introduzioni e discorsi*. Milan: Bompiani.

———. 1974 [1938]. *L'avventura novecentista*. Florence: Vallecchi.

Borgese, Giuseppe Antonio. 1923. *Tempo di edificare*. Milan: Fratelli Treves.

———. 1962. *La città assoluta e altri scritti*. Milan: Arnoldo Mondadori Editore.

Bottai, Giuseppe. 1927. Resultanze dell'inchiesta sull'arte fascista. *Critica fascista* 5 (4): 61–64.
———. 1931. La tessera e l'ingegno. *Critica fascista* 9 (8): 142.
———. 1932. Italianità e modernità. *Critica fascista* 10 (20): 392–393.
———. 1933. Totalità, perennità, universalità della rivoluzione fascista. *Quadrante* 1 (8): 1–2.
———. 1940a. Il coraggio della concordia. *Primato* 1 (1): 1.
———. 1940b. Il regime per l'arte' (Interview). *Il Corriere della sera* (24 January).
———. 1943. *Fronte dell'arte*. Florence: Vallecchi.
———. 1992. *La politica delle arti. Scritti 1918–1943*. Ed. Alessandro Masi. Rome: Editalia.
Bottoni, Piero, Mario Cereghini, Luigi Figini, Guido Frette, Enrico A. Griffini, Piero Lingeri, Gino Pollini, et al. 1933. Un programma d'architettura. *Quadrante* 1 (1): 5–6.
Bouchard, François. 2009. 'L'acqua oscura delle grotte': il realismo sperimentale di Dino Terra. In *La figura e le opere di Dino Terra nel panorama letterario ed artistico del '900*, ed. Daniela Marcheschi, 39–52. Venice: Marsilio.
Bragaglia, Anton Giulio. 1926. Lo stile è l'epoca. *Critica fascista* 4 (22): 417–418.
Braun, Emily. 2000. *Mario Sironi and Italian Modernism: Arts and Politics Under Fascism*. Cambridge: Cambridge University Press.
Briganti, Alessandra. 1984. Umberto Barbaro dall'avanguardia al neorealismo. *Letteratura italiana contemporanea* 5 (11): 187–209.
———. 1988. Occidente e la capitale delle avanguardie. *Letteratura italiana contemporanea* 9 (25): 1–24.
Brunetta, Gian Piero. 1976. Introduzione. In *Neorealismo e realismo*, ed. Umberto Barbaro, 11–40. Rome: Editori Riuniti.
Buchignani, Paolo. 1987. Avanguardie durante il fascismo: Umberto Barbaro, il realismo, l'immaginismo. *il Mulino* 36 (313): 724–749.
———. 2012. Scrittori e intellettuali fascisti. In *La sabbia e il marmo: la Toscana di Mario Tobino*, ed. Giulio Ferroni, 47–76. Rome: Donzelli.
Buonanno, Enrico. 2003. Il Novecento immaginario di Massimo Bontempelli. *Studi Novecenteschi* 30 (66): 239–262.
Busoni, Jaurès. 1934. Il romanzo collettivo. *Corriere Padano* (20 September).
Cadioli, Alberto, and Giuliano Vigini. 2004. *Storia dell'editoria italiana dall'unità ad oggi: un profilo introduttivo*. Milan: Bibliografica.
Carli, Carlo Fabrizio, ed. 1980. *Architettura e fascismo*. Rome: G. Volpe.
Carli, Carlo F., and Elena Pontiggia, eds. 2006. *La grande Quadriennale 1935. La grande arte italiana*. Milan: Electa.

Bibliography 211

Carpi, Umberto. 1981a. *Bolscevico immaginista: comunismo e avanguardie artistiche nell'Italia degli anni venti*. Naples: Liguori.

———. 1981b. Gli indifferenti rimossi. *Belfagor* 36 (6): 696–709.

Carrà, Carlo. 1932. Il Fascismo e l'arte. *L'Ambrosiano* (22 October).

Castronovo, Vittorio. 1988 [1976]. Strutture economico-sociali e fascismo tra le due guerre. In *Il Razionalismo e l'architettura in Italia durante il fascismo*, ed. Danesi Silvia and Luciano Patetta, 12–16. Milan: Electa.

Celant, Germano, ed. 2018. *Post Zang Tumb Tuuum. Art Life Politics Italia 1918–1943*. Milan: Fondazione Prada.

Cennamo, Michele. 1973. *Materiali per l'analisi dell'architettura moderna*. Naples: Fausto Fiorentino editore.

Cioli, Monica. 2011. *Il fascismo e la 'sua' arte. Dottrina e istituzioni tra futurismo e Novecento*. Florence: L. S. Olschki.

Ciucci, Giorgio. 1982. L'autorappresentazione del fascismo. La mostra del decennale della marcia su Roma. *Rassegna* 4 (10): 48–55.

———. 2002 [1989]. *Gli architetti e il fascismo: architettura e città 1922–1944*. Turin: Einaudi.

Ciucci, Giorgio, and Silvio Pasquarelli. 1986. Un documento inedito. La ragione teorica del Danteum. *Casabella* 522 (March): 40–41.

Colarizzi, Simona. 2000. *L' opinione degli italiani sotto il regime 1929–1943*. Rome-Bari: Laterza.

Conforti, Claudia, Roberto Dulio, and Marzia Marandola. 2016. La stazione di Firenze è bellissima. In *La stazione di Firenze di Giovanni Michelucci e del Gruppo Toscano, 1932–1935*, ed. Claudia Conforti, Roberto Dulio, Marzia Marandola, Nadia Musumeci, and Paola Ricco, 11–41. Milan: Electa Architettura.

Corner, Paul. 2012. *Popular Opinion in Totalitarian Regimes: Fascism, Nazism, Communism*. Oxford: Oxford University Press.

Cresti, Carlo. 1986. *Architettura e Fascismo*. Florence: Vallecchi Editore.

———. 2015. *Architetti e architetture dell' 'Era Fascista'*. Florence: Angelo Pontecorboli editore.

Curtis, William J.R. 1982. *Modern Architecture since 1900*. Oxford: Phaidon.

Dal Falco, Federica. 2002. *Stili del razionalismo: anatomia di quattordici opere di architettura*. Rome: Gangemi.

Danesi, Silvia, and Luciano Patetta. 1988 [1976]. *Il Razionalismo e l'architettura in Italia durante il fascismo*. Milan: Electa.

De Begnac, Yvon. 1990. *Taccuini mussoliniani*. Ed. Francesco Perfetti. Bologna: il Mulino.

De Grand, Alexander J. 1978. *Bottai e la cultura fascista*. Rome-Bari: Laterza.
De Sabbata, Massimo. 2007. *Tra diplomazia e arte. Le Biennali di Antonio Maraini (1928–1942)*. Udine: Forum.
———. 2012. *Mostre d'arte a Milano negli anni Venti: dalle origini del Novecento alle prime mostre sindacali, 1920–1929*. Turin: Allemandi.
De Seta, Cesare. 1982. "Gaddus": oltre l'architettura degli anni Trenta. In *Annitrenta: arte e cultura in Italia*, 213–216. Milan: Mazzotta.
———. 1988 [1976]. Cultura e architettura in Italia fra le due guerre: continuità e discontinuità. In *Il Razionalismo e l'architettura in Italia durante il fascismo*, ed. Danesi Silvia and Luciano Patetta, 7–11. Milan: Electa.
———. 1998. *La cultura architettonica in Italia tra le due guerre*. Naples: Electa Napoli.
———. 2008. Introduzione. In *Architettura e città durante il fascismo*, ed. Giuseppe Pagano, xix–xci. Milan: Jaca Book.
———. 2012 [2000]. Introduzione. In *Gli architetti di Olivetti: una storia di committenza industriale*, ed. Rossano Astarita, 11–20. Milan: Franco Angeli.
Di Giovanna, Maria. 1992. *Teatro e narrativa di Umberto Barbaro*. Rome: Bulzoni.
Doordan, Denis. 1988. *Building Modern Italy: Italian Architecture, 1914–1936*. Princeton: Princeton Architectural Press.
Durante, Lea. 2000. Avanguardia e realismo in *Luce fredda* di Umberto Barbaro. *Critica letteraria* 28 (1): 111–127.
Eisenstadt, Shmuel. 2002. *Multiple Modernities*. London: Routledge.
Esposito, Roberto. 1978. *Il sistema dell'indifferenza: Moravia e il fascismo*. Bari: Dedalo libri.
Etlin, Richard A. 1991. *Modernism in Italian Architecture, 1890–1940*. Cambridge, MA: MIT Press.
Fabre, Giorgio. 1998. *L'Elenco. Censura fascista, editoria e autori ebrei*. Turin: Silvio Zamorani editore.
Fabbri, Marcello, and Antonella Greco, eds. 1988. *La comunità concreta: progetto ed immagine. Il pensiero e le iniziative di Adriano Olivetti nella formazione della cultura urbanistica ed architettonica italiana*. Rome: Fondazione Adriano Olivetti.
Fagone, Vittorio. 1982. Arte, politica e propaganda. In *Annitrenta: arte e cultura in Italia*, 43–52. Milan: Mazzotta.
———. 2001. *L'arte all'ordine del giorno. Figure e idee in Italia da Carrà a Birolli*. Milan: Feltrinelli.
Fillìa. 1929. Futurismo e Fascismo. *La città Futurista* 1 (1): 1.
Finocchi, Luisa, and Ada Gigli-Marchetti, eds. 1997. *Stampa e piccola editoria tra le due guerre*. Milan: Franco Angeli.

Forti, Umberto. 1934. Tecnica e mondo moderno. *Occidente* 3 (9): 7–13.
Fossati, Paolo. 1972. *L'immagine sospesa. Pittura e scultura astratte in Italia, 1934–40*. Turin: Einaudi.
Galateria, Marinella Mascia. 1997. Il viaggio di una Fiat 522 in un racconto novecentista di Massimo Bontempelli. In *Letteratura e industria: atti del XV Congresso A.I.S.L.L.I., Torino, 15–19 maggio 1994*, ed. Giorgio Barberi Squarotti and Carlo Ossola, 707–719. Florence: L.S. Olschki.
Gallian, Marcello. 1933. Tradimento. *Quadrante* 1 (1): 3–4.
Gennaro, Rosario. 2010. I manifesti di '900' tra politica e letteratura. *Bollettino 900* 1–2. https://boll900.it/numeri/2010-i/Gennaro.html.
Gentile, Emilio. 1982. *Il mito dello stato nuovo dall'antigiolittismo al fascismo*. Rome-Bari: Laterza.
———. 1988. Il futurismo e la politica. Dal nazionalismo modernista al fascismo (1909–1920). In *Futurismo, cultura e politica*, ed. Renzo De Felice, 105–159. Turin: Fondazione G. Agnelli.
———. 1990. Fascism as Political Religion. *Journal of Contemporary History* 25: 229–251.
———. 1996 [1975]. *Le origini dell'ideologia fascista (1918–1925)*. Bologna: il Mulino.
———. 1997. *La grande Italia. Il mito della nazione nel XX secolo*. Rome-Bari: Laterza.
———. 2003. *The Struggle for Modernity*. Westport: Praeger.
———. 2009. *Il culto del Littorio. La sacralizzazione della politica nell'Italia fascista*. Bari-Rome: Laterza.
Ghelardini, Armando. 1932. Idee uomini opere attraverso la stampa internazionale. *Occidente* 1 (1): 121.
Ghirardo, Diane. 1992. Architects, Exhibitions, and the Politics of Culture in Fascist Italy. *Journal of Architectural Education* 45 (2): 67–75.
———. 2013. *Italy: Modern Architectures in History*. London: Reaktion Books.
Giacomelli, Milva. 2003. I progetti di Mazzoni per la stazione ferroviaria di Santa Maria Novella. In *Angiolo Mazzoni: architetto ingegnere del Ministero delle Comunicazioni*, ed. Mauro Cozzi, Ezio Godoli, and Paola Pettenella, 155–166. Milan: Skira.
Giuntini, Andrea. 2003. Management e progetto nelle ferrovie italiane tra le due guerre. In *Angiolo Mazzoni: architetto ingegnere del Ministero delle Comunicazioni*, ed. Mauro Cozzi, Ezio Godoli, and Paola Pettenella, 99–110. Milan: Skira.
Golomstock, Igor N. 1990. *Totalitarian Art: In the Soviet Union, the Third Reich, Fascist Italy and the People's Republic of China*. London: Collins Harvill.

Gramsci, Antonio. 2014. *I quaderni del carcere*. Ed. Valentino Gerratana. Turin: Einaudi.
Greenblatt, Stephen. 2004. *Will in the World. How Shakespeare Became Shakespeare*. London: Jonathan Cape.
Gregotti, Vittorio, and Giovanni Marzari. 1997. *Luigi Figini, Gino Pollini: opera completa: [1927–1991]*. Milan: Electa.
Griffin, Roger. 1993. *The Nature of Fascism*. London: Routledge.
———. 1998. The Sacred Synthesis: The Ideological Cohesion of Fascist Cultural Policy. *Modern Italy* 3 (1): 5–23.
———. 2007. *Modernism and Fascism: The Sense of a Beginning Under Mussolini and Hitler: The Sense of a New Beginning Under Mussolini and Hitler*. Basingstoke: Palgrave.
Griffin, Roger, and Matthew Feldman, eds. 2004. *Fascism. Volume III: Fascism and Culture*. London: Routledge.
Gruppo 7. 1927. Architettura II. Gli stranieri. *La rassegna italiana* 29 (February): 129–137.
Guglielmi, Guido. 1963. Lingua e metalinguaggio di Gadda. *Rendiconti: Rivista di Letteratura e Scienza* 2 (2): 71–78.
Herf, Jeffrey. 1986. *Reactionary Modernism: Technology, Culture, and Politics in Weimar and the Third Reich*. Cambridge: Cambridge University Press.
Iannaccone, Giuseppe. 1999. *Il fascismo sintetico*. Milan: Greco & Greco.
Irace, Fulvio. 1982. La casa sospesa. In *Annitrenta: arte e cultura in Italia*, ed. Vittorio Fagone, 217–221. Milan: Mazzotta.
———. 1994. *Giovanni Muzio 1893–1982: Opera*. Milan: Electa.
Isastia, Alessandro. 2017. Giovanni Muzio, Ca' Brutta. In *Case milanesi 1923–1973. Cinquant'anni di architettura residenziale a Milano*, ed. Isastia Alessandro and Orsina Simona Pierini, 478. Milan: Hoepli.
Isastia, Alessandro, and Orsina Simona Pierini, eds. 2017. *Case milanesi 1923–1973. Cinquant'anni di archittettura residenziale a Milano*. Milan: Hoepli.
Isnenghi, Mario. 1979. *Intellettuali militanti e intellettuali funzionari*. Turin: Einaudi.
Jacobbi, Ruggero. 1974. Introduzione. In Massimo Bontempelli, *L'avventura novecentista*, ed. Ruggero Jacobbi, ix–xxii. Florence: Vallecchi.
Jacopini, Alberto. 1926. A proposito di arte fascista. *Critica fascista* 4 (24): 454–456.
Jewell, Keala. 2008. Magic Realism and Real Politics: Massimo Bontempelli's Literary Compromise. *Modernism/Modernity* 15 (4): 725–744.

Kallis, Aristotle. 2014. *The Third Rome, 1922–43. The Making of the Fascist Capital*. Basingstoke: Palgrave.
Kirk Rossi, Terry. 2005. *The Architecture of Modern Italy/Visions of Utopia, 1900–Present*. Vol. 2. New York: Princeton Architectural Press.
Lazzari, Marino. 1940. *L'azione per l'arte*. With a Preface by Giuseppe Bottai. Florence: Le Monnier.
Lewis, Pericles. 2000. *Modernism, Nationalism, and the Novel*. Cambridge: Cambridge University Press.
Lima, Antonietta Iolanda. 2003. Il palazzo delle Poste di Palermo. In *Angiolo Mazzoni. Architetto, Ingegnere del Ministero delle Comunicazioni*, ed. Mauro Cozzoli, Ezio Godoli, and Paola Pettenella, 243–254. Milan: Skira.
Lista, Giovanni. 2013. *Enrico Prampolini futurista europeo*. Rome: Carocci.
Longatti, Alberto. 1969. Massimo Bontempelli e l'architettura "naturale". *L'eredità di Terragni e l'architettura italiana*. Special issue of *L'Architettura. Cronache e storia* 15 (193): 34–36.
Lu, Andong. 2010. The Telling of a Spatial Allegory: The Danteum as Narrative Labyrinth. *ARQ: Architectural Research Quarterly* 14 (3): 237–246.
Lucie-Smith, Edward. 1985. *The Art of 1930s. The Age of Anxiety*. London: Weidenfeld and Nicolson.
Maccari, Mino. 1926. Arte fascista. *Critica fascista* 4 (21): 396–398.
Malaparte, Curzio. 1926. Botta e risposta. *Critica fascista* 4 (22): 419–420.
Malgeri, Francesco. 1980. *Giuseppe Bottai e 'Critica fascista'*. S. Giovanni Valdarno: L. Landi.
Malvano, Laura. 1988a. *Fascismo e politica dell'immagine*. Turin: Boringhieri.
———. 1988b. La peinture murale, lieu privilégié de la politique fasciste de l'image. *Ligeia* 1 (1): 56–68.
Mancini, Susanna. 2004. L'avventura europeista di "900". In *Le letterature straniere nell'Italia dell'entre-deux-guerres*, ed. Edoardo Esposito, vol. 2, 365–381. Lecce: PensaMultimedia.
Mangione, Flavio, and Cristiano Rosponi. 2009. *Angiolo Mazzoni e l'architettura futurista*. Rome: CE.S.A.R.
Mangoni, Luisa. 1974. *L'interventismo della cultura: intellettuali e riviste del fascismo*. Rome-Bari: Laterza.
———. 1999. *Pensare i libri*. Turin: Bollati e Boringhieri.
Maraini, Antonio. 2001 [1934]. La nuova gestione della Biennale di Venezia. Speech pronounced on 20 December. Reprinted in *Istituzioni politiche e culturali in Italia negli anni Trenta, volume 1*, ed. Vincenzo Cazzato, 43–46. Rome: Istituto poligrafico e zecca dello Stato.

Marazzi, Martino. 2015. *Danteum: studi sul Dante imperiale del Novecento*. Milan: Franco Cesati Editore.
Marcheschi, Daniela, ed. 2014. Introduzione. In Dino Terra *Ioni* [1929], vii–xxvii. Venice: Marsilio.
Mariani, Riccardo. 1989. *Razionalismo e architettura moderna: storia di una polemica*. Milan: Edizioni di Comunità.
Masi, Alessandro. 1992. Giuseppe Bottai: dal futurismo alla legge del 2 per cento. In Giuseppe Bottai, *La politica delle arti. Scritti 1918–1943*, ed. Alessandro Masi, 7–56. Rome: Editalia.
Maulsby, Lucy. 2014. *Fascism, Architecture, and the Claiming of Modern Milan, 1922–1943*. Toronto: University of Toronto Press.
Micali, Simona. 2002. *Miti e riti del moderno: Marinetti, Bontempelli, Pirandello*. Florence: Le Monnier.
Milelli, Gabriele. 1996. 1938–1940. Progetto per il Danteum a Roma. In *Giuseppe Terragni: opera completa*, ed. Giorgio Ciucci, 565–575. Milan: Electa.
Minnucci, Gaetano. 1926. L'architettura e l'estetica degli edifici industriali. *Architettura e Arti decorative* 5 (11–12): 481–583.
Mondello, Elisabetta. 1990. *Roma futurista: i periodici e i luoghi dell'avanguardia nella Roma degli anni Venti*. Milan: Angeli.
Monotti, Francesco. 1933. Antiletteratura. *Quadrante* 1 (1): 5–6.
Moravia, Alberto. 1964. *L'uomo come fine e altri saggi*. Milan: Bompiani.
Moravia, Alberto [Pincherle, Alberto]. 1927. C'è una crisi del romanzo? *La Fiera Letteraria* 3 (41): 1.
Mozzoni, Loretta, and Santini Stefano, eds. 2009. *Architettura dell'eclettismo: il rapporto tra l'architettura e le arti (1930–1960)*. Naples: Liguori.
Murphy, Richard. 1999. *Theorizing the Avant-Garde: Modernism, Expressionism, and the Problem of Postmodernity*. Cambridge: Cambridge University Press.
Mussolini, Benito. 1933. Certezza nelle forze dello spirito e dell'intelligenza italiana. *Quadrante* 1 (2): 1–2.
———. 1934. *Scritti e discorsi dal 1925 al 1926*. Ed. Valentino Piccoli. Milan: Hoepli.
Napolitano, Giorgio. 1928. Difesa di una generazione. *I lupi* 1 (2) (10 February).
Neudecker, Edith. 2007. *Gli edifici postali in Italia durante il fascismo (1922–1944)*. Latina: Casa dell'architettura edizioni.
Nicoloso, Paolo. 2008. *Mussolini architetto: propaganda e paesaggio urbano nell'Italia fascista*. Turin: Einaudi.

Olivetti, Adriano. 1935. Razionalizzazione e corporazioni. *Quadrante* 3 (21): 5–6.

———. 1936. Architettura al servizio sociale. *Casabella* (101): 4–5.

———. 1960. *Città dell'uomo*. Milan: Ed. di Comunità.

Olmo, Carlo, ed. 1994. *Il Lingotto, 1915–1939: l'architettura, l'immagine, il lavoro*. Turin: U. Allemandi.

Ori, Eva. 2014. *Enrico Prampolini tra arte e architettura: teorie, progetti e Arte Polimaterica*. PhD diss.: University of Bologna.

Orpheus (Editorial). 1933. I giovani e la nuova cultura. *Orpheus* 2 (10): 1–6.

Paci, Enzo. 1933. In margine ad un'inchiesta. *Orpheus* 2 (6–8): 1–4.

Pagano, Giuseppe. 1934. Mussolini salva l'architettura italiana. *Casabella* (78) (June): 2–3.

———. 1935. Architettura nazionale. *Casabella* (85) (January).

———. 1937. Tre anni di architettura in Italia. *Casabella* (110) (February).

———. 1939. Architettura industriale in Italia. *Le arti* 1 (4): 358–364.

———. 2008 [1976]. *Architettura e città durante il fascismo*. Ed. Cesare De Seta. Milan: Jaca Book.

Palazzolo, Maria Iolanda. 1993. L'editoria verso un pubblico di massa. In *Fare gli italiani*, ed. Simonetta Soldani and Gabriele Turi, vol. 2, 287–317. Bologna: il Mulino.

Pampaloni, Geno. 1980. *Adriano Olivetti: un'idea di democrazia*. Milan: Edizioni di Comunità.

Pannunzio, Mario. 1932. Del romanzo. *Il Saggiatore* 2 (11): 432–438.

Parisi, Roberto. 2011. *Fabbriche d'Italia. L'architettura industriale dall'Unità alla fine del Secolo breve*. Milan: Franco Angeli.

Parlato, Giuseppe. 2000. *La sinistra fascista. Storia di un progetto mancato*. Bologna: il Mulino.

Patetta, Luciano. 1972. *L'architettura in Italia 1919–1943. Le polemiche*. Milan: Clup.

———. 2009. Introduzione. In *Architettura dell'eclettismo*, ed. Lorella Mozzoni and Stefano Santini, 1–4. Naples: Liguori.

Pavolini, Alessandro. 1926. Dell'arte fascista. *Critica fascista* 4 (21): 393–395.

Pederson, Sanna. 2016. From Gesamtkunstwerk to Drama Music. In *The Total Work of Art: Foundations, Articulations, Inspirations*, ed. David Imhoof, Margaret Eleanor Menninger, and Anthony J. Steinhoff, 39–55. New York and Oxford: Berghahn.

Pensabene, Giuseppe. 1933. Significato estetico del razionalismo. *Quadrante* 1 (1): 6–7.

Piacentini, Marcello. 1928. Prima internazionale architettonica. *Architettura e arti decorative* 7 (12): 544–561.

———. 1996. In *Architettura moderna*, ed. Mario Pisani. Venice: Marsilio.

Pieri, Elisabetta. 2003. Architetture per il carbone: le centrali termiche delle stazioni di Firenze e Venezia. In *Angiolo Mazzoni: architetto ingegnere del Ministero delle Comunicazioni*, ed. Mauro Cozzi, Ezio Godoli, and Paola Pettenella, 123–135. Milan: Skira.

Pollini, Gino. 1988. Fabbrica e quartiere a Ivrea. In *La comunità concreta: progetto ed immagine. Il pensiero e le iniziative di Adriano Olivetti nella formazione della cultura urbanistica ed architettonica italiana*, ed. Marcello Fabbri and Antonella Greco, 155–159. Rome: Fondazione Adriano Olivetti.

Ponti, Pio. 1933. Architettura e aderanza alla realtà. *Orpheus* 2 (4–5): 14–15.

Pontiggia, Elena. 1990. *Mario Sironi: Il mito dell'architettura*. Milan: Mazzotta.

———. 2003. *Il Novecento italiano*. Milan: Abscondita.

Pozzetto, Marco. 1975. *La Fiat-Lingotto: un'architettura torinese d'avanguardia*. Turin: Centro studi piemontesi.

Prosperi, Giorgio. 1932. Realismo e impersonalità. *Il Saggiatore* 2 (12): 486–494.

Ratti, Marzia. 2003. Il palazzo delle Poste della Spezia e i mosaici futuristi di Prampolini e Fillìa. In *Angiolo Mazzoni. Architetto, Ingegnere del Ministero delle Comunicazioni*, ed. Mauro Cozzoli, Ezio Godoli, and Paola Pettenella, 283–294. Milan: Skira.

Riccio, Attilio. 1931. In margine all'ultimo Borgese. *Il Saggiatore* 2 (9): 334–341.

Rifkind, David. 2012. *The Battle for Modernism: Quadrante and the Politicization of Architectural Discourse in Fascist Italy*. Vicenza: Centro internazionale di studi di architettura Andrea Palladio; Venice: Marsilio.

Roberts, David. 2011. *The Total Work of Art in European Modernism*. Ithaca: Cornell.

Rocca, Enrico. 1933. Hermann Kesten o delle trasfiguraizoni del cuore. *Occidente* 2 (2): 53–58.

Rochat, Giorgio. 1982. Due mostre sugli anni fascisti. *Italia contemporanea* (146–147): 153–157.

Romanelli, Romano. 1932a. La stazione ferroviaria di Santa Maria Novella. *La Nazione* (17 June).

———. 1932b. Monumento o stazione ferroviaria? *La Nazione* (10–11 July).

Rundle, Christopher. 2001. *The Permeable Police State. Publishing Translations in Fascist Italy*, PhD diss.: University of Warwick.

Sabatino, Michelngelo. 2010. *Pride in Modesty. Modernist Architecture and the Vernacular Tradition in Italy*. Toronto: Toronto University Press.

Sagramora, Alessandro, ed. 2008. *I futuristi e la Quadriennali*. Milan: Electa.

Salaris, Claudia. 1985. *Storia del futurismo*. Rome: Editori Riuniti.
———. 1990. Immaginismo e neorealismo. In *Luce fredda*, ed. Umberto Barbaro, 229–239. Montepulciano: Editori del Grifo.
———. 2004. *La Quadriennale. Storia della rassegna d'arte italiana dagli anni Trenta ad oggi*. Venice: Marsilio.
Salvagnini, Sileno. 1988. L'arte in azione. Fascismo e organizzazione della cultura in Italia. *Italia contemporanea* (173): 5–21.
———. 2000. *Il sistema delle arti in Italia, 1919–1943*. Bologna: Minerva.
———. 2015. L'arte in azione. Quando gli archivi diventano vita. In *Patrimoni da svelare per le arti del futuro: 1*, ed. Giovanna Cassese, 175–183. Rome: Gangemi.
Santomassimo, Gianpasquale. 2006. *La terza via fascista: il mito del corporativismo*. Rome: Carocci.
Santoro, Marco. 2008. *Storia del libro italiano*. Milan: Editrice Bibliografica.
———. 2009. *Storia del libro italiano. Libro e società in Italia dal Quattrocento al nuovo millennio*. Milan: Editrice bibliografica.
Saporta, Isaac. 1933. Architettura razionale. *Orpheus* 2 (4–5): 10–12.
Sarfatti, Margherita. 1925. *Segni colori luci*. Bologna: Zanichelli.
Sartoris, Alberto. 1933. Significato estetico del razionalismo. *Quadrante* 1 (1): 6–7.
Savinio, Alberto. 1984 [1944]. *Ascolto il tuo cuore, città*. Milan: Adelphi.
Scarsella, Alessandro. 1993. Bontempelli nella casa di vetro: letteratura e architettura in Italia negli anni Trenta. In *Materiali per comprendere Terragni e il suo tempo*, ed. Alberto Artioli and Gian Carlo Borellini, 31–37. Viterbo: Betagamma edizioni.
Schettino, Franca Rita. 1974. Oggettività e presenza del narratore ne *Gli indifferenti* di Moravia. *Revue des Etudes Italiennes* (20): 300–324.
Schnapp, Jeffrey. 1993. 18 BL: Fascist Mass Spectacle. *Representations* (43) (Summer): 89–125.
———, ed. 2000. *A Primer of Italian Fascism*. Lincoln: University of Nebraska Press.
———. 2003. *Anno X: la Mostra della rivoluzione fascista del 1932*. Pisa: Istituti editoriali e poligrafici internazionali.
———. 2004. *Building Fascism, Communism, Liberal Democracy*. Stanford: Stanford University Press.
———. 2012. *Modernitalia*. Ed. Francesca Santovetti. Bern: Peter Lang.
Schnapp, Jeffrey, and Barbara Spackman, eds. 1990. Selections from the Great Debate on Fascism and Culture: *Critica Fascista* 1926–1927. *Stanford Italian Review* 8 (1–2): 238.

Schumacher, Thomas L. 1983. *Terragni e il Danteum*. Roma: Officina.
———. 1991. *Surface & Symbol: Giuseppe Terragni and the Architecture of Italian Rationalism*. New York: Princeton Architectural Press.
———. 2004. *Terragni's Danteum*. New York: Princeton Architectural Press.
Schwartz, Alberto F. 1933. La nuova Architettura in Francia. *Orpheus* 2 (1): 10–14.
Sechi, Mario. 1980. "Critica Fascista" 1929–1932. Idealismo politico e fermenti di cultura nuova alla svolta del regime. *Lavoro critico* (19): 271–322.
———. 1984. *Il mito della nuova cultura: Giovani, realismo e politica negli anni trenta*. Bari: Lacaita.
Sinopoli, Franca. 2017. Il tema "razionalista" tra le arti da "900" a "Quadrante". In *I modernismi delle riviste. Tra Europa e Stati Uniti*, dal falcoy by Caroline Patey and Edoardo Esposito, 181–192. Milan: Ledizioni LediPublishing.
Sironi, Mario. 1932. Pittura murale. *Il Popolo d'Italia* (1 January).
———. 1980. *Scritti editi ed inediti*. Ed. Ettore Camescasca. Milan: Feltrinelli.
Sironi, Mario, Massimo Campigli, Carlo Carrà, and Achille Funi. 1933. Manifesto della pittura murale. *Colonna: Periodico di civiltà italiana* 1 (1): 11–12.
Solari, Piero. 1933. L'Europa letteraria: Orpheus dalla Germania. *Occidente* 2 (5): 41–47.
Stone, Marla Susan. 1997. The State as Patron: Making Official Culture in Fascist Italy. In *Fascist Visions: Art and Ideology in France and Italy*, ed. Matthew Affron and Mark Antliff, 205–238. Princeton: Princeton University Press.
———. 1998. *The Patron State: Culture and Politics in Fascist Italy*. Princeton: Princeton University Press.
Storchi, Simona. 2007. *Il fascismo è una casa di vetro*: Giuseppe Terragni and the Politics of Space in Fascist Italy. *Italian Studies* 62 (2): 231–245.
———. 2012. Costruire il moderno. Bontempelli, "Quadrante", e il fronte unico dell'estetica. *Bollettino 900* 1–2. http://www3.unibo.it/boll900/numeri/2012-i/Storchi.html.
Talarico, Elio. 1933. Coefficienti nuovi nel romanzo. *Occidente* 2 (3): 7–9.
Talbot, George. 2006. Alberto Moravia and Italian Fascism: Censorship, Racism and *Le ambizioni sbagliate*. *Modern Italy* 11 (2): 127–145.
Tarquini, Alessandra. 2011. *Storia della cultura fascista*. Bologna: il Mulino.
Tempesti, Fernando. 1976. *Arte dell'Italia fascista*. Milan: Feltrinelli.
Tentori, Francesco. 1990. *P.M. Bardi: con le cronache artistiche de "L'Ambrosiano" 1930–33*. Milan: Mazzotta.
———. 1996. Terragni e Bontempelli, architettura e letteratura. In *Giuseppe Terragni: opera completa*, ed. Giorgio Ciucci, 207–217. Milano: Electa.

Terragni, Giuseppe. 1931. Per un'architettura italiana moderna. *La Tribuna* (23 March).
Toffanello, Marcello, ed. 2017. *All'origine delle grandi mostre d'arte in Italia (1933–40)*. Mantova: il Rio.
Tongiorgi, Duccio. 1994a. Il mestiere di scrittore: episodi di una *letteratura Fiat* degli anni 30. In *La strada e il volante*, ed. Pietro Maria Bardi, 7–30. Turin: Scriptorium.
———. 1994b. Scrittori e industria: L'immagine della fabbrica nelle riviste aziendali (1913–1957). In *Scritture di fabbrica: dal vocabolario alla società*, ed. Carlo Ossola, 385–511. Turin: Scriptorium.
Tranfaglia, Nicola, and Albertina Vittoria. 2000. *Storia degli editori italiani. Dall'Unità alla fine degli anni Sessanta*. Rome-Bari: Laterza.
Trivellin, Eleonor. 1996. *1933, la villa razionalista: BBPR, Terragni, Figini e Pollini*. Florence: Alinea.
Tschumi, Bernard. 1996. *Architecture and Disjunction*. Cambridge, MA: MIT.
Turi, Gabriele. 1980. *Il fascismo e il consenso degli intellettuali*. Bologna: il Mulino.
———. 1990. *Casa Einaudi. Libri, uomini, idee oltre il fascismo*. Bologna: il Mulino.
———. 1995. *Giovanni Gentile. Una biografia*. Florence: Giunti.
Vittoria, Albertina. 1980. Le riviste di regime: "Gerarchia", "Civiltà fascista", "Critica fascista". *Studi romani* 28 (3): 312–334.
———. 1983. *Le riviste del duce*. Turin: Guanda.
Vivarelli, Pia. 1993. La politica delle arti figurative negli anni del Premio Bergamo. In *Gli anni del premio Bergamo. Arte in Italia intorno agli anni Trenta*, ed. AA. VV, 24–38. Milan: Electa.
Voza, Pasquale. 1981. Il problema del realismo negli anni Trenta: *Il Saggiatore, Il Cantiere*. *Lavoro critico* (21–22): 65–105.
———. 1982. Nel ventisette sconosciuto: Moravia intorno al romanzo. *Belfagor* 37 (2): 207–212.
———. 1997. *Moravia*. Palermo: Palumbo.
———. 2007. Scrivere dentro: Moravia e la villa-teatro dell'indifferenza. In *Interni familiari nella letteratura italiana*, ed. Maria Pagliara, 146–153. Bari: Progedit.
Zunino, Pier Giorgio. 1985. *L'ideologia del fascismo*. Bologna: il Mulino.

Index[1]

NUMBERS AND SYMBOLS

522: racconto di una giornata, see Bontempelli, Massimo
900, 12, 42, 51, 97–117, 149, 154, 194n1, 203
  See also Bontempelli, Massimo

A

Accademia delle Belle Arti di Pesaro, 91n43
Aero painting, 80, 90n23
Aero sculpture, 80
Alpes, 38, 57n42
Alvaro, Corrado, 41, 42, 57n35, 63, 103, 104, 131, 133, 141
Ambrosiano, L, 177, 198n35
Anceschi, Luciano, 128, 136, 137, 141, 146n28
Angela, see Fracchia, Umberto
Anthropological revolution, viii, 2, 8, 34, 49, 117, 125, 126, 135, 165, 166, 172, 201, 203, 204
Anti-rhetorical style, 86, 179
Architettura, 10, 78, 79, 91n36, 92n51, 120n18, 174, 176, 178, 179
Architettura rurale (ruralist architecture), 41, 42

B

Bacchelli, Riccardo, 43, 53
Banfi, Gian Luigi, 84, 121n29, 198n41

---

[1] Note: Page numbers followed by 'n' refer to notes.

© The Author(s) 2019
F. Billiani, L. Pennacchietti, *Architecture and the Novel under the Italian Fascist Regime*, https://doi.org/10.1007/978-3-030-19428-4

Barbaro, Umberto, 43, 48, 130–134, 141, 153–159, 167
Bardi, Pietro Maria, 45, 71, 76, 78, 80, 92n51, 93n62, 93n63, 109–111, 115, 116, 121n27, 122n33, 136, 141, 159–161, 163–166, 168, 169, 172, 175–177, 185, 203
Bazzani, Cesare, 175
BBPR, 63, 70, 71, 82, 86
Belli, Carlo, 82, 121n24, 177
Bompiani, Valentino, 49–51, 83
Bontempelli, Massimo, 20, 21, 35–36, 41, 42, 45–47, 50, 51, 53, 57n40, 57n42, 76, 80, 83, 94n70, 98–116, 118n2, 118n4, 118n8, 119n11, 120–121n21, 121n27, 122n30, 122n33, 130, 131, 141, 142, 145n13, 152, 159–164, 171–173, 177, 180, 190, 191, 203
Borgese, Giuseppe Antonio, 37–39, 69, 142, 143, 151, 152
Bottai, Giuseppe, 12, 16–18, 20–23, 27n2, 29n16, 29n18, 32, 36, 45–47, 49, 59n57, 87, 117, 131, 144n7, 144n10, 153, 191, 202
Bottoni, Piero, 72, 114, 121n29
Bragaglia, Anton Giulio, 20, 21, 40, 63, 131, 140
Brasini, Armando, 76, 175
Buzzati, Dino, 43, 57n48

C

Calligrafisti *vs.* contenutisti, 45
Cappa, Benedetta, 81
Carabba, publishing house, 37, 43
Cardarelli, Vincenzo, *see Ronda, La*
Carella, Domenico, 59n59, 140, 141, 143
Carrà, Carlo, 26, 91n42
Casabella, 68, 82, 84, 94n82, 95n90, 171, 177, 185, 199n45
Casa Bragaglia, 47
Casa del fascio (Como), 65, 73, 90n34, 187
Casa della Meridiana, *see* De Finetti, Giuseppe
Casa elettrica, 72, 73, 80, 135
Casa Pizzigoni, 67
Castello di Udine, see Gadda, Carlo Emilio
Cereghini, Mario, 121n29
CIAM, *see* Congrès internationaux d'architecture moderne
Cicognani, Bruno, 40, 48, 52
Ciocca, Gaetano, 198n41
Città corporative, *see* Corporativist city; New town; Littoria-Latina; Sabaudia; Tresigallo
Città nuova, La, 80
Città universitaria (La Sapienza), 65, 79, 80
Colloqui con Mussolini, 90n25
Colonia Rosa Maltoni Mussolini, 65
Congrès internationaux d'architecture moderne (CIAM), 77
Contro i ritorni in pittura, *see* Sironi, Mario
Convegno, Il, 131, 146n26
Corporativist city, 185
Corrente, group, 128, 144n4
Corrente, journal, 128
Corrente movement, 128

Critica fascista, 10, 12, 17, 18, 20, 23, 24, 26, 35, 59n59, 99, 126, 127, 136, 153
Croce, Benedetto, 45, 48, 133, 135, 139, 140

D

D'Annunzio, Gabriele, 37, 133, 135, 195n6
De Chirico, Giorgio, *see* Valori plastici
De Crecchio, Parladore Luigi, 38, 140, 143
De Finetti, Giuseppe, 67, 68, 91n39
De Renzi, Mario, 78, 93n60
De Stijl, 77
Decadentism, 2, 39, 133, 140, 195n6
Del Debbio, Enrico, 65, 84, 86
Depero, Fortunato, 54n3, 59n61, 63, 76, 92n51, 179
Di Belgioioso, Lodovico B., 121n29, 198n41
Döblin, Alfred, 50
Domus, 86, 94n82, 145n26
Dos Passos, John, 49, 131, 143

E

Edificio-tipo, 81
E42 (Esposizione Universale), 4, 86, 87, 186
Esposizione internazionale d'arte decorative e industriali moderna, 72, 82
Esposizione italiana di architettura razionale, I, 93n56, 93n57

F

Fabbrica Olivetti, 167, 199n43
Festa del libro (book fair), 49
Fiera letteraria, La, 39, 48, 49, 149, 153
Figini, Luigi, 71–73, 82, 121n29, 135, 167, 181–184
Fillìa (Colombo, Luigi), 63, 76, 80, 81, 93n70
Flores, Paolo, 144n10, 154
Fontana, Lucio, 82, 85, 86
Ford, Henry, 198n40
Foschini, Arnaldo, 84
Fracchia, Umberto, *see Fiera letteraria, La*
Frette, Guido, 71, 82, 121n29
Funi, Achille, 66
Futurist architecture, 63, 70, 79–82, 94n70

G

Gadda, Carlo Emilio, 38, 43, 53, 75, 128
Gallian, Marcello, 43, 57n40, 57n42, 112
Gamberini, Italo, 174
Garofano rosso, Il, 43
Gente in Aspromonte, *see* Alvaro, Corrado
Gentile, Giovanni, 12n2
Gherardini, Armando, *see Occidente*
Giornale d'Italia, 76
Gramsci, Antonio, 45, 51, 52
Granata, Giorgio, 57n35, 140, 142
Grassi, Bonaventura, 154
Griffini, Enrico A., 121n29, 167

Gropius, Walter, 71, 73, 78, 92n52, 139, 182, 184
Gruppi universitari fascisti (GUF), 126
Gruppo 7, 61, 63, 65, 68, 70, 71, 92n51, 109, 113, 180, 197n28
Gruppo Foschini, Il, 84
Gruppo Toscano, 65, 84, 174, 176–179
GUF, see Gruppi universitari fascisti

I

Immaginismo (Immaginist movement), 43, 127, 154, 155
Inchiesta del Saggiatore (inquiry), 140
Indifferenti, Gli, 38, 40, 41, 53, 57n35, 57n42, 143, 149–153, 157, 166–170, 180
Interplanetario, 10, 43, 126, 130, 149, 170
Italia letteraria, L, 10, 48, 57n40, 90n25, 94n78, 122n33, 126, 135

L

Larco, Sebastiano, 71
Lazzari, Marino, 29n18, 32, 191
Le Corbusier, 71, 73, 77, 78, 83, 92n51, 92n52, 198n37
Levi-Montalcini, Gino, 80
Libera, Adalberto, 71, 75, 78, 82, 86, 93n60
Lingeri, Pietro, 121n29, 186, 188, 189, 191, 192
Lissitzky, El, 77
Littoria-Latina, 65
Loos, Adolf, 68, 135
Luce fredda, 43, 153–159, 166–170, 184
Lupi, I, 43, 121n28, 149

M

Maccari, Mino, 20, 21, 24, 25, 33, 36, 41, 44
Magical realism, 42, 54, 102, 118n2, 119n10, 162, 190, 203
Malaparte, Curzio, 20, 21, 36, 48
Manifesto della pittura murale, 82
Manzoni, Alessandro, 108
Marinetti, Filippo Tommaso, 20, 21, 33, 56n23, 63, 65, 69, 79, 80, 82, 131, 140, 144n4, 175
Martini, Arturo, 63
Matteotti, Giacomo, 3, 39
Mazzoni, Angiolo, xii, 63, 65, 80, 81, 88n7, 174, 175, 177, 197n32
Medusa (book series), see Mondadori publisher
Michelucci, Giovanni, 65, 84, 86, 94n81, 174, 178
Mies van der Rohe, Ludwig, 73, 77
Minnucci, Gaetano, 75, 76, 181, 182, 197n28
Minucci, Giovanni, 76
Modernism, vii, 13n7, 33, 55n14, 131, 140
Mondadori, Arnoldo, 52, 53
Mondadori publisher, 4, 37, 38, 41, 50, 52, 53, 56n27
Monotti, Francesco, 112, 113
Monumentalism, 11, 24, 61, 65, 79, 84–87, 95n90, 188

Moravia, Alberto (Pincherle, Alberto), 38, 40–42, 63, 134, 143, 149–154, 157, 169, 194n3
Morpurgo, Vittorio, 84
Mostra del Decennale, 4, 78
Movimento Italiano per l'Architettura Razionale (MIAR), 75, 77, 80, 174
Munari, Bruno, 63
Mussolini, Benito, 3, 16, 19, 20, 25, 33, 34, 62, 64, 66, 76, 78, 87, 91n43, 93n66, 103, 111, 115, 160, 172, 175, 176, 185, 186, 191, 193, 194n5
Muzio, Giovanni, 63, 65–70, 73, 83, 86, 122n34

N

Neoclassicism, 21
 See also neo-Palladian style
Neo-Palladian style, 68
New Man, vii, ix, 3, 34, 45, 125, 139, 202–204
New objectivity, 37–38, 71, 131, 133, 140, 143, 146n35
New realism (Neorealism), 149, 170
New town, 17, 85, 108
Novecento, 19, 21, 24, 29n15, 33, 38, 55n9, 61, 65–70, 78, 91n39, 91n42, 91n43, 101, 118n4, 133, 154

O

Occidente, 12, 42, 47, 53, 126, 129–135, 137, 141, 146n26
Ojetti, Ugo, 78, 90n36, 94n84, 175

Olivetti, Adriano, 105, 135, 167, 173, 181–186, 193, 198n38, 198n40
Oud, J. J., 72, 78

P

Paci, Enzo, 128, 136, 137, 139
Pagano, Giuseppe, 41, 65, 70, 71, 83–87, 93n62, 93n68, 95n90, 107, 108, 167, 171, 172, 175–177, 185, 187, 197n28
Paladini, Vinicio, 43, 79, 93n65, 130, 144n10, 154
Palazzeschi, Aldo, 44
Palazzo dei Congressi, *see* Libera, Adalberto
Palazzo della civiltà, 87
Palazzo dell'Arte, *see* Muzio, Giovanni
Palazzo delle poste di La Spezia, *see* Mazzoni, Angiolo
Palazzo delle poste di Palermo, *see* Mazzoni, Angiolo
Palazzo delle poste di Pola, *see* Mazzoni, Angiolo
Palazzo del Littorio (Farnesina), 84, 90n36, 186
Palazzo dell'Ina, 87
Pannaggi, Ivo, 154
Pannunzio, Mario, 142, 143
Pavolini, Alessandro, 21, 36, 79, 173
Pavolini, Corrado, 131, 141
Pègaso, 136
Pensabene, Giuseppe, 114, 115
Peressutti, Enrico, 121n29, 198n41
Perrotti, Nicola, 59n54, 140
Persico, Edoardo, 70, 85, 86, 94n78

Pesaro, Lino, 91n43
Pestelli, Gino, 160
Piacentini, Marcello, 10, 65, 75, 76, 78–80, 84–87, 90n36, 93n60, 119–120n14, 171, 175
Pirandello, Luigi, 142
Planetario Hoepli, *see* Portaluppi, Piero
Pollini, Gino, 71–73, 76, 82, 121n29, 135, 167, 181–185
Ponti, Giò, 65, 67, 86, 93n68
Popolo d'Italia, Il, 82, 91n43
Portaluppi, Piero, 69, 75, 82
Poss, Alessandro, 186
Prampolini, Enrico, 63, 76, 80, 81, 88n7, 90n23, 94n73
Premio Bagutta, 40, 43, 49
Premio Mediterraneo, 43
Premio Mussolini, 49
Premio Viareggio, 49
Primato, 29n16, 35, 87
Prosa d'arte, 2, 38, 68, 75, 128, 137, 146n28, 157, 158
Prosperi, Giorgio, 142
Puccini, Mario, 36, 131, 141

Q

Quadrante, *see* Bardi, Pier Maria; Bontempelli, Massimo

R

Rapporto sull'architettura (per Mussolini), *see* Bardi, Pier Maria
Rassegna italiana, 71, 73, 92n52
Rationalist architecture, 3, 9, 61, 62, 65, 75, 76, 78, 79, 85, 114, 115, 119n14, 127, 132, 140, 164, 170, 171, 174, 177, 193
Rava, Carlo Enrico, 71
Rebbio, 65
Riccio, Attilio, 141, 142
Rocca, Enrico, 131, 134
Rogers, Ernesto N., 121n29, 198n41
Romanelli, Romano, 175, 180
Romanzi della Palma (book series), *see* Mondadori publisher
Romanzo Fiat, 159–166
Ronda, La, 38, 40, 131, 137
Rosai, Ottone, 179
Ruota dentata, La, 10, 47, 57n42, 126, 130, 155

S

Sabaudia, 65
Saggiatore, Il, 10, 12, 38, 42, 48, 57n35, 59n54, 59n56, 126, 129, 130, 133, 136–138, 140–144
Sant'Elia, Antonio, 69, 78, 81
Sarfatti, Margherita, 10, 24, 33, 52, 65, 66, 76, 91n42, 127, 140
Sartoris, Alberto, 92n53, 114, 115, 167
Sassu, Aligi, 128, 144n4
Savinio, Alberto, 180, 181
See also Valori plastici
Scacchiera davanti allo specchio, La, *see* Bontempelli, Massimo
Serra, Renato, 37
Sironi, Mario, 10, 25, 55n15, 66, 82, 97
Soffici, Ardengo, 20, 45, 177
Solari, Pietro, 133

Solaria, 38, 40, 43, 131, 136, 146n26
Solaria edizioni, 43
Sonzogno, publisher, 37
Sorelle Materassi, Le, see Palazzeschi, Aldo
Spettatore italiano, Lo, 131
Stazione dei treni, Firenze (Santa Maria Novella), *see* Gruppo Toscano
Stile littorio, 3, 11, 85
Strada e il volante, La, see Bardi, Pier Maria
Strapaese, *see* Maccari, Mino

T
Talarico, Elio, 130, 133
Tato, 81, 94n73
Tavola degli orrori, 76, 78
Taylor, Frederick, 198n40
Taylorization, 167
Tecchi, Bonaventura, 141
Tecnica e organizzazione, 198n40
Terra, Dino, 47, 141, 144n10, 154
Terragni, Giuseppe, 65, 70, 71, 73, 76, 78, 83, 84, 86, 90n33, 93n62, 95n86, 110, 121n29, 186–193
Thayaht (Ernesto Michahelles), 63
Tinti, Mario, 97
Titta Rosa, Giovanni, 48, 49
Torchi, Pietro, 136
Torre Ina, *see* Piacentini, Marcello

Total work of art, viii, ix, 62–64, 88n10, 115
Tozzi, Federigo, 39, 131
Translations, 4, 5, 11, 47, 48, 50–53, 59n53, 68, 70, 77, 78, 128, 131, 136, 202
Treccani, Ernesto, *see Corrente*, journal; *Corrente* movement
Tresigallo, 65
Treves, publishing house, 37, 38, 43
Triennale, V, 81, 115

U
Umbertine style, 68
Universale, L, 42, 126, 144n8

V
Valdameri, Rino, 186
Valori plastici (movement), 66, 91n42
Viani, Lorenzo, 39
Villa Malaparte, *see* Libera, Adalberto
Villa razionalista, 83
Villa-studio per un artista, *see* Portaluppi, Piero
Vittorini, Elio, 43, 63, 128, 131, 137, 141

W
Wilde, Oscar, 134

The manufacturer's authorised representative in the EU is Springer Nature Customer Service Centre GmbH, Europaplatz 3, 69115 Heidelberg, Germany. If you have any concerns regarding our products, please contact ProductSafety@springernature.com

Printed and bound by CPI Group (UK) Ltd, Croydon, CR0 4YY
28/03/2026
02080358-0001